D1824192

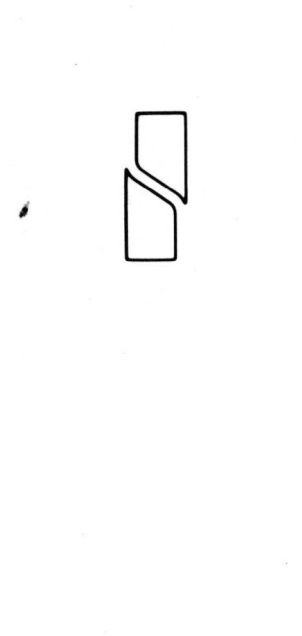

MODERNIZING LIVES

Experiments in English Biography, 1918–1939

RUTH HOBERMAN

FOREWORD BY A. O. J. COCKSHUT

SOUTHERN ILLINOIS UNIVERSITY PRESS
Carbondale and Edwardsville

Library of Congress Cataloging-in-Publication Data

Hoberman, Ruth.
Modernizing lives.
Bibliography: p.
Includes index.
1. Biography (as a literary form). 2. Great Britain—
Biography. I. Title.
CT21.H59 1987   808'.06692   86-4004
ISBN 0-8093-1288-3

for Richard

Contents

Foreword

Responding with pleasure to the invitation to write a foreword to Ruth Hoberman's book, I recall that in my own
book on biography, *Truth to Life*, I wrote, "The student
who attempted to summarize the course of biography
from 1900 to 1940 would confront difficulties not encoun-
tered in the present task." The "present task" was to trace
the history of biography in the nineteenth century, and it
was not an easy one; but it was, as I said then and as I still
think, less difficult than that which Professor Hoberman
has attempted with such fine and fruitful results.

Essentially, her subject—and a particularly fascinating
one it is—is the impact of literary modernism on the art of
biography. We all know, of course, that literary periods are
never precise. Biographies of the traditional type continued to flourish down to 1914, and a few (like G. M.
Trevelyan's *Grey of Fallodon*, 1937) continued to appear
long afterwards. But such anomalies need not deter us
from seeing the period as a coherent whole; and, in particular, its latter half, after World War I, has an unrepeat-
able flavor. It is the achievement of this book to capture
that flavor very well.

It would be absurdly oversimple to deny that Victorian
biographers could criticize people severely. Froude's *Carlyle*, perhaps the finest of all Victorian biographies, is sufficient evidence of that. But as Hoberman says, in Froude's
work "The flaw or conflict becomes evidence not of human
weakness but of a titanic destiny." And in her discussion of
Mill's *Autobiography*, she sums up that characteristic of Vic-

torian biography which is most unlike the works that form her own subject: "The key word is *will*: Ulysses has it, Arnold seeks it, Mill discovers it, and Carlyle praises it." In contrast, early twentieth century biographers prefer to show either that will is almost powerless in the grip of the terrible forces of life and of the unconscious mind (as in Cecil's Cowper) or that the exercise of a strong will will led to the suppression of unadmitted drives, and thus to unconscious hypocrisy (as in Strachey's Manning).

Placed as we are now, nearly half a century after modernism, we can appreciate the full force of the reaction against it. Biography today may be considered, if you like, as a synthesis of the Victorian and the modernist; but there can be no doubt that the reaction against modernism has gone very far, and that the Victorian again has the upper hand. Sexual and financial reticence, certainly, have been largely dropped. But in place of the impressionistic, and often unhistorical, sketches of Strachey and Virginia Woolf, we have once again the biography dominated by documents, strong on facts, and wary of too much interpretation. Edel's *James*, Bullock's *Bevin*, Crick's *Orwell* are, in many respects, natural developments of the Victorian, and one would look in vain in them for any hint of modernism. If a decadent modernism is still to be found, it is usually in the work of journalists, with their "brilliant" psychological reconstructions.

No one can fairly be held responsible for the short-comings of his successors. But Hoberman is not really being too severe when she writes, "Strachey's pretense of merely 'exposing' the facts seems, finally, disingenuous." But as far as her own book is concerned, this rapid decline and disappearance of modernist biography is by no means a disadvantage. It gives the subject an attractive and manageable unity, as a brief and distinctive phase of literary taste.

Naturally, as in any phase of taste, there was room for

striking variation. Cecil's sense of sympathy and pity is not at all like Strachey's ironic detachment. Cecil wants to find out about Cowper and tell us what he was like. Strachey is fundamentally incurious—he hardly ever did any research, but picked up facts magpie-like from the Victorian biographers—and, above all, he is conscious of himself as an artist. He was right: biography is an art. The great age of our drama in the seventeenth century, and of our novel in the nineteenth, might be quoted in support of this. But Strachey never shows that great virtue of all high art, self-forgetfulness before the object contemplated. His main subject is always himself. Against this we may place Cecil's sense of the drama of Cowper's life, as described in Hoberman's words: Cecil "paints the domestic life of Cowper and Mrs Unwin as a kind of cozy nook in a furiously dangerous, disordered world," and so creates "a gripping tension between the reader's identification and his omniscience."

Perhaps it was, in part, a reaction against Strachey's too conscious art that led Virginia Woolf, in an essay in *The Death of the Moth,* to question the status of biography as art, and to remind us that "Micawber and Miss Bates will survive Lockhart's Sir Walter Scott and Lytton Strachey's Queen Victoria." But we may question whether she was right, and leave the final decision to the (perhaps unlikely) day when we have a biographer with genius equal to that of our two greatest novelists. Perhaps her essay also reflects a justified uneasiness about the balance of power between the author of biography and its subject. The classic Victorian biographer—Buckle, say, or Morley—aimed to efface himself and allow Disraeli or Gladstone to speak for himself; to create, as it were, his own life. The early twentieth century reaction against this is seen in its extreme form in what is here called "mediated biography," especially in Symons's *Quest for Corvo.* Here the interviews with people who knew Corvo are the essence of the book, and the reader may be excused for wondering whether he is reading a biography or an autobiography. And no doubt some read the book (which was surprisingly popular) as a detective story of real life.

Nevertheless, Symons did preserve what Strachey, in his petty bumptiousness, so completely lacked, a sense of humility before the mystery of his subject. This essential feature of a great biography, present in the work of Boswell and Froude, for instance, can be lost in more ways than one. It may be lost in a painstaking Victorian biography by excess of documentation, by over-complete explanation of every act and every episode; or it may be lost by tidy psychological explanations, and by the biographer's cheap self-admiration at the expense of his subject. Some biographers of the early twentieth century were guilty of forgetting that the subject of a biography is normally of greater stature than its author. Reading Strachey, I am sometimes reminded of a grubby little boy making faces behind the headmaster's back. In this respect, too, the pendulum has swung back. The best recent biographers assume that we want to know about the book's ostensible subject, and that our interest in the biographer's personality is secondary. They are no longer doing what Hoberman, in a telling phrase, calls "constantly inviting the reader's collusion."

But in another way, it might be argued, the early twentieth century biographers did put their finger on a weakness in the work of their predecessors. They rightly saw that piling up facts was not enough. There must be a creative act of insight. But the wiser among them knew that this insight could be no substitute for hard work with facts. A mathematician told me once that the points of real significance in his work were sudden and extraordinarily brief flashes of insight. But, he added, you don't get those flashes without months of hard work beforehand: a perfect image, it seems to me, of the relation between facts, documents, and insights for the biographer. It was this unseen center, or "figure in the carpet," that Virginia Woolf, in implied criticism of Strachey, was seeking for in her comments on Roger Fry. "Instead of a unity firmly fixed in a family life and career, Fry's self is a texture superimposed on the reality." But unless we are given facts and documents, we cannot judge how far the figure in the carpet represents the truth; and if we are given very few, we are liable to suspect the biographer of arbitrarily imposing his own view. Worse, the biographer may invent things that never happened, like Strachey's invention of a conversation between Pius IX and Manning, or his purely novelistic deathbed of Queen Victoria.

Some of the biographers discussed in this book broke new ground, too, in their treatment of failure. To regard failure as interesting, significant, even sometimes in a paradoxical way as a triumph, may be more true to reality than to celebrate heroes. The great truth that every man is his own worst enemy cannot be said to be completely absent from the work of the traditional biographers. Boswell dealing with Johnson's anger and temptations to despair, Lockhart with Scott's fatal extravagance, Froude with Carlyle's perverse egoism—all these powerfully showed their awareness of it. Yet cases like these stand out as exceptions; and one can read many thousands of pages of nineteenth century biography with an impatient sense that it is all too good to be true. The reality of human weakness really was due for an innings. In the hands of some, though by no means all, of the biographers with which this book deals, this reality can be felt as liberating. I do not mean merely in the superficial sense that it came as a breath of air after much evasion and pretence. A deeper defence of the new method could be mounted on the lines of Ruskin's defence of the imperfections of Gothic. A perfect, well-rounded life made out of what was really no such thing, may suffer from the stifling over-completeness which Ruskin attributed to classic form. An imperfect life is not only more true to experience, but more suggestive of the largeness of human possibility, like the pinnacles of Ruskin's cathedrals. Such a life, too, may be felt to be more open to Divine

Mercy. Sometimes deliberately (as in *The Stricken Deer*), sometimes quite unconsciously, the new form of biography was actually more religious than its predecessors. It substituted the more easily forgivable sins for the pharisaism that too easily invaded the judgments of the Victorian Age.

Hertford College, Oxford   A. O. J. Cockshut

Acknowledgments

For permission to quote from two of A. J. A. Symons's unpublished letters, I would like to thank Julian Symons and the Henry W. and Albert A. Berg Collection, the New York Public Library, Astor, Lenox, and Tilden Foundations. I am also grateful to the Mrs. Giles Whiting Foundation and to Columbia University for financial support, to Professor Carl Woodring for his encouragement and suggestions, and to Professor Carolyn Heilbrun for her comments, criticism, and huge quantities of moral support.

Modernizing Lives

I

Introduction

*Apparently life-writing is the last major
discipline uncorrupted by criticism.* (Clifford,
Puzzles 102)

Lytton Strachey, Geoffrey Scott, David Cecil, Percy Lubbock, A. J. A. Symons, Virginia Woolf, E. M. Forster, and
Harold Nicolson form an odd collection of the famous and
the not so famous, an apparently motley crew who are, collectively, the subject of this study. All were distinguished
writers in England between World Wars I and II, and all
wrote biographies of note. If their subjects are miscellaneous—ranging from Queen Elizabeth to Roger Fry—as
writers they are nonetheless linked by common concerns,
primarily the reshaping of traditional biography into a
more flexible, more artful form, able to accommodate
modern ideas of the self, of time, and of narration. Yet
these writers are rarely perceived as a group, in part because biographies are rarely read as literature, offering a
style and treatment particular to the author and worthy of
literary analysis. Arranged on the library shelves by subject
rather than by author, biographical texts are thought to
offer themselves as nontexts, as transparent receptacles
for their content.

Such a view is rather obviously naive. The unmediated

transmutation of life into language is utterly impracticable. When readers exclaim of a biography that it is "realistic," that it "really brings the subject to life," what they mean is that its choice of literary conventions exactly matches their own preconceptions, their own past experience of how reality is to be represented. E. H. Gombrich makes the same point about pictorial representation in *Art and Illusion*. The artist's own perception is structured by what he already knows about painting: "The schemata he has learned to handle," Gombrich writes, "will leap forward as centers of attention" (85). Similarly, in recreating what he sees for a viewer, his task is not one of technical precision but of psychological second-guessing; he must convey, according to Gombrich, a "convincing image despite the fact that no one individual shade corresponds to what we call 'reality'" (49). "Reality" is perceptible only through internalized schemata, which have a history of their own.

No one would dispute the fact that there is a big difference between the way Rembrandt and Cézanne portray people and that that difference is worth analyzing and talking about. Yet life-writing, in some ways a verbal equivalent of portrait-painting, has received little critical attention; its varying representational schemata have been, for the most part, overlooked.

How much weight are friendships and family given? Is it assumed that the subject's letters reveal or belie an inner self? How much authority does the narrator claim to have in speaking of his subject? The answers are not obvious. How they are answered will depend to a large extent on the biographer's intellectual and social milieu. Richard Altick points out that Galton and Taine led to a greater biographical interest in the subject's heredity and environment (222). The nineteenth-century autobiographers brought new prominence to childhood. Freud made the automatic acceptance of a subject's self-image unthinkable. What's convincing to one generation will suddenly seem lopsided or laughable to another. Thus Virginia Woolf writes of Victorian biographies that they have a "depressing similarity; very much overworked, very serious, very joyless, the eminent men appear to us to be, and already strangely formal and remote from us in their likes and dislikes" (*Contemporary Writers* 29).

Shaped to a large extent by historically determined concerns, biographies have had a heavy ideological burden to bear. From hieroglyphic accounts of dead pharoahs to modern official biographies, they have served to recuperate the particularities of a life into the social norm. Particularly in the late nineteenth century, series of lives—Eminent Women, for example, and Great Men of Letters—and the massive *Dictionary of National Biography* both reflected and shaped a particular sense of what matters in life, and what makes for greatness. Biography as a genre was, according to Georges Gusdorf, "reviewed and corrected by the demands of propaganda and by the general sense of the age" (31). The post-Victorians recognized, to some extent, its ideological content and often sought to revise, in their own terms, the old versions of great lives to convey new assumptions and messages. A new series of lives of women was published, and in 1937 the Hogarth Press began issuing World-Makers and World-Shakers, a series of brief biographies whose subjects included Socrates, Joan of Arc, Mazzini, Garibaldi and Cavour, and Darwin. Leonard Woolf writes: "It was a series of short biographies for young people which would attempt to explain history to them through the lives of great men and women, and at the same time present history from a modern and enlightened point of view" (*Journey* 98).

The life described is the life noticed. Again and again in *Three Guineas* Virginia Woolf turns to biography for evidence that women have been excluded from their cultural inheritance and, to speed the reclaiming of it, calls for more biographies in the future. If novelists fail to portray the realities of female experience, she writes in *The Par-*

giters," this is largely because the biographers and auto-biographers also ignore it, and thus reduce the material which the novelist has to work upon to a minimum" (*Par-giters* 51). In her 1939 essay "The Art of Biography," Woolf argues that the biographer provides a lesson in the percep-tion of reality, more so than any but the greatest novelist (*Death* 195).

Yet biographers have tended to deny their own power. When James Clifford asked contemporary biographers about their theoretical assumptions, they insisted in reply that they were simply "objective," an insistence that gives biography an extraordinary power to define the real and makes it essentially un-analyzable (*Puzzles* 103).

That biographical methodology and structure are, in fact, discussable becomes obvious during the period be-tween 1918 and 1939. The dates are borrowed from E. M. Forster, who characterizes that period as a "long week-end" between two wars (*Two Cheers* 272). The aftermath of one war, the premonition of another, technological devel-opment, Proust, psychoanalysis, and the theory of rela-tivity, he says, all had an impact on English prose (272–77). The result was a feeling of insecurity, according to Forster. Certainly the old schemata by which human beings were portrayed had come to seem inadequate.

This inadequacy triggered the famous announcement made by Virginia Woolf in "Mr. Bennett and Mrs. Brown," an announcement as relevant to biography as to fiction. Woolf cites 1910 (perhaps because of the Post-Impressionist Exhibition in London that year) as her turning point. In any case the sense that something happened around this time to affect both fictional and nonfictional characteriza-tion is pervasive. Altick mentions the impact of Henry James and post-Jamesian literary theory, as well as Freud, whose impact on biography peaked he says, between 1920 and 1930 (352, 338). For John Garraty, another literary historian of biography, the major factors were Freud and World War I, in part because the phenomenon of shell shock forced people to recognize the existence of an unseen, irrational, yet powerful inner life ("Interrelations" 570). I would add Pater, Dostoievsky, Conrad, and feminism as important intellectual currents affecting biography.

Amid the atmosphere of insecurity and change described by Forster and others, the traditional biographical method seemed outdated. The compilation of letters and autobiographical fragments, which allowed the subject to depict himself with minimal intervention from the biographer, was no longer convincing; childhood tended to be neglected in such works, and totally ignored was the unconscious, unwilled element in character—the social forces one takes too much for granted to notice, and the psychic forces one has too great a stake in refusing to notice (Cockshut 17–18). In 1918, with *Eminent Victorians*, Strachey provided an alternative.

Although Samuel Butler's *The Way of All Flesh* (1903) and Edmund Gosse's *Father and Son* (1907) are cited as forerunners, Strachey is generally credited with having articulated the goals and methodology of modern biography. He did so in his much-quoted preface to *Eminent Victorians*, where he rejected the clumsiness, the moral earnestness and awestruck hero-worship of Victorian biography. Strachey insisted that biography required literary skill, that even the greatest of subjects requires a great biographer in order to come alive. The great biographer, he argued, selects, limits, even interprets his data. He has, in other words, a method.

The assumptions Strachey was battling against stem in part, oddly enough, from Boswell's *Life of Johnson*, unanimously acclaimed as the masterpiece of English biography. Joseph Reed points out that Boswell was viewed condescendingly in the early nineteenth century; in response to Croker's 1831 edition of *The Life of Johnson*, Macaulay derided the author, while Lockhart suggested that Boswell was "unconscious of the facts he is narrating" (Reed 5–6). Even Strachey persists in denying Boswell artistic control and deliberation: "Boswell triumphed," he writes, "by dint of abandoning himself, through fifty years, to his instincts" (*Biographical Essays* 147). It was not until 1929, when Geoffrey Scott, editor of Boswell's private papers, described the care and artfulness with which Boswell worked, that he came to be seen as something other than a bumbling syco-phant who had, virtually by accident, produced the great-est English biography.

If an inept author can produce a biographical master-piece, the inevitable implication is that method is insignifi-cant compared to subject. Under such circumstances biog-raphy could scarcely be viewed as an art, nor could critics offer more than a judgment as to whether the subject was well or badly chosen, the data true or inaccurate.

Strachey's major contribution, then, was that, despite his view of Boswell, he forced readers to recognize an artful authorial presence in biography. His approach, though, had its opponents, of whom the most ferocious was Bernard DeVoto, whose 1933 "The Skeptical Biographer" lashed out at the new, literary biography. "God help the man who comes to Strachey ignorant and desirous of learning the truth," he declares, accusing him of deliberate inaccuracy for the sake of literary effects (182). He goes on to indict the use of psychoanalysis by biographers and lit-erary biography in general: "Literary people should not be permitted to write biography," he suggests. "The liter-ary mind may be adequately described as the mind least adapted to the utilization of fact" (181).

The literary biography attacked by DeVoto came to be called the "new biography." The term was the title of Vir-ginia Woolf's 1927 review of Harold Nicolson's *Some People* and has been used since by countless commentators to mean slightly different things: most generally, the wave of biographical experimentation in Europe during the nine-teen twenties and thirties; more specifically, the work of Strachey, Cecil, Nicolson and their followers.[1] *Some People*, a collection of essays on figures from the author's past, which mingled changed names and invented incidents with factual reportage, was not typical of what has come to be known as new biography, but it dealt with similar, now central questions about biographical method. The essays aim at capturing a particular mood or a person, generally prominent, out of the author's past, and for the most part include a reversal or surprise whereby the narrator's initial perception of the facts is revealed to be false. The effect is thus to indicate a psychological reality behind the apparent "facts" of history and experience. Woolf was critical of the work, but sympathetic to its aims: "Truth of fact and truth of fiction are incompatible," she writes, "yet [the biographer] is now more than ever urged to combine them. For it would seem that the life which is increasingly real to us is the fictitious life; it dwells in the personality rather than in the act" (*Granite* 155).

Representational schemata suited to the portrayal of acts, Woolf is suggesting, are no longer convincing, but the new schemata, those capable of evoking the *inner* life, have not yet been sufficiently absorbed by either writer or reader. Woolf uses the word *fictitious* here in rather a broad sense. Personality and fiction are equated in opposition to fact and action because the only way a writer can convey personality is through techniques associated with fiction: "arrangement, suggestion, dramatic effect" (155).

Once personality is seen as something not entirely manifest in action, it becomes a kind of artifact, something *made* as opposed to enacted, and in that sense, too, it is fiction. Aristotle had written that character is manifested and shaped by action; the new biography needed a new Aristotle to serve as its theoretical basis, for the relationship between character and action—as indicated by Conrad's *Lord Jim*, for example (published in 1900)—had by now become extremely problematic.

Even the relation of action to action was problematic. As Strachey points out, the writing of biography involves making connections, which involves using the imagination. In

Jean-Paul Sartre's 1938 novel *La Nausée*, Antoine Roquentin records his growing despair over his biography-in-progress of a man of action, the Marquis de Rollebon:

Je commence à croire qu'on ne peut jamais rien prouver. Ce sont des hypothèses honnêtes et qui rendent compte des faits: mais je sens si bien qu'elles viennent de moi, qu'elles sont tout simplement une manière d'unifier mes connaissances. Pas une lueur ne vient du côté de Rollebon. Lents, paresseux, maussades, les faits s'accommodent à la rigueur de l'ordre que je veux leur donner mais il leur reste extérieur. J'ai l'impression de faire un travail de pure imagination. (26)

The radical split he sees between matter and consciousness forces him first to discard the past as pure imagination; all that's real, he says, is the bundle of yellow papers covered with ink, not the story created there by his imagination. When he finally accepts his own consciousness, he discards the biography and decides to write a novel. The biographer complains unhappily when he writes, "Seulement ce n'était qu'une image à moi, une fiction," while the novelist can echo the same words cheerfully (139).

The Victorian biographer had no such dizzying sense of his own ability to create a life. Even the agnostics, according to A. O. J. Cockshut, read the "*evidence* of the life as if it were a novel and God were the novelist" (21). The Victorian biographer could borrow the life's unity—presumably intrinsic in a creation of God—announcing that his text's shape merely reflected the shape "found" in the life. For them there was no tension between the demands of art and of truth. As God's work, the great life incarnated their fusion. Take away God, and unless he is to produce a random accumulation of data, the Author must take his place. Three works, by Sidney Lee, Virginia Woolf, and André Maurois, indicate three attempts to come to terms with these issues. Woolf's "The New Biography," besides discussing Nicolson, decisively rejects the old methods, for her symbolized by Lee. Maurois's *Aspects of Biography* is very much a response to the dichotomy posed by Woolf in that essay between the "granite" of fact and the "rainbow" of personality.

In 1911, Sidney Lee, Leslie Stephen's replacement as editor of the *Dictionary of National Biography*, delivered the Leslie Stephen lecture at Cambridge. Published as *The Principles of Biography*, the lecture was the final and most sophisticated word of the late-Victorian biographers. Lee argues that the aim of biography is to "transmit personality" by describing the character of its subject as manifested in its exploits: "Character which does not translate itself into exploit," he writes, "is for the biographer a mere phantasm" (8, 9).

For Woolf, on the other hand, that "phantasm" is precisely what personality is:

> "The aim of biography," said Sir Sydney [sic] Lee, who had perhaps read and written more lives than any man of his time, "is the truthful transmission of personality," and no single sentence could more neatly split up into two parts the whole problem of biography as it presents itself to us to-day. On the one hand there is truth; on the other there is personality. (*Granite* 149)

Lee's refusal to recognize as real any element in personality that exists apart from its enactment in deeds spares him the essential problematic of biographical writing—and according to Woolf, makes his biographies hopelessly dull, because though his books "are stuffed with truth, he failed to choose those truths which transmit personality" (149–50). Nor does Lee find the detection of facts or their conversion into language difficult; the biographer, he writes in *Principles*, "submits [his subjects] to minute examination, and his record of observation becomes a mirror of their exploits and character from the cradle to the grave" (27).

Seventeen years after Lee's *Principles*, André Maurois,

the French writer known as a Stracheyan and new biographer, delivered six lectures, also at Cambridge, published as *Aspects of Biography*. The title was chosen to recall Forster's *Aspects of the Novel*, which had grown out of
the same lecture series the previous year. Maurois's aim,
clearly, was to establish the characteristics of a "modern"
biography, as Forster had for the novel. Working from the
Forsterian assumption that personality is like an iceberg,
with the greater part submerged, he establishes as the goal
of a new biography the depiction of just that phantasm dismissed by Lee and described as ungraspable by Woolf. Ad-
mitting the plausibility of Woolf's granite/rainbow dichotomy, he insists that reconciliation is possible. To support
his view, Maurois questions the graniteness of truth: "It
is impossible, in history, to arrive at scientific truth," he
writes (100). Even documents are not trustworthy, and different witnesses arrive at widely varying conclusions (83).
Also accommodating the reconciliation of external and internal view of the subject is the common human tendency
to invent and live out an artificially coherent self. Especially a prominent person, he points out, will simplify himself to suit his role: "Unconsciously he aims at making his
life a work of art" (55).

The granite, then, is itself suffused with rainbow (the element of subjectivity, and uncertainty accompanying "facts")
while the rainbow may itself be fortified by granite (the deliberate effort to be what circumstance demands). The biographer achieves knowledge of this mixture through
identification with his subject; to a certain extent, according to Maurois, biography is "autobiography disguised"
(125). At the heart of the biographer's task is intuition: "We
cannot understand a human being by an exhaustive compilation of detail. . . . We get our understanding by a coup
d'état" (133).

Lee and Leslie Stephen represent the most progressive
of Victorian biographers: like their heirs they argue for
concision, for skill, for honesty. It is in their treatment of

human personality that they were judged by those who followed to have failed most abysmally. In search of psychologically complex models, Maurois turns away from biography altogether, to Proust and Dostoievsky, who revealed the multiplicity and terrific energy within the self.

In exploring this rejection of Victorian biography, it is easy to exaggerate the contrast between nineteenth- and twentieth-century conceptions of life-writing. In fact, there are important continuities linking the two centuries, but these are continuities more evident to later generations than to those still in revolt against their immediate predecessors. In large part Strachey and his followers applied to biography the insights already evident in the great Victorian autobiographies and essays: insights into the complex relation between the past and our memory of it, between the environment and our own psyches, between history and imagination. Carlyle's 1830 essay "On History" suggests the arbitrariness of clock time (as opposed to experienced time), the unrecordability of change, the conflict between "linear" narrative and "solid" action, and past overemphasis on wars as historical subject matter—all issues taken up by Virginia Woolf nearly a century later (*Critical Essays* 2: 83–95). Pater's "The Child in the House" portrays the impact of sense perception on a developing mind much as Woolf does in her depictions of Orlando, of Roger Fry, and of herself. His *Imaginary Portraits,* in which he places individuals at crucial historical moments, clearly anticipates Nicolson's *Some People* and Woolf's *Orlando.* Browning's *The Ring and the Book,* with its variant versions of an uncertain "truth," produces a sense of mystery and tension redolent of A. J. A. Symons's *Quest for Corvo.* "How one organicizes empirical knowledge," William Buckler argues in *The Victorian Imagination,* a process which mingles "epistemology and imagination," was a central concern of Victorian literature as it was of post-Victorian biography (22).

Complicating matters is a transitional movement intervening between "Victorianism" and its detractors: Samuel

Butler (1835–1902); Leslie Stephen (1832–1904); then, a generation younger, Edmund Gosse (1849–1928) and, even younger, Sidney Lee (1859–1926). Butler and Gosse were, with qualifications, embraced by post-Strachey biographers as demolishers of Victorian myths, while Stephen and Lee, though equally iconoclastic in their way, stood for outdated methodology. When Woolf first described the new biography, she chose Sidney Lee, her father's successor, to represent the old, yet he and Stephen before him had both insisted, as Strachey was to do in 1918, that biography should "again be considered as a work of art" (Stephen, *Men* 143). There are those who argue Stephen directly influenced Strachey's style (Rosenbaum, "Edu-cated" 49), and that Woolf was herself in many ways "Vic-torian" (Lyndall Gordon 12).

What integrity, then, does the time period finally have? Certainly there was a wave of controversy and innovation sweeping Europe between the wars. It included France, where Maurois wrote biographies of Shelley and Disraeli, and Germany, where Emil Ludwig dismissed academic his-tory as pedantry in his *Die Kunst der Biographie*. Theoretical issues raised were closely related to those generally asso-ciated with literary modernism—formulated by David Daiches as a newly uncomfortable relation between writer and audience; a new idea of time; and a new idea of con-sciousness (814). A. A. Mendilow, in *Time and the Novel*, ar-gues that in the modern novel, life becomes a "sequence of non-causal impressions," unsuited to an Aristotelian con-cept of plot (8). His conclusion, that "more importance is being attached to what the characters think and how they think, less and less to what they do," serves equally well to describe modernistic biography (202).

There are continuities between any two periods of liter-ary history. It is more useful, though, in studying biogra-phy, to begin by understanding the contrasts, for it was on this contrast that the post-Victorian experimenters based their identity and aims. And the contrasts are there. Leslie

Introduction

Stephen felt biography should be an art, but his idea of art differed from his daughter's; Carlyle recognized the existence of a complex inner life in *The Life of John Sterling*, but he declined to explore it. From Strachey on, biography is aestheticized and psychologized. How this tendency affects its narrative structure is the subject of this book.

In choosing my subjects, I have limited myself to England and to the more literary of those experimenting with biography: to those who were most likely to take seriously the representational problems posed by modern notions of narration, selfhood, and time. I have therefore been particularly interested in those who were also novelists and theoreticians. Those who saw themselves merely as historians or polemicists and their task as the straightforward representation of the truth have been excluded. Given an era of changing characterizational schemata and a generation of biographers intensely aware of their artistic freedom, I have asked myself, what are the variations on traditional biographical narration that will emerge? While including in my discussion a broader range of experimental methods than a strict understanding of "new biography" would permit, I have omitted those who refused to claim their freedom at all and those for whom (as Paul Fussell writes in *Abroad*), "the dimension of delight in language and disposition, in all the literary contrivances, isn't there" (197). Finally, for reasons of time and space, I have not dealt for the most part with the biographical essay, a fertile subject in itself.

The narrative variations produced by biographical experimenters have fallen into three general categories: novelistic, mediated, and psychosociological. In novelistic biography (Leon Edel's term), the narrator is virtually omniscient and the subjects' inner lives are open to scrutiny, their motives depicted and interpreted (*Literary Biography* 82). In mediated biography, the biographer's own perceptions are dramatized, the narrator's insight limited by his own particular viewpoint; influenced by post-Jamesian theory, mediated biographers dramatize their relation to their material, so that the biography unrolls in their perceptions, much as Strether's experiences in *The Ambassadors* are depicted through his consciousness of them. Finally, in psychosociobiography, the narrator's voice is suppressed, and narrative, subject, and environment seem a continuous web of texts, bound less by causal chains than by rhythmic recurrences.[2] One of the most overlooked yet strongest forces altering biography during this time was the effort of women to establish themselves as the authors and subjects of historical and biographical writing. Woolf's contribution to biographical theory was on a much larger scale than her rejection of Lee, or her description of granite and rainbow. She recognized the huge impact biographies have on the construal of reality, and she bemoaned the absence of women from the biographical record. She links the faulty depiction of character to imperialism, to patriarchy, and to war. Those who follow her seek, as she did in *Roger Fry*, to depict the self without exalting egotism, without asserting an exaggerated narrative authority, without simplifying the complex rhythms of a life.

Novelistic biography as I define it has much in common with "new biography," but is by no means synonymous with it; I use "novelistic" to designate a type of biography, "new biography" to designate an historical phenomenon. All three categories define themselves against the massive compilations of the nineteenth century, their air of moral authority, their emphasis on outward achievement. All three suggest greater equality in the stature of subject and author. There is less concern with the subject's discovery of a vocation and no sense that the life has been divinely shaped. For the novelistic biographer, the shape is there, but imposed by the narrator; for the mediated, the shape is deliberately created by the subject in relation to others; for the psychosociological, the shape emerges only out of the larger picture of transpersonal influences. But for none of these writers is the coherence of the life they depict a given, a divine plan lived out by the subject and glossed by the biographer.

To find a way of talking about biography analytically, I have turned to theoretical discussions of autobiography, biography, history, and fiction. While past writing on biography has, for the most part, overlooked the broad range of choices faced by the nonfiction writer, autobiography has received a tremendous amount of critical attention, particularly in the last decade. To a certain extent, similar issues are involved. Roy Pascal's *Design and Truth in Autobiography*, for example, serves much the same critical purpose as A. O. J. Cockshut's *Truth to Life* in putting aside questions of factual accuracy for discussion of artistic strategies. But the major commentators of recent years—among them Olney, Starobinski, Spengemann, and Fleishman—all tend to rely on one of two premises, both irrelevant to biography: the autobiographer's characteristically double role as narrator and subject, and his frequent use of St. Augustine's *Confessions* as paradigm.[3] Olney's emphasis on the "isolated uniqueness" of personal experience is typical. While for the autobiographer this uniqueness provides substance and motivation, for the biographer it provides only a problem: an insuperable barrier between his own subjectivity and his ostensibly objective story. While suggestive then, recent commentary on autobiography is by no means definitive for the critic of biography, who may conclude with Cockshut that "The difference between biography and autobiography is fundamental" (195).

Until recently, biographical commentary has lacked the critical sophistication characteristic of these autobiographical studies. Book-length works on biography have tended to be either all-inclusive historical overviews or anecdotal discussions of problems faced by the biographer.[4] Only a few published works gather together, as I do, a group of contemporaneous biographies and examine their common elements. Joseph W. Reed Jr.'s *English Biography in the Early Nineteenth Century* and Dennis Petrie's *Ultimately Fiction: De-*

sign in *Modern American Literary Biography* deal, obviously, with different eras. Mark Longaker's *Contemporary Biogra-phy* itself emerges from the period under discussion: pub-lished in 1934, it provides a chapter apiece on Strachey, Gamaliel Bradford, Maurois, Ludwig, Guedalla, and Hi-laire Belloc. By spreading his attention among four differ-ent countries, however, and accepting uncritically his sub-jects' theoretical explanations rather than reading their biographies closely, Longaker fails to move beyond de-scription to analysis.

A. O. J. Cockshut's *Truth to Life*, on the other hand, con-sisting of in-depth discussion of six Victorian biographies, provides me with a precedent and a valuable backdrop against which to define a characteristically modern biogra-phy. He himself disowns the task of providing a sequel, suggesting that the period from 1900 on lacks "a common frame of reference" (16). On this particular point, I dis-agree; a common frame of reference does emerge—one suggested as early as 1957, when Leon Edel, in *Literary Bi-ography*, singled out major twentieth-century biographers for notice, classified biographies according to their struc-ture, and analyzed, brilliantly, Woolf's *Orlando* as a "fable for biographers."

Since the 1974 publication of *Truth to Life*, there has been increasing agreement that the narrative and rhetori-cal strategies of biography are discussable. Ira Nadel, in his 1984 *Biography: Fiction, Fact and Form*, proposes the analy-sis of tropes, narrative strategy, and "personal myth" (151). Insisting that "language and modes of narrative, not con-tent, structure a biography," Nadel provides support for the treatment of biography as literature (9).[5] Recent essays by James Clifford *fils* (son of the author of *From Puzzles to Portraits*), Park Honan, and William Epstein also insist on treating biography analytically, though from widely vary-ing critical viewpoints.

The discussion of biography in literary terms is based on the assumption that historical data, no matter how well

Introduction

supported by documents, do not dictate their own self-evident shape and language, and that therefore it is useful to discuss the shape and language in which they are presented. The point has long been made and argued by philosophers of history. R. G. Collingwood, for example, though he sharply differentiates between history and biography because the bounds of biography are determined by the natural processes of birth and death rather than thought, discusses evidence and coherence in terms relevant to biography (304). In *The Idea of History*, Collingwood insists not only that "the historian's picture of his subject . . . appears as a web of imaginative construction between certain fixed points," but that the fixed points are themselves the result of critical thought; there is in history no such thing as pure data (242–43). As a result, the "historian's picture of the past is . . . in every detail an imaginary picture" (245). Novelistic and historical writing resemble each other, he concludes. But they are not the same thing, for history must be written in relation to evidence. This evidence may be unverifiable in an absolute sense, but the historian's task is to ask not whether a fact is true or false, but what it means (275).

Collingwood thus provides an excellent case for the reading of biography as literature; as an "imaginative picture," it will bear the same mark as fiction of personal vision and style. But the question then arises, Why discuss biography, or even history, as a genre separate from fiction? Mark Weinstein has criticized Collingwood's distinction between history and fiction as insufficient (267), and numerous later attempts at formulating the difference have left unsettled the question of whether history is not, in Petrie's words, "ultimately fiction."

The critic of biography must read it, in many ways, as if it were indeed fiction, attentive to stylistic, narrative, and even thematic choices, aware above all that these are choices and not givens. But she must also read it differently. For if there are many fuzzy boundaries on the history-fiction spectrum and few distinctions intrinsic to one category or the other, there is a vastly different extratextual relation- ship between the biographical/historical writer and his ma- terial and audience.

Paul Ricoeur, listing the various elements of historical writing that preclude objectivity (choice of what's impor- tant; decisions about causality; the author's distance from his subject in time and as a separate human being) insists nonetheless that historical subjectivity is not "adrift," but bound by ethical if not logical considerations (31).[6] Biogra- phy gains the trust of its readers quite differently from fic- tion; if disbelieved, the biographer risks ignominy or pros- ecution. His narrative persona is differently presented and differently understood; as Paul Hernadi points out, "the historian endorses the narrator's credibility to the point of turning the ontological distinction between the author and narrator of fiction as creator and creature into the psycho- logical distinction between the historian's actual persona and the person he would like to be or at least appear" ("Clio's Cousins," 252).

The ethical, legal, and psychological context in which bi- ography is read places peculiar pressure on its practition- ers. When they do borrow new techniques and conceptual- izations from modern fiction, they do so self-consciously, often thematizing within the text their own difficulties as biographers. They tend to strain against the tradition within which they work and against their readers' expecta- tions. The strain is increased by the tendency of modernist fiction to challenge precisely those narrative and charac- terizational assumptions that novelists had traditionally borrowed from nonfiction: the pretense, that is, that nar- rator and author are the same, that the narrator knows the "truth," and that he expects to be believed. "Modern art," writes Lionel Gossman, "radically challenges the artistic ideals from which the general historian draws his inspira- tion" (26). Modernist biography, then, is an extremely paradoxical notion, seeming to reject all that would distinguish it as what it pretends to be. No wonder it met with anger, disbelief and controversy, followed by neglect. But for all its paradoxicality, it remains a clearly distinguishable entity.

If it retains its generic independence, biography is nonetheless read most revealingly in the light of a feature shared by biography, history, and fiction alike: their narrativity. It is for this reason that my categories reflect an author's choice of narrative strategy, while chapter headings generally suggest the relationship between that choice and the author's conception of the self. I have assumed that experimental biographies can be read as stories emerging from a peculiarly intense and contradictory narrative situation. I have asked of them how that situation has affected their narrative structure and thematic emphasis. In what relation does the narrator stand to his story? What assumptions has he made regarding the interaction of consciousness and time? What aspects of his subject's life or imagination attract his attention? How does the biographer depict his own quandaries within the text?

In the process, I have found that biographers working between 1918 and 1939 shared some common concerns, most notably the impact of Freud and modernist fiction. They also, to a large extent, responded to their predecessors and each other: the earliest Georgian effort, as indicated by *Eminent Victorians,* was to dismantle Victorian tropes; Strachey and his followers were then free to investigate the implications of their new narrative self-consciousness. Paralleling the novelistic response was the dramatizing of the narrative act itself by the mediated biographers. Woolf's association of referential narration as traditionally conceived with patriarchy and imperialism was followed by a further drive to destabilize the relation of text to reality, leading to a perception of the life as an intersection of texts which determine, as much as they are determined by, biographical events. Throughout I seek to discover how each writer's attitude to biography as a genre shapes his treatment of the life, and how, in responding to the pressures of modernism, each writer looks to modern fiction for new representational strategies.

II

The Revolt against Victorianism

"We smile to-day at our Victorians," Harold Nicolson writes at the start of his 1923 biography of Tennyson (1). This bold and immediate assumption that writer and reader share the same condescending attitude toward the subject reveals just how pervasive anti-Victorianism had become. Anger apparently was no longer necessary: the Victorians are no longer a "them" opposing "us," but "ours." With that bold first sentence, Nicolson appropriates not only a Victorian hero, but a Victorian genre as well. That he can put biography here to so deflating a purpose is due in part to three books: Samuel Butler's *The Way of All Flesh,* Edmund Gosse's *Father and Son,* and Lytton Strachey's *Eminent Victorians:* an autobiographical novel, an autobiographical biography, and a collection of four brief biographies.[1]

Both Butler and Gosse depict an authoritarian father who justifies his dominance by asserting his own disinterest and his intimacy with God. But in the eyes of the son, the authority is based either on hypocrisy or self-delusion, since the father seems ignorant of the very nature of reality, as well as of his own actual motivations. The son exposes the father by subjecting his supposedly pure intentions and free will to strenuous examination. His weapons are force of circumstance, ulterior motivation, and hereditary tendencies, for all compromise the freedom of the will. Eager to dismantle the pretenses of his

21

eminent Victorians in a similar way, Strachey, following Butler, aligned himself with empiricism and eighteenth-century skepticism. "Je n'impose rien; je ne propose rien; j'expose," he concludes in his preface to *Eminent Victorians*, arguing that to tell the facts truthfully is all he intends (ix). E. M. Forster, in his 1920 essay "Notes on English Character," describes the English in terms that echo Butler and Strachey. The English, he writes, are "the people who have built up an Empire with a Bible in one hand, a pistol in the other, and financial concessions in both pockets" (*Abinger Harvest* 11). This "muddle-headedness," attacked less generously as hypocrisy by Butler and Strachey and viewed by many as typical of Victorianism, had been facilitated by biographies that accepted their subjects' own view of them-selves and had come, finally, in the eyes of the new biog-raphers—particularly of Strachey—to represent the Vic-torian era as a whole. Thomas Arnold punishing boys for their own "good," Manning becoming a Catholic for the good of his "soul," England intervening in Africa for the Arabs' "good," if described only through letters and overt actions, will appear justified, without the ironizing quota-tion marks. Only a new kind of biography, one that goes behind the subject's self-concept, would be sufficient to expose what William Gerhardie, a novelist admired by Strachey, calls the uniquely English talent for "accumulat-ing social and material stock with both eyes glued reso-lutely—and, what is more remarkable, sincerely—on eter-nal values . . ." (29).

A great deal of what the Georgians objected to in "their" Victorians was their lack of self-knowledge, as revealed by the very sincerity with which they managed to make the best of both spiritual and material worlds, ignoring the un-comfortable implications of either their religiosity or their ambition. When they should have looked inward, they looked to others, proselytizing when they should have been questioning. Thus Nicolson's complaint about Ten-nyson is that he became with time more prophet than poet, choosing to assert a shallow intellect when his talent was for lyricism (5). Five years later Hugh Kingsmill writes of Matthew Arnold in identical terms: "The theme of this book is the collapse of a poet into a prophet" (2). And Herbert Read writes of the nineteenth-century confusion by which "Poets were made prophets, and willy-nilly out of their verse a gospel was extracted" (26).

The emphasis on prophecy, according to the Georgians, led Victorian narrators to affect impersonality if not invisibility to give their utterances an air of objective truth. Arnold in particular, suggests Kingsmill, had a tendency to leave himself entirely out of the picture. "The critic's business," Arnold argued, according to Kingsmill, "is to get himself completely out of the way, to lay the actual facts before the reader, and leave it to the reader to form his own conclusions" (2). So also was the traditional biographer's. But Kingsmill argues that the goal of self-suppression is a ruse—one that only biography can expose, and that will necessarily transform biography as it is exposed. Arnoldian self-suppression, Kingsmill writes,

> sounds modest, until we ask on what grounds Arnold assumes himself to be in possession of the actual facts. It then becomes clear that Arnold's desire to vanish into a cavern, from which his voice will presently emerge with the authority of something abstract and impersonal, is due not to modesty but to prudence. The omniscient like a certain distance between themselves and their audience. (2–3)

The best way to attack this pretense of disinterested omniscience is clearly biography, which reveals the particular and inevitably limiting circumstances out of which the prophetic voice arises. The biographer enters the prophet's cavern with a flashlight, and the resultant vision belies the voice.

Kingsmill's complaint is central to Strachey's *Eminent Victorians* and to the new biographies that followed. The crime of the Victorians as perpetuated by their biographers was that their tremendous authority had been based on self-delusion—but on self-delusion so pervasively shared that it worked. "General advisers to the universe are usually at a loss in front of the easiest problems in their own lives," Kingsmill writes of Arnold (80), but they have a frustrating tendency not to notice and to get along perfectly well nonetheless. Eventually, though, somebody pays the price of that self-delusion: Butler's Ernest Pontifex, Gosse's Son, Strachey's Arabs.

All the figures in *Eminent Victorians* locate themselves in relation to spiritual, wholly selfless aims. These higher aims legitimate their authority without challenging it—a paradox made even more paradoxical by the intrinsic un-reality of the view of human nature presupposed by the aims themselves. This delusory higher authority allows the eminent to insist on their own selflessness while achieving their egotistic ambitions. The initial task of the new biog-raphers, then, is to expose this double paradox of the de-lusory belief that works and the selflessness that empowers. But skepticism has its limits, as Mark Rutherford, an earlier skeptic, discovered: "'The older I got,' he writes in William Hale White's fictional autobiography, another late nineteenth-century expression of revolt, "the less I ap-peared to believe. Nakeder and nakeder had I become with the passage of every year, and I trembled to anticipate the complete emptiness to which before long I should be reduced" (84). The disbeliever in free will leaves little room for originality and artistic creation. If Strachey's first impulse, in *Eminent Victorians*, was to expose as a sham the Victorian notion of will by explaining, with a vengeance, the actual reasons for things, his second impulse (and that of his followers) was to invite a reclamation not of will but of imagination. The new biographers—or, more correctly in this context, the novelistic biographers—continued to insist on the predetermined element in their subjects' fail-ures, on a self-destructive pattern played out again and again, on a persistently dual self belying the subject's pretense of unity. But they also suggest that the tragedy is not inevitable, that it derived from a failure of the imagination, a failure to recognize the extent to which the self is self-created, even if the raw material of circumstance, psyche, and heredity is not. The novelistic biographers' reclamation of imagination will be the subject of chapter 3. Here I want merely to explore their initial rejection of Victorian biography and their use of explanation and empiricism to dismantle the Victorian versions of will and achievement.

> I am well aware that in these days Hero-worship, the thing I call Hero-worship, professes to have gone out, and finally ceased. This . . . is an age that as it were denies the existence of great men; denies the desirableness of great men. Show our critics a great man, a Luther for example, they begin to what they call "account" for him . . . (Carlyle, *On Heroes* 12).

Thus Thomas Carlyle in 1840 bemoaned the tendency of historians to emphasize heredity, environment, and historical circumstance at the expense of individual greatness. History, he argues, in *On Heroes, Hero Worship, and the Heroic in History*, is "the Biography of Great Men," and hero-worship, "the life-breath of all society" (12–13). Carlyle was not long in an adversary position, however: "In the fifty years after 1830," Walter Houghton writes, "the worship of the hero was a major factor in English culture" (310).[2]

Historians of biography have pointed out that the Victorian love of biography—and particularly laudatory, commemorative biography—was in part a response to the threateningly impersonal natural forces posited by Darwinism (Altick 86). In *The Victorian Frame of Mind* Houghton writes in addition of a general sense of spiritual dislocation and political uncertainty that encouraged hero-worship and led Victorian writers like Carlyle, Kingsley, and Tennyson to describe men of towering stature, providing at once an escape into a grander world and a model for imitation (340). Tennyson's "Ulysses," then, could be read as a response to the pain of "In Memoriam":

> Are God and Nature then at strife,
> That Nature lends such evil dreams?
> So careful of the type she seems,
> So careless of the single life.

And Matthew Arnold, according to Houghton, who complains in "The Scholar-Gypsy," of "this strange disease of modern life," in "Rugby Chapel" thanks his father (one of Strachey's "Eminent Victorians") for inspiring him with recognition of individual greatness: "Through thee I believe/In the novel and great who are gone," he writes (339). Besides Darwinism and general despair, there were the remnants of eighteenth-century philosophy, with its tendency to "account" for greatness rather than worship it, oppressing the nineteenth-century sense of human potential. "... The doctrine of what is called Philosophical Necessity," John Stuart Mill writes in his *Autobiography*, "weighed on my existence like an incubus" (175). He longs to escape his father's conception of character as wholly formed by circumstance, which has forced on him a depressing sense of his own helplessness. As he drifts closer to the views of John Sterling, Frederick Maurice, and even Carlyle, he reformulates his father's doctrine to allow more room for individual effort:

> I saw that though our character is formed by circumstances, our own desires can do much to shape those circumstances; and that what is really inspiriting and ennobling in the doctrine of freewill, is the conviction that we have real power over the formation of our own character; that our will, by influencing some of our circumstances, can modify our future habits or capabilities of willing. (177)

26

The key word is *will:* Ulysses has it, Arnold seeks it, Mill discovers it, and Carlyle praises it.

Life, for Carlyle, is a "chivalrous battlefield" on which men are judged according to their effort at self-assertion (*Sterling* 52). His metaphors are insistently military, for the task of man is to engage as fully as possible in the struggle to establish himself—his work and personality—against the flux of his environment. In Samuel Johnson, he writes, for example, "lay the true spirit of a Soldier," and his life was "the victorious Battle of a free, true Man" (*Critical Essays* 3: 120). Thomas Huxley, in his 1894 essay "Evolution and Ethics," describes life as a "Sisyphean process" and the ethical progress of society as a "combat" with the forces of nature (48). Suitably, he concludes his essay by quoting the final lines of Tennyson's "Ulysses." The portrayal of this struggle is *the* subject of nineteenth-century biography, as Carlyle demonstrates in *The Life of John Sterling* and argues in his essay "Biography," where he writes of the importance of understanding "how, in short, the perennial Battle went, which men name Life, which we also in these new days, with indifferent fortune, have to fight, and must bequeath to our sons and grandsons to go on fighting . . ." (*Critical Essays* 3: 47).

This does not mean the Victorians were unaware of a further, mysterious element in the human psyche. But as Paul Kendall points out, their insight into psychology was limited by their assumptions about life (106). In his *Life of John Sterling*, Carlyle recognizes the existence of introspection and self-doubt, but he lacks the conceptual framework that would allow him to explore them, and most of all, he does not find them worthy of exploration. Psychological problems are to be conquered, not analyzed. George Landow has written of the Victorian dislike of introspection for its own sake; personal insights were to serve, above all, public purposes (xiv). Sterling's great achievement, in Carlyle's view, was that despite ill-health and doubts he was a "victorious believer," and under great difficulties a vic-torious doer" (6).

In *Truth to Life*, A. O. J. Cockshut writes of this charac-teristically Victorian respect for willed action, pointing out that the result is biography favoring the latter part of its subject's life, when outward achievement and inner life are presumably at their most consonant (17). The heavy dependence of Victorian biography on letters and docu-ments, he points out, similarly assumes that manifest and inner selves coincide, that intention moves smoothly from willed to completed action.

The biographer, then, described primarily the outward events of a man's life. If he recognized the existence of an inner life, as Stephen does in his 1893 essay "Biography," he denied his ability to present it, or dismissed it, as does Lee, as mere phantasm. He wrote from a fixed moral standpoint while nonetheless aspiring to narrative unob-trusiveness.[3] The biographical plot emphasized chronologi-cal development, as it portrayed its subject's progressive self-differentiation, and its focal point was the discovery and pursuit of vocation. "How was this conjured spirit to find occupation?" Stephen asks of Swift (12), and Carlyle's John Sterling wonders, "How unfold one's little bit of tal-ent; and live, and not be sleeping, while it is called Today?" (121). While both admit the possibility of confusion and self-deception, they assume that at bottom lies a path to-ward self-realization, if only one discerns it properly. Di-vine plan and evolutionary struggle alike posit a given life-course which man has only to discover and fulfill.

Commentators have tended to dismiss as hagiography the biography that grew out of this view of life. Lytton Strachey ridicules those "two fat volumes," and John Gar-raty writes in *The Nature of Biography* of a "regressive re-turn to panegyric" during the Victorian Age (98). Robert Gittings detects only three exceptions to the Victorian rule of moralism and concealment, in the works of Carlyle, Elizabeth Gaskell, and James Anthony Froude (35–36). Of these, the latter two aroused storms of protest by their frankness. Certainly, though, Carlyle on Sterling is brief and insightful; Froude on Carlyle is lively and even ironic; Stephen's biographies for the English Men of Letters series are concise and direct; even debunking was not solely a post-Victorian prerogative. Victorian biography was heavily censored by survivors and often ridiculously circumspect, but it was Carlyle who raged against its "mealy mouth" (*Critical Essays* 4: 29).

Nineteenth-century biography, then, was a more various form than twentieth-century critics have tended to allow. But just as Mill had felt crushed by his father's view of man's position in the world, the Georgians found the Victorian admiration for action and will and the Great Man a heavy burden to bear. "Veneration of great men is perennial in the nature of man," according to Carlyle (*Critical Essays* 4: 24), but Virginia Woolf suggests that such veneration exacts a price. In *Night and Day,* whose heroine helps research a biography of her grandfather (paralleling Woolf's own assistance of Frederick Maitland with his biography of her father), Woolf writes, "The glorious past, in which men and women grew to unexampled size, intruded too much upon the present, and dwarfed it too consistently, to be altogether encouraging to one forced to make her experiment in living when the great age was dead" (39). A similar view is voiced by Sidney Lee of Woolf's father: "Stephen belonged to a notable generation," he writes in *Principles of Biography,* "a generation the heroes of which seem to have been cast in a larger mould than those of my own" (3). The genre most suited to the expression of this view—that great men are more than human, defined not by circumstance, but by some spark of divine fire that they express through the exercise of gigantic wills—was the traditional biography, massive, adulatory, "objective."

Biography borrowed its structure from the life it portrayed. In affirming its own unity and coherence, it af-

firmed also that of its subject. The genre's drama was precisely this testing of unity: did the subject stand up to
scrutiny? Did the life support the work? Did the content of
the biography, in other words, justify its inception? These
are the questions implicit at the start of Froude's life of
Carlyle (published in four volumes, in 1882 and 1884), a
work which gains its power from the intensity of the testing, while affirming from the start that the answer to all
these questions is yes. "Such faults as these," he writes, ad-
mitting his subject's flaws at the start of *Life in London* 1
"were but as the vapours which hang about a mountain,
inseparable from the nature of the man" (5). The same nature, he writes, operated in both life and work.

The word *nature* is important here; it appears again and
again to designate what Gosse tended to call *temperament*
and Woolf, *personality*. It suggests the vastness of the self
and its consonance with vast forces. It provides, in its suggestion of the world of nature, a reservoir of metaphors to
explain and transcend the duality that Froude was forced
to concede. For there was, according to Froude, a gap between Carlyle's knowledge of himself and his knowledge of
the world; a gap between private pettiness and public grandeur, between his intentions and his actual behavior. Into
this gap creep flickerings of irony foreshadowing Strachey,[4]
even a touch of Stracheyan *style indirecte libre*: Jane, he writes
of Carlyle's wife, "could not hide from herself that he was
selfish—extremely selfish" (*First Forty Years* 276). But Carlyle's lack of self-knowledge is linked to his great powers, the
forces in him he can't understand (*First Forty Years* 39, 290),
but that blossom into greatness. His split soul, torn between
heaven and hell (*In London* 1: 277), is transposed into the
natural, unitary metaphor of mountain-peak (high but
craggy [*First Forty Years* 286]), diamond (beautiful but hard
[*First Forty Years* 147]), vapour about a mountain or a fire
with sparks (*In London* 1: 5), a flower with thorns (*In London* 1: 150)—even Christ, whose laurel wreath is also a

crown of thorns (*In London* 1: 62). Always Carlyle's divid-
edness, then, is seen in the context of the larger unity of
his genius, which is itself continuous with pervasive natural forces, even with an overarching, divine scheme of
salvation.

Froude's Carlyle has a Faustian quality, and like *Faust,*
the biography is part Greek tragedy, part romance.[5] Before the domestic Carlyle, the biographer as Greek chorus
(*First Forty Years* 231) shakes his head ominously (283) and
compares the marriage to the sacrifice of Iphigenia at
Aulis: victory followed, but there was a victim (299). No
Greek fate, but Providence rules the professional Carlyle,
however, and for this figure his biographer has nothing
but wonder. Cockshut argues in *Truth to Life* that Froude's
divided view was motivated by his discipleship; wanting to
see the public Carlyle as perfect, he relegates all his flaws to
his private life (149). The overall effect, though, of what
Cockshut calls Froude's dialectical method is not conflict
but synthesis. As in *Faust,* the tragedy ends in redemption,
the ascension of the flawed man into "the hearts of all
to whom truth is the dearest of possessions" (*In London*
2: 406).

That Froude allowed himself to criticize Carlyle, then,
and the fury he thus aroused against himself, are not alone
evidence of the work's modernity. Certainly, there is, in the
book's concern with self-knowledge, a hint of things to
come. But flawed self-knowledge is seen, finally, not as a
fissure in the self, but as a kind of halo, emanating from a
divine spark. Cockshut's description of the critical difference between nineteenth- and twentieth-century biography
is relevant here: "There is, almost always," he writes, "a further idea present, sometimes overtly expressed, sometimes
vaguely adumbrated, of spiritual formation by forces beyond man's control, and indeed beyond his full understanding" (21). Such an assumption allowed the biographer to turn away from contradictions and posit their

solution on a divine plane, paralleled in his own work by redemptive metaphors. The flaw or conflict becomes evidence not of human weakness but of a titanic destiny.

Edmund Gosse's initial biography of his father, *The Naturalist of the Seashore* (1890), is similar in some ways to Froude's life of Carlyle. It, too, tests the unity of his father's life and with it the integrity of his own biographic enterprise, and finds coherence, despite evidence to the contrary. Like Froude's Carlyle, Gosse's father does not know himself, but is redeemed by the mystery and force of his vocation, which comes to him less through the influence of his aunt and cousin (also collectors of specimens), than through the intercession of a great white bird:

At the age of four, the instinct of the future naturalist was first aroused, as in later years he was fond of repeating, by a vision which imprinted itself upon his memory with perfect clearness. Being alone in Springwell Fields, from amidst the tall ripening wheat he saw rise, close to the footpath, and within a few yards of him, a large white grallatorial bird . . . (10–11).

But Gosse is no disciple of his father, as he indicates by interjecting into the bird story a distancing phrase, "he was fond of repeating." To his father's story of divinely sent vocation, immunity to circumstance, lack of social relations, and direct relation to God, Gosse appends a negative subtext, the story of what his father lacked: maturation by experience, friendship, the intellectual discovery offered by Darwinism, and self-awareness. "It must be said," he writes, "that he was never a very subtle judge of man, and always a very bad critic of himself" (44). The flaw that Froude more than forgave Carlyle is here more problematic, and in *Father and Son* will be a source of great bitterness, for in not knowing himself, Philip Gosse fails even more seriously to know his son. It is the accusation Virginia Woolf will bring against her father in "A Sketch of the Past" and that Strachey will hurl against Carlyle in *Portraits in Miniature*. It is the means by which the Georgians will shatter their forebears' pretense of titanic scale and integrity, for they need only find physical or psychological mechanisms underlying ostensibly freely willed or spiritually dictated behavior, and the meaning their subjects attributed to their own lives evaporates. When Philip Gosse sees visions and is racked by religious agony, Edmund detects malaria, and if pathos still prevents ridicule, nonetheless the potential for *Eminent Victorians* is there in embryo: "His diary is full of self-upbraidings, penitential cries, vows of greater watchfulness in the future; and it is downright pathetic to read these effusions, and to know that it was quinine that the poor soul wanted in its innocent darkness" (114–15).

In *Father and Son*, an autobiographical and artful rewriting of the earlier biography, Gosse ventures further in his filial revolt, following in the footsteps of Butler's *The Way of All Flesh*. Both works are frequently cited as Strachey's precursors, and both reject the father's authority along with the father's sense of who he is on the grounds that what he said differed from what really was. Empirical reality becomes a weapon against paternal authority.

Where the Victorians reacted, via biography and hero-worship, against Darwinism and its implied belittlement of human achievement, these two works embrace evolutionary concepts, painting their heroes as survivors at the expense of their fathers. Both suggest that there is more to life than what is consciously willed—not in the Victorian sense of divine mysteries, but in the pre-Freudian sense of instincts and innate characteristics. Nor do they, like Carlyle in his *Life of Sterling*, recognize an unknown psychic realm only to do battle with it. Instead they embrace it, recognizing it as an ally against the encroaching power of the father. Corresponding to Gosse's "inner self" refusing to be abolished is Butler's "instinct." For both, success is not the imposition of self on world, but a process of social accommodation. "All our lives long," Butler writes, "every day and every hour, we are engaged in the process of accommodating our changed and unchanged selves to changed and unchanged surroundings; living, in fact, is nothing else than this process of accommodation" (264). Gosse is less explicit, but he too sends his hero off to London at the book's end. Rejecting his isolated father, who insists on a personal relation to God, the Son immerses himself in gregarious London, where every fixed idea is modified by its relation to others. "He is the most per-fect saint who is the most perfect gentleman," comments Butler's narrator, Overton (258), and Gosse, I suspect, would agree.

Attempting to crystallize the difference between nine-teenth- and twentieth-century biographers, Cockshut writes that *all* biographers have "some sense of a man strug-gling to achieve something, and of some other forces, sepa-rate from his will, at work to help or hinder him." But the Victorian biographer, he argues, "whether Christian or not, inherited and seldom questioned an assumption that these forces could not be summed up simply in physical law and social pressure" (21). The eighteenth century, on the other hand, Carlyle had complained, tended to "ac-count" for people, to explain what happens to them in ra-tional, causal terms. Butler is a forerunner of Strachey in this respect for he, too, returns to the eighteenth-century school of rationality—much as his hero, Ernest Pontifex, is a throwback of sorts to his great grandfather. Like Strachey, Butler expresses his revolt against spiritual dictatorship by materializing the spirit, by explaining things with a ven-geance. "Perhaps some men are independent of anteced-ents and surroundings and have an initial force within themselves which is in no way due to causation," Overton says at the start of *The Way of All Flesh*, but he adds skep-tically, "this is supposed to be a difficult question and it may be as well to avoid it" (18). This view of the self as a nexus of hereditary tendencies, circumstantial necessity, and innate drives was not an uplifting conceptualization, but was precisely that most suited to the dismantling of Victorian exaltation of individual achievement.

Late Victorian biography, then, suggested a helpful methodology for Strachey's revolt. But with their "perfect gentlemen" evolving by way of social interaction, Butler and Gosse remain clearly pre-Georgian—and in fact Strachey complained to Woolf of Butler's "Victorian taint" (Woolf and Strachey 60). For Strachey it was precisely the conventionality of his subjects' delusions that made them so dangerously powerful. Ernest Pontifex and Gosse's Son find in London's cosmopolitan culture a welcome relief from paternal authority. Strachey, on the other hand, sees only varying degrees of irrationality masquerading as truth, of self-interest masquerading as renunciation. Responding to *Eminent Victorians*, Gosse complains in "The Agony of the Victorian Age" that Strachey is too lacking in "imaginative insight," too critical toward the Victorians who had, after all, a "deep consciousness of the guiding restraint of tradition upon character" (*Diversions* 326). Strachey seemed to be dismantling the Victorian ideas of spiritual and moral development without replacing them. If accommodation to a changing society is not a constructive, evolutionary impetus, if a direct relation to God does not define the individual and his vocation, how are human beings to grow, change, achieve? To a certain extent Strachey will find in the imaginative life of his subjects an answer to these questions. But in doing so he will transform the reader's relation to biography from trust to wary skepticism.

In her 1924 essay "Mr. Bennett and Mrs. Brown," Virginia Woolf groups *Ulysses, Queen Victoria,* and "Mr. Prufrock" as the extenuated creations of writers alienated from their age. Joyce, Strachey, and Eliot, she argues, attempt to express a Georgian sense of character by manhandling Edwardian conventions, and as a result, "where so much strength is spent on finding a way of telling the truth, the

truth itself is bound to reach us in rather an exhausted condition" (*Captain's Deathbed* 117). As characters they share,
perhaps, an unnervingly physical quality; Bloom's taste for
inner organs, Prufrock's bald spot, and Victoria's too-visible
gums fix them aggressively as flesh and blood. But they
remain, nonetheless, an odd trio, partly because, while
Strachey has long been acknowledged a major innovative
force in modern biography, he has rarely been viewed as a
modernist comparable in any way to Joyce, Eliot, or, for
that matter, Woolf.

Strachey gets his taste for irony and reason from eighteenth-century French and English literature, but his choice
and treatment of his subjects reveal a characteristically
modern, anti-heroic stance that explains Woolf's incongruous grouping. Prufrock is not Prince Hamlet; Bloom is
not Ulysses; Strachey's subjects are, in a similar sense, not
themselves. The disciplined and deliberate biographee becomes, in Strachey's hands, an ambivalent figure torn by
conflicting drives and buffeted by circumstance. Strachey's
similarities to eighteenth-century historians are thus not
archaisms, but reapplications of old weapons. Carlyle complained of the tendency of earlier writers like Hume and
Gibbon to account for their subjects by denigration of
their accomplishments; in reaction to Carlyle, Strachey accounts for his with a vengeance.[6]

The accounting gains some of its power from World War
I, which went on while Strachey, a pacifist, was writing
Eminent Victorians. In an angry 1918 essay on Lord Morley, Strachey writes, "We begin to long for a little of the
cynicism and scepticism of, precisely, the age of Diderot,
Rousseau, and Voltaire [of whom Morley had written biog-
raphies]" as antidotes to the misguided idealism and self-
deception responsible, he hints, for the war: "Perhaps—
who knows?—if Lord Morley and his contemporaries had
been less devoid of those unamiable and unedifying qualities, the history of the world would have been more fortu-
nate. The heartless, irreverent, indecent eighteenth cen-

tury produced the French Revolution. The Age of Victoria produced—what?" (*Biographical Essays* 283). David Garnett, listening in 1918 to Strachey reading *Eminent Victorians*, "soon realized that Lytton's essays were designed to undermine the foundations on which the age that brought the war about had been built" ("Keynes" 53). For the gap between abstract principles and everyday reality noted by Butler in *The Way of All Flesh* was turned by World War I into a gaping abyss. Idealistic intentions met with hideous results, and when the disillusionment was chronicled, a peculiarly modern kind of irony became, according to Paul Fussell in *The Great War and Modern Memory*, the "one dominating form of modern understanding" (35). *Eminent Victorians* can be read as a reflection of this post-World War I irony, the "first and finest piece of sharp-shooting through the crack that the Great War had made," John Raymond calls it (164). For World War I was the ultimate proof that, as Strachey says of Thomas Arnold, "Teachers and prophets have strange afterhistories" (*Eminent Victorians* 241). If the fanatic enthusiasm for sports at public schools was a strange thing to grow out of Arnold's reforms, how much stranger was the war, which seemed to grow in turn out of the sports?

Teachers and prophets have strange afterhistories, according to Strachey (and Nicolson and Kingsmill), because their incessant moralizing precludes self-knowledge and underestimates the complexity of human motivation. Obsessed with acting and judging the actions of others, they fail to grasp the particularity of each man's position in the world; they fail to grasp how limited is the perspective on which they base their generalizations. They fail, most of all, to look within themselves. Carlyle's "reckless moral sense," Strachey points out, did not require, until it was too late, that he treat his wife like a human being (*Biographical Essays* 252).

At the core of *Eminent Victorians* is a paradox central to the age it portrays. All of its subjects have a peculiarly intense relation to absolute values, derived unpragmatically, without regard for actual experience, yet which sanction and even promote their egotistic ambitions. Faith, in other words, is for these figures at once delusory and self-serving. Strachey is most explicit in his discussion of General Gosse's extreme religiousness, where "egotism and renuncia-tion melted into one another" (*Eminent Victorians* 260). Putting one's faith entirely in God can also mean exalting one's own desires as the desire of God—as the Son dis-covers in Gosse's *Father and Son* when he tells his father that it is God's wish that he go to the Browns' party. What emerges in the course of *Eminent Victorians*, as a hint in "Manning," as bitter truth in "Gordon," is that this same mingling of power, abstract principle and egotistic ambi-tion is at the bottom of English imperialism, with its self-serving yet idealistic notion of the "white man's burden."

The post-Victorian attack discerned by Gerhardie on any group "attempting to justify its hegemony by identifying its interests with the supposed good of others" (26), strik-ing at the family, class system, established church, and im-perialism is there, almost *in toto*, in *Eminent Victorians*. Only the class system escapes intact; "Nightingale," "Manning," and "Gordon" take care of the rest.

The content of *Eminent Victorians*, then, grew out of a late Victorian and Edwardian tradition of revolt against hypocrisy, complacency, and self-delusion. Like *The Way of All Flesh*, it derived much of its ammunition from eigh-teenth-century skepticism, from the Voltairean argument, as cited by Strachey, that the "prime factor in the world's history has always been *la chaise percée*" (*Biographical Essays* 52). This skepticism drew added force from the War, which accentuated the gap between the truths of the *chaise percée* and the lies of the self-righteous. But what were the im-plications of this content for biographical technique? To what extent did it force a redefinition of the self and of hu-man development, and thus of the proper subject of biogra-phy itself? Or had modern fiction and Victorian autobiog-raphy already so redefined the self that biography would have changed without the War and the desire to debunk Victorian heroes?

These questions are impossible to answer with any certainty. Even before the start of World War I, Strachey's intellectual predispositions—his skepticism, his love of Voltaire, the impact of G. E. Moore's *Principia Ethica*—led him to take an unconventional view of biographical plot and narration. In "Godfrey, Cornbury, or Candide?" a paper read to the Cambridge Apostles, he argues that the purpose of life may well be ambitious achievement, but that the achievement is not subsumed in the act or product (*Interesting Question* 64). Happiness as experienced by Voltaire, for example, is not contained in the various volumes he produced, but in the intangible sense of being alive, of being Voltaire, and of writing. By implication, then, a biography that described only accomplishments would not go far toward recreating its subject. Nor could the biography's narrator aspire to invisibility if, as Strachey and his Bloomsbury friends believed, the inner, unmanifested life was much more important and much more complex than had hitherto been recognized. Valuing states of being for their own sake and deeply distrusting the "man of action," Strachey could not but radically alter the form of biography at the same time that he exposed that form's heroes.

Strachey's only explicit description of his own biographical technique is in his preface to *Eminent Victorians*. Unfortunately, as one of the few documents of modernist biography, the preface has been quoted to death, in varying contexts, in support of contradictory views. The preface is, in fact, so concise as to be enigmatic. The two duties of the biographer, according to Strachey, are to be brief and to be detached. He should not be careless, unselective, or sycophantic, as were earlier biographers. And, faced with the overwhelming quantity of data provided by the all too prolific and newly dead Victorians, he should be subtle, focusing his attention on "obscure recesses, hitherto undivined" (vii).

The biographer, Strachey writes, "will row out over that great ocean of material, and lower down into it, here and there, a little bucket, which will bring up to the light of day some characteristic specimen, from those far depths, to be examined with careful curiosity" (ix). "Haphazard visions" are what Strachey says he presents in *Eminent Victorians*, "certain fragments of the truth which took my fancy and lay to my hand." The references to vision and to light are quite striking, derived in part, I suspect, from Conrad's concern with making the reader see. There is also a clever pairing of aesthetic and scientific impulses, of subjectivity and objectivity. The specimens appear to be hauled up at random, yet they are "characteristic"—i.e., selected. The fragments of truth "took my fancy"—i.e., pleased me aes-thetically—and "lay to my hand"—i.e., were randomly chosen specimens. And the fragments, of course, are to be shaped into artful wholes. The result of this art-science pairing has been that those supporting wholly objective bi-ography cite Strachey in support, and those supporting expressivist biography cite Strachey in support, both argu-ing he has been misunderstood.[7] Strachey's aim becomes clearer, though, if his preface is juxtaposed with Conrad's 1897 preface to "Nigger of the Narcissus," which it re-sembles. Describing the aim of the artist, Conrad writes: "To snatch in a moment of courage, from the remorseless rush of time, a passing phase of life, is only the beginning of the task. The task approached in tenderness and faith is to hold up unquestioningly, without choice and without fear, the rescued fragment before all eyes in the light of a sincere mood" (xiv).

Both writers suggest that mere exposure of the frag-ment and its presentation as aesthetically coherent are consonant, equating the artist's intervention with the reve-lation of the fragment's own internal relations. Strachey wants to "lay bare the facts of the case"; Conrad looks for "the stress and passion within the core of each convincing moment." The logical inconsistency is disguised by the emphasis on the artist's exalted task; for both, the meeting ground of artistry and truth is the artist's own self: his sincerity, his "careful curiosity."

The preface to *Eminent Victorians* is not an argument in favor of or opposed to biographical objectivity, for it presupposes the harmony of (or at least blurs the distinction between) artistic intervention and scientific detachment. "History is not the accumulation of facts," Strachey writes in a 1928 essay on Gibbon, "but the relation of them"; it is an omelette, not an assortment of "butter, eggs, salt and herbs" (*Biographical Essays* 142). But omelettes vary according to who makes them; the historian-as-chef is inevitably a more visible and self-conscious figure than the historian-as-shopping basket. Strachey's pretense of merely "exposing" the facts seems, finally, disingenuous.

Perry Meisel has argued that Strachey's pretense of scientific interest involves him in logical inconsistencies so obvious as to seem "almost intentional" ("Counterplot" 5). There is a certain hilarity in presenting so Conradian a preface to a collection of biographical essays. Conrad's talent is for illuminating that aspect of truth which is most indecipherable, for exposing the haze that covers the truth, not the truth itself. This paradoxical mingling of exposure and obfuscation is Strachey's aim, though it emerges only gradually during the course of his career.

Strachey's method is, above all, indirect. He suggests that the biographer "attack his subject in unexpected places . . . fall upon the flank, or the rear" (vii). Fussell suggests that this is a response to the failed tactics of World War I generals who persisted in facing the enemy head-on and whose troops were mowed down as a result (*Great War* 188). It is mainly, though, an attempt to shift the narrative viewpoint from alignment with the subject's self-image to a new, independent standpoint: the oblique attack is performed by a "sudden, revealing searchlight" shot "into obscure recesses" (*Eminent Victorians* vii). The searchlight's aim is not merely the seeking out of petty weaknesses, but the subjection of the central figure to a point of view other than his own. Strachey's writing is full of theatrical figures of speech; Gordon's catastrophe, for example, is compared to a puppet show, Disraeli to a comedian. Strachey's subjects are actors denying their artifice, and as long as the only lights on them are footlights, the stage set will be mistaken for reality. This repressed theatricality is for Strachey synonymous with Victorian self-delusion. "The old comedian," he writes of Disraeli, "preferred not to question the solidity of the fairy palaces in which he played his marvellous part" (*Biographical Essays* 267). But thanks to Buckle and Monypenny's biography, readers "have been provided with seats in the wings [and] can see only too clearly what lies on the other side of those flimsy erections. Such is the doom of the egoist." Strachey's sudden searchlight has a similarly deflating effect, revealing the stagy unreality of his subjects' self-concepts.

The eminent Victorian chooses to ignore his own complicity in the creation of the fictions by which he lives. Strachey as biographer is similarly complicitous, but ridiculously so. He seems to be presenting the facts at face value, but he also points continually behind them—inevitably drawing attention to his own and his audience's role in construing them. Occasionally omniscient, occasionally protesting his ignorance, the narrator, even when silent, renders his subjects' versions of themselves incredible. The reader acquires a habit of looking behind characters that does not cease merely because the narrator has briefly aligned himself with one of them.

Strachey's insistence on indirection shapes his biographical technique in yet another way: it seems to move him in the direction of Freudian interpretation of the apparently insignificant or even nonexistent action. There is no precise information as to when Strachey first read Freud's *Psychopathology of Everyday Life*, which was translated into English in 1914, but Holroyd's guess is that "According to Freud," Strachey's dialogue about parapraxis in which

Rosamund and Arthur discuss just how accidental the forgetting of the fountain pen really was, was written at about
that time (*Interesting Question* 112). This would suggest that
Strachey had read some Freud by the time he completed
Eminent Victorians. In any case the importance he grants
Manning's omission from his diary of a detailed account of
his interview with the Pope indicates a readiness for if not
a familiarity with Freudian theory. Earlier biographers had
acknowledged that apparent reasons were not always real
reasons; Carlyle, for example, recognizing the complexity
of Sterling's inner life, suggests in *The Life of John Sterling*
that a professed cause might be "the summing-up of innumerable far deeper conscious and unconscious causes"
(103). But to infer from a manifest action a meaning exactly opposite to it is a more radical questioning of conscious behavior. Manning fails to describe the meeting;
therefore something important took place: such reasoning
suggests an understanding not merely of psychological
confusion, but of repression.[8]

Strachey is fascinated by causal relationships and ulterior motives, but undercutting his announced aim of exposure is a stance of awed incomprehension. By alternat-
ing between extremes of reductionism and mystification,
he subverts the credibility of his own story, but also utterly
demolishes the pretenses of his subjects, exposing the ma-
terialist subtext underlying Victorian abstractions and the
authoritarian implications of Victorian actions.

In Hayden White's terms, Strachey mingles the tropes of
irony and metonymy, using satiric and tragic emplot-
ments. Metonymy, for White, is mechanistic, reducing one
phenomenon to being a function of another, extrinsic one
(*Metahistory* 35–36). His definition differs from the standard one in that the same expression ("He is all heart"
is his example) can be either synecdochic or metonymic,
depending on whether it is essentially integrative (heart
meant figuratively) or reductive (heart meant less symbolically, as vital organ). "In Metonymy," White writes,

"phenomena are implicitly apprehended as bearing relationships to one another in the modality of part-part relationships, on the basis of which one can effect a *reduction* of
one of the parts to the status of an aspect or function of the
other" (*Metahistory* 35). Thus Strachey repeatedly suggests
that the Church of England evolved out of Henry the
Eighth's taste in women. Hurrell Froude, he writes, was
"possessed by the ideals of saintliness, and convinced of the
supreme importance of not eating too much" (*Eminent Victorians* 14). (The Victorian equation of religious devotion
and fasting is here split apart into two extremes: the gran-
diose spiritual idea of saintliness and the material aim of
not eating too much. The metaphorical whole has been
broken into parts whose presumed relation to each other
now appears ridiculous.) Similarly, he breaks down Manning's spiritual aspirations into their constituent parts, as
he describes his conscientious attempt to suppress his ambition to be cardinal:

. . . what are words, and thoughts, and even prayers, to the
mysterious and relentless powers of circumstance and character? Cardinal Wiseman was slowly dying; the tiller of the
Church was slipping from his feeble hand; and Manning was
beside him, the one man with the energy, the ability, the courage, and the conviction to steer the ship upon her course. (72)

But Strachey does not merely deflate. Manning's attempt at self-suppression is not simply hypocritical, and
it continues to coexist with his ambition. "Plain duty," the
unifying concept that would bring together circumstance
and divine will, continues to hover as a possible redemptive metaphor. But as often as it appears, it is broken up.
The final blow comes with the essay's conclusion, when all
of Manning's life and achievement is reduced to the absurdly material hat, "the incongruous, the almost impossible object which, with its elaborations of dependent tas-
sels, hangs down from the dim vault like some forlorn and

"Panmure" entirely, he is not, as Nadel argues, transforming biography by replacing "naming" with interpretation
(147).[9] He is transforming biography by blurring boundaries between narrator and character, between narrator and
reader. The term Bison originated not in Strachey's artistry, but among Panmure's friends, and in borrowing it,
Strachey is like a ventriloquist speaking, for a moment, in
another's voice.

This ventriloquism is subtle but pervasive. Nightingale
writes in a letter that advising her to rest is "*de rigueur*";
several pages later the same phrase turns up in the narrator's commentary. Strachey's frequent use of words like
"surprising," "perplexing," and "curious" blur the bound-
ary between narrator and reader by anticipating and echoing, in his responses to his characters, his reader's responses
to his narrative. Strachey's much-discussed use of clichés
serves the same purpose, by suggesting that Strachey's narrator is speaking in the very voice of conventionality.

Traditionally biography adjudicates between its extraordinary subject and its ordinary readers. The biographer
places his subject, made anomalous by his achievement
and his past-ness, in a context contemporary with and reflecting the norms of his reader. But Strachey tampers
with this process of adjudication. He adopts his readers'
conventions even to the point of writing banal prose. Shirk-
ing his own role as go-between, he portrays his subjects as
part-cliché, part-mystery: whatever is not trite is inexplicable. The point has been made before, as evidence of
Strachey's bad writing and simplistic psychology.[10] I see it,
however, as part of his rhetorical strategy. Those deeds
which ought to demonstrate the subject's greatness are
made to seem commonplace, while the process of spiritual
and intellectual growth through which the reader might
identify with him becomes inaccessibly singular and implausible. It is no wonder that Woolf felt he had strained
his relationship with his audience.

In "Manning," the two extremes of triteness and inex-

47

plicability are suggested by clichés and fairy-tale transitional phrases. Brimming cups are dashed from lips, old scores are wiped out, shoes are stepped into and gnats strained at, all time-worn expressions for oft-repeated and oft-described behavior. The fairy tale motif, on the other hand, is suggested by transitional phrases devoid of any apparent plausibility or logic. "It was at this time" (8); "Just then"; "At this time there was living in a country parish a young clergyman of the name of John Keble" (13); "It so happened that it was at this very time . . ." (86). In fairy tales, events are recounted and heard with a sense of wonder at their having occurred; their significance is in their having happened *once,* and they are ordered only by spatial or temporal relationships, not by the logical and psychological connections implicit in clichés.

The gap, then, between the accumulated cultural wisdom of clichés, which turn all phenomena into familiar, repetitive, and well-understood occurrences, and fairy tales, which turn all phenomena into strange one-of-a-kind occurrences, is disturbingly wide. It is the kind of gap bridgeable only by an imaginative use of figurative language: analogies, metaphors, comparisons to bring together the familiar and strange aspects. But Strachey's goal of dismantling the Victorians' own metaphors leads him to eschew his own, and the result is a kind of narrative metonymy, associating the obvious and the obscure, without integrating them.

The method of "Manning," if effective, is constricting, and during the course of *Eminent Victorians,* which was composed in the same order as that in which the essays now appear, Strachey's method evolves (Stratford 93). The fairy tale motif disappears, while an oddly modulated narrative voice increases its range. Strachey's apparent penetrations into his subjects' minds have long been noted, and characterized sometimes as interior monologue, sometimes *style indirecte libre.* The second term is the more accurate; but what is most interesting about Strachey's narrative

voice is the varying degree to which it speaks for the subject—what I call its modulations. Particular characters can
sometimes seem to influence the narrative style, or they
can appear actually to take over the narrative role, or they
may be speaking to themselves, their conversation without
quotation marks simply because it is unpronounced. And
the lines between these possibilities are none too clear. The
description of Lord Hartington's conscience is perhaps the
subtlest example, as the narrator gradually, unobtrusively
takes on the not-too-bright English gentleman's tonality
(322). General Gordon provides a more obvious example:
"He was Gordon Pasha, he was the Governor-General, he
was the ruler of the Sudan. He was among his people—his
own people, and it was to them only that he was responsible—to them, and to God. Was he to let them fall without
a blow into the clutches of a sanguinary imposter? Never!"
(301). The use of the third person indicates this is not interior monologue, but the repetitious insistence on Gordon's importance, the choppy sentence structure, the melo-
dramatic diction, even the overemotional punctuation by
dashes, question mark, and exclamation point suggest that
the narrator has, for the moment, identified himself with
Gordon's emotional state.

The gradations by which this apparent identification
takes place are so subtle that the character's voice may seem
to have accidentally seeped into the narration, without the
author's knowledge. In fact, of course, the modulated voice
is a deliberately chosen narrative strategy allowing Strachey
a tremendously broad range of possible attitudes toward
his subjects, including sympathy.[11] It is particularly useful
in suggesting the various encapsulated imaginative constructs different people make of the world and in dramatizing the relation between these constructs and history.

In "The End of General Gordon," these narrative modulations are particularly prevalent and serve to dramatize
the isolation of various consciousnesses from each other
and from history itself. Lord Hartington, Gladstone, the

Mahdi, and especially Gordon are defined by their limited vision, by their questions—to which they want no answers but their own—and by their characteristic prose rhythms. "Of course, the whole thing was a nuisance—an obvious nuisance," the narrator suggests in Lord Hartington's voice, "and everyone else must feel just as he did about it" (322). The bland conventionality of Hartington is not summarized by an omniscient narrator (whose summary would be a relief from and transcendence of his stupidity), but dramatized as an eruption into the narration, which thus appears vulnerable to the claustrophobically constricted viewpoints of self-involved individuals.

The narrator says of the Mahdi, temporarily triumphant:

> He was master of Kordofan; he was at the head of a great army; he was rich; he was worshipped. A dazzling future opened before him. No possibility seemed too remote, no fortune too magnificent. A vision of universal empire hovered before his eyes. Allah, whose servant he was, who had led him thus far, would lead him onward still, to the glorious end. (275).

Strachey's extraordinarily subtle movement here from external description of the Mahdi's triumph and circumstances to a narrative alignment with his delusions dramatizes the interaction of imagination and history.

The narrator's alignment with the Mahdi is the act of a ventriloquist; he remains in control throughout. Similarly, history never quite yields to any particular person's version of it. The Mahdi's vision of the "glorious end" is a delusion since he dies six months after his victory at Khartoum. Nor is Gordon's end the one he had imagined. To a large extent, in fact, "The End of General Gordon" is about the difference between *end* meaning intention and *end* meaning simply the cessation of the story. The essay begins with one apparent end, in Jerusalem, where "it might have seemed that a life of inordinate activity had found at last a longed-for, a final peacefulness" (246). But Gordon returns to England, is sent to Egypt, and "it was not in peace and rest, but in ruin and horror, that he reached his end." The apparently appropriate end is not to be realized.

Even though Gordon does manage to further imperialist aims and to achieve legendary status, it is after his death and to the advantage of others. Gordon's is a "tragic history" (246), ending in defeat. But Strachey's story continues beyond Gordon's end, to the future, which "lay with Major Kitchener and his Maxim-Nordenfeldt guns" (349). Thirteen years after the fall of Khartoum, the Mahdi's empire was destroyed, and so, Strachey concludes, "At any rate it had all ended very happily—in a glorious slaughter of twenty thousand Arabs, a vast addition to the British Empire, and a step in the Peerage for Sir Evelyn Baring" (350). That final sentence has a hint of Flaubert's *Madame Bovary* in it; Charles Bovary dead, his daughter working in a cotton mill, one character has yet triumphed, the ultimate mediocrity, M. Homais, of whom the book's last line speaks: "Il vient de recevoir la croix d'honneur" (324). In both books' conclusions, history is seen to grind on in meaningless banality, profiting the shallow—Sir Evelyn Baring, for example—while the somewhat deeper are isolated and deluded by their own limited consciousnesses.

"The End of General Gordon" appears to align history itself with the convention of the "happy ending." History seems an endless process of recuperation: of the uncolonized into the Empire, of the strange into the hackneyed, of the haphazard into an ordered climb to the top. It is a process from which the individual consciousness is forever excluded. The appointment of Gordon, the exactly wrong person to command a withdrawal, serves the interests of the imperialists yet appears almost accidental; at most Lord Hartington "instinctively, perhaps subconsciously, apprehended the elements of a situation which he never formulated to himself" (294). Why does Gladstone intervene to prevent Gordon's rescue? Metaphor is piled on metaphor; Gladstone is a snake, a cloud, a labyrinth, a crater . . . each equation less revealing than the one preceding. Personal actions wind up counting for little: "Gordon once gone, events had taken their own course; the policy of the government began to slide, automatically, down a slope at the bottom of which lay the conquest of the Sudan and the annexation of Egypt" (309). Nor does Gordon himself fully understand what is happening (312). To write history is to give that slide the shape of a story, and thereby, as Hayden White points out, an aura of inevitability, even desirability.[12] For the "happy ending" of "Gordon" finally suggests that the writing of history itself is an act of collusion with convention, with what actually happened transmuted into what had to happen, and thus with imperialism.

The writing of biographies, on the other hand, if they serve to explore an individual consciousness, can be viewed as a rejection of collusion. Such biographies would make no pretense of conveying what happened and how and why. But if history remained elusive, the depiction of consciousness would at least suggest its potential for imaginative transformation. This was preferable, for Strachey, to implicit endorsement of history's happy endings. The most likely consciousness to depict, in fact, would be those most necessarily in opposition to the ostensibly inevitable, those whom convention allowed no active role at all, and whose very achievement, therefore, had to involve first the imaginative construction of an apparently implausible alternative, then its enactment to transform what was: the consciousness, that is, of women.

"Shut out by the social disabilities of women from any adequate exercise of her highest faculties in action on the world without," John Stuart Mill had written in his *Autobiography* of Harriet Taylor, "her life was one of inward meditation" (195). Women of action offered Strachey a fascinating paradox: their lives moved forcibly inward, their impulses mediated by societal resistance to their impact, they nonetheless acted, but in doing so redefined themselves and the very notion of action. "The cliché that women, more consistently than men, turn inward for sustenance," writes Patricia Spacks, "seems to mean, in practice, that women have richly defined the ways in which imagination creates possibility: possibility that society denies" (315). The Victorian model of achievement had been predominantly male, the actions it valued based on metaphors of chivalry and battle. Reality itself seemed to be a male domain; Leslie Stephen valued above all else a "masculine grasp of facts" (Annan 307). Lytton Strachey was aware of the stultifying role such a view forced on women, but he was even more interested in the implicit critique ambitious women offered the Victorian cult of masculinity and action and the technical innovations they forced, as a result, on their biographers. Florence Nightingale, and later Strachey's Queen Elizabeth, triumph by reinventing their roles in explicit opposition to male-conceived alternatives of traditional heroism and feminine submission. To match their reinvention, Strachey must create a biography that conveys without compromising the implausibility of their acts. In the bulk of *Eminent Victorians* Strachey is occupied in deflating nineteenth-century metaphors—the delusions in which they muffled their ambition and egotism. In "Florence Nightingale" he begins to suggest the transformative power of metaphor, when used *against* rather than in collusion with convention.

Michael Holroyd, in *Lytton Strachey by Himself*, writes that Strachey "took the nineteenth-century cult of homosexuality and turned it into a weapon of twentieth-century revolt" (105). Certainly his own failure to fit into a traditional sexual role, along with the influence of his politically active sisters, allowed him to see beyond the narrow confines of "masculinity" or "femininity." In his 1904 dialogue "He, She, and It," he even has the two discussants exchange sexes for the duration of the dialogue, one telling the other, "I can't believe that your minds are radically different from ours" (*By Himself* 94). But Strachey does not merely question traditional sexual roles; he uses this questioning to inject into the biography a typically modern concern with the importance and difficulty of describing the inner workings of the psyche. His later interest in Freud and his use of Freudian terminology in *Elizabeth and Essex* grow out of this early insistence on the importance of the inner life. For just as a childhood psychic trauma turns the neurotic's life drama inward, the woman stifled by societal expectations must turn inward, imagining for herself a life that does not yet exist, before she can act.

Strachey's Nightingale, Queen Victoria, and Queen Elizabeth are not completely immune to the ridicule he pours on the male subjects of *Eminent Victorians*. To the extent that they succeed, that they manage to impose their wills on others, that they become respected representatives of their society's values, they are as liable to be satirized as Manning, Arnold, and Gordon. But to the extent that they violate socially defined roles and are excluded from the exercise of genuine power, they gain his sympathy. The more imagination they are forced to use in rejecting "reality" and reformulating their relations to the world, the more their unconventional life-plots mirror Strachey's reformulation of biography. "She was heroic," Strachey writes of Nightingale, "yet her heroism was not of that simple sort so dear to the readers of novels and the compilers of hagiologies . . ." (155), and of Queen Elizabeth he writes, "She succeeded by virtue of all the qualities which every hero should be without" (*Elizabeth* 10). To the extent that they replace conventionally defined roles with their own imagined self-concepts, they offer a radical alternative to Victorian hero-worship, and a more positive alternative than post-Victorian skepticism.

More so even than Manning, Florence Nightingale is described in terms of a fairy tale. A "delicate maiden of high degree" (135), her duty is "living happily ever afterwards"

(136). But unlike her male counterparts, Nightingale consciously rejects that story and replaces it with her own. In an odd reversal, her dreams are granted the reality Strachey denies to her circumstances, and her triumph is that she manages to impose those dreams on the world. Nancy Miller has recently cited the connection made by Genette between "plausibility" and "propriety": "What defines plausibility," Genette writes, "is the formal principle of respect for the norm" (Miller 36). Miller goes on to suggest that the plots of women writers have frequently been criticized as implausible because of their rejection of such a norm—their rejection in particular of the choice described by Freud between ambitious (male) and erotic (female) longing (Miller 40). Strachey's reception as a biographer, it seems to me, has been affected by just such culturally defined notions of plausibility (a frequent charge against him is that one simply does not believe what he says); even more clearly, though, this is precisely the problem faced by Nightingale. She daydreams about becoming a nurse and building hospitals, but "The whole scheme was summarily brushed aside as preposterous" (137). "Preposterous" is a favorite word of Strachey's, generally applied by narrator to subject, indicating ironic distance. But Florence Nightingale is up against institutionalized incredulity, which bears the brunt, in her stead, of the narrator's irony.

Nightingale rejects marriage, choosing instead "the chance of forming for myself a true and rich life" (140). At times the decision seems to indicate, as Martin Kallich argues in *The Psychological Milieu of Lytton Strachey,* a neurotic repression presaging Queen Elizabeth's (58). Strachey's insistence on her "Demon," which drives her to wear out Sidney Herbert and go mad herself with overwork, does suggest that she is just one more man of action, overachieving and self-deluded, her ambition fueled by repression. But just as Nightingale defines herself against conventional expectations, Strachey's version of her defines itself against traditional versions. "Everyone knows the popular conception of Florence Nightingale," the portrait begins, ". . . but the truth was different" (135). She appeared a perfect lady, he writes, but "It was not by gentle sweetness and womanly self-abnegation that she had brought order out of chaos in the Scutari Hospitals . . ." (156).

It was, Strachey writes, "an almost unimaginable thing in those days for a woman of means to make her own way in the world" (138). Nightingale managed to imagine it, and then to do it. Popular history then, with its vast recuperative powers, converted the once-unimaginable into the trite legend of the "angel of mercy," the Lady with the Lamp. Strachey's task is to make the legend seem once more unimaginable.[13] This he does by devoting slightly more than half his portrait to the years after the Crimean War, the years when she was dominated by her "Demon" of maniacally hard work. "Her real life began," he writes, "at the very moment when, in the popular imagination, it had ended" (164).

The Demon suggests not merely the fierce results of sexual repression, but the imaginative transcendence of her culturally determined role. It is not the evil demon of Christianity, but the Greek *daimon,* meaning divine power or inspiration. Just as, as a child, Nightingale had to use her imagination to contest her family's expectations, she must, as an adult, use her Demon to contest her society's disregard. Because she is a woman, she cannot work at the War Office; so she becomes an invalid, free because she is outside the world to reimagine her place in it.[14]

"Miss Nightingale was not at the War Office," Strachey writes, "and for a very simple reason: she was a woman" (166). The explanation has an air of plausibility. It sounds a little like an adult explaining something to a child, the language is so simple, the causal relationship so clear. But it is, of course, this very clarity and simplicity that Strachey is ridiculing; the "reason," after all, is immeasurably complex and not the least bit reasonable. The sentence shows how closely related are Nightingale's and Strachey's positions. Both challenge conventional plots and plausibility—the one in her conception of herself, the other in his conception of biography.

In *Eminent Victorians,* then, Strachey begins by using irony and skepticism as a weapon against nineteenth-century metaphorizing. The blend of self-interest and self-abnegation so often disguised as "plain duty" is analyzed and exposed, as is, in "Gordon," the complicity of history itself. The interplay between narrative voice and the characters' inner lives offered Strachey a way of writing about the past that was not solely deflating, and it had the added advantage of avoiding complicity with historical sense-making—the placing of events within a context that makes them seem logical, comprehensible, even normal in the reader's terms. In the opposition of consciousness to time, in the exploration of the imagination at the expense of historical explanation, he found a way of depicting the past without rationalizing it. This was the way he would pursue in *Queen Victoria,* and the way that others would follow—borrowing his irony and his anti-Victorian assumptions, but especially borrowing his mingling of narrative voice and inner life, his view of experience as something made from within.

III

Weaving the Self:
Novelistic Biography

In madmen, artists, and women, Strachey and his followers found their most congenial subjects. The accounts, in *Eminent Victorians*, of Gordon's mysticism, Newman's *Apologia*, and Nightingale's fantastic ambition suggest the power of imagination to transform experience. Even without the impulse provided by these figures, Strachey's ironizing would have pushed him in the direction of fiction, for the ironic commentator, constantly inviting his reader's collusion, suggests that the apparent is not the actual, and that the actual can be construed only by a collaborative act of the imagination on the part of reader and writer. But in describing the sealed-off inner life of Gordon and the stifling conventionality opposed by Nightingale, Strachey found an additional impetus. It is primarily in these essays that he uses his modulating narrative voice that dramatizes while describing his subjects' emotions. His own imaginative entry into his subjects' minds, in other words, is most prevalent where the action of his subjects' minds constitutes their experience.

Nightingale's life in particular, then, becomes something very much *made*. Particularly when seen in opposition to the convention it ignored, Nightingale's story seems an implausible construct superimposed on the "real" world. But that this world is itself unreal has become clear through the portraits of Manning and Arnold, whose versions of reality seem more "realistic" only because they are more widely promulgated. Because their version is the conventional one, they need never acknowledge its imaginative element. Their stories, unlike Nightingale's, will never be dismissed as preposterous daydreams—except, of course, by the narrator of *Eminent Victorians*.

Had he *only* exposed the preposterousness of Manning and Arnold, contrasting professed belief with actual motivations and outcomes, Strachey could have painted himself into a corner, describing a world rigidly split between predetermined mechanisms and the incomprehensibility of Fate. For as Hayden White points out, where everything is explained in terms of causality, no overall unity of meaning is possible, except the absence of such unity—Fate (*Metahistory* 66). This was the problem faced by Enlightenment philosophers, according to White, who saw imagination only as a threat to reason. "They did not believe in their own prodigious powers of dreaming," White writes in *Metahistory,* with the result that they "never rose to full awareness of the creative possibilities contained in their own Ironic apprehension of the 'fictive' nature of historical reflection" (69). In *Queen Victoria,* Strachey contrasts the power of dreaming with the Victorians' overmaterialized imaginations and the mysterious mechanisms of history.

Published in 1921, *Queen Victoria* was the first and seminal example of novelistic biography. Novelistic biographies are not novel*ized*. There are no invented occurrences; letters and diaries provide evidence for the depiction; and attributions of thoughts are often qualified by a "perhaps" or a "might" or phrased as questions. But they are novel*istic,* primarily because of the access they provide to their subjects' inner lives. In *Aspects of the Novel,* E. M. Forster writes of the difference between *homo fictus* and *homo sapiens.* The novelist's function, he says, is "to reveal the hidden life at its

source." But the historian has no knowledge of unex-
pressed emotion; had Queen Victoria not said, "We are not
amused," he argues, no one would have known that she
wasn't. *Homo fictus,* then, is by definition one whose inner
life is visible, while *homo sapiens,* the historian's subject, retains his secrets (38). But, Forster argues, the chronicling
of plot alone, of life as seen from the outside, leaves people
"shadowy and intractable and three quarters hidden like
an iceberg" (59). Biographers like Strachey, believing as
did Forster that the bulk of human experience resides not
in action but in inward experience, must necessarily turn
to the devices of fiction in order to depict that experience.
The connection was made by Forster himself, who writes
of Strachey that he "makes his people move; they are alive,
like characters in a novel: he constructs or rather recon-
structs them from within" (*Two Cheers* 281). It is in this Forsterian sense, then, that Strachey and his followers write
novelistic biographies.[1] The insight they display into their
subjects' minds is more characteristic of the modern psychological novel than of traditional biography.

Depicting the inner life of an historical personage does
involve the biographer in speculation. Such speculation is
eagerly defended by Ludwig and Maurois, both of whom,
following Croce and Collingwood, insist on the importance of intuition in understanding others, the understanding by coup d'état that Maurois describes in *Aspects of
Biography.*[2] The novelistic biographers allow this theoretical issue to shape their books. They dramatize in the text
the interplay between the knowable and the unknowable
as the subject's own struggle to understand and to create
himself. Their shaping of the life into a biographical unit
is thematized as the subject's own propensity to pattern
himself. Again and again, however, the subject's battle is
lost: he fails to know himself; he is trapped in a pattern of
his own conceiving; most of all, he fails to recognize the
power of his own imagination. Queen Victoria tries to lit-
eralize her memories in a series of memorials to her hus-

band, and so loses their substance. Geoffrey Scott's Zélide sacrifices her passionate nature to her relentlessly analytic reason. David Cecil's Cowper alternates between the madness entailed by taking his imagination literally and the circumscribed domesticity he gains by rigidly controlling it. Cecil's Melbourne, torn between eighteenth-century rationalism and nineteenth-century melancholy, mistakes his profession as a philosopher and goes into politics.

The novelistic biographers are obsessed with the pattern taken by human personality. In part, their obsession results from the technical problems they face as biographers: a patterned life will make an aesthetically unified biography. A patterned life will also be more knowable, since what is not known can then be extrapolated from what is. Cecil makes the connection explicit in his biography of Cowper: "Tracing a man's history through the records time and chance have left to us," he writes, "is like reading a novel from which important pages have been torn out at random" (53). The deletions are mystifying, but the assumption that the life has a novel's coherence at least allows the biographer to guess, to "put two and two together," and so give the portrait "that completeness which is as necessary to history as to other arts" (54).

This patterning is not merely a biographer's trick, but also an intrinsically human propensity to play a role, to construct one's own self as a pattern with a kind of fictive coherence. Maurois argues that this tendency is typical of the prominent figure, but I would argue that this patterning takes place on a particularly large scale in novelistic biography and that underlying it is an essentially Paterian— and typically modern—sense of the self in relation to time.[3]

In his conclusion to *The Renaissance*, Pater questions the physical and mental integrity of individual human beings. Our bodies, he says, are made of elements and ruled by laws that extend far beyond us, through the entire natural world: "That clear, perpetual outline of face and limb is but an image of ours," he writes, ". . . a design in a web, the actual threads of which pass out beyond it" (234). Our minds are even less certainly defined, as they turn perceived objects into a flow of impressions, which we receive in isolation, "each mind keeping as a solitary prisoner its own dream of a world" (235). What is left, finally, of personal identity, is only movement, the constant interplay of flow and experienced moment:

> To such a tremulous wisp constantly re-forming itself on the stream, to a single sharp impression, with a sense in it, a relic more or less fleeting, of such moments gone by, what is real in our life fines itself down. It is with this movement, with the passage and dissolution of impressions, images, sensations, that analysis leaves off—that continual vanishing away, that strange, perpetual weaving and unweaving of ourselves. (236)

Perry Meisel has pointed out the paradox by which a nonexistent self, whose unity is wholly imaginative, is at the same time a prisoner behind a "thick wall of personality" (*Absent Father* 114).[4] The paradox is at the heart of Strachey's, Scott's, and Cecil's biographies, all of which portray the self establishing a fictive unity by which it is then entrapped.[5]

Strachey himself was not fond of Pater; ". . . after all," he writes of him in a 1901 letter, "does he say so very much worth hearing?" (Meisel, *Absent Father* 34). But Strachey was fond of Virginia Woolf, to whom he dedicated *Queen Victoria*, and while Pater may not have been the overpowering influence on Woolf described by Meisel in *The Absent Father*, he is certainly present in such scenes of Woolf's as Rachel Vinrace's abrupt awareness of the contrast between momentary transcendence and ceaseless change: "It seemed to her that a moment's respite was allowed," Woolf writes in *The Voyage Out*, "a moment's make-believe, and then again the profound and reasonless law asserted itself, moulding them all to its liking, making and destroying" (263). The Paterian self is by definition fictive—a design in a web, a weaving, a moment's make-believe. But it is also continuous with a world of chemical elements and natural forces. This dual vision of make-believe and determinism underlies Rachel's moment of horror and the structure of novelistic biography.

Insisted upon in opposition to flux, imagination becomes a trap. Aligned with flux as an endless act of weaving and unweaving, it is a potential source of power. This is the theme of *Queen Victoria* and the implication of Scott's and Cecil's work as well. For the binary divisions that novelistic biographers so frequently detect in their subjects are at once reflections of their own ambiguous role and fissures in their subjects that could be mended only by their imaginative acknowledgment and enactment of apparently contradictory characteristics.

Paul Hernadi has described a dual perspective typical of both historical and fictional narration: the narrator, he points out, balances a retrospective viewpoint with the perspective of one immersed in events as they occur. The two angles correspond to what Hernadi calls logos and myth: the depiction of events in terms of causality versus their depiction in terms of intention or teleology ("Clio's Cousins" 249–50).[6] While implicit in all narrative, this duality is present in its extremest and most self-conscious form in the novelistic biographies. For the novelistic biographers, in aligning themselves with their subjects' psyches, do not sacrifice their superior knowledge of how things will work out. It is as if James in *The Ambassadors* had accompanied Strether's ruminations with periodic hints of his final renunciation. The biographies' internal focalization coexists somewhat uncomfortably with a deterministic subtext suggesting narrative omniscience.

This subtext surfaces in frequent references to fate, in theatrical imagery suggesting that life is as tightly plotted as tragedy, in occasionally overblown diction and an obtrusively overmodified style, and in a narrative so obsessed by causality that each effect is determined by multiple circumstances. This determinism, operating structurally, sty-listically, and thematically, is in constant tension with the transformative potential of imagination—the subject's and the biographer's. Lytton Strachey's *Queen Victoria*, pub-lished in 1921; Geoffrey Scott's *Portrait of Zélide*, published in 1925, and Lord David Cecil's *The Stricken Deer*, published in 1929, are generally agreed to be particularly successful examples of new biography. I will argue that they also ex-emplify the issues I have discerned underlying the more narrowly defined novelistic biography.

When *Queen Victoria* was published in 1921, Strachey's readers were surprised by its sympathetic treatment of the queen. The narration is so closely aligned with her view-point that Michael Holroyd compares it to a subjective novel (2: 403). Victoria is portrayed as essentially power-less, and that powerlessness is, as Holroyd suggests, one explanation for the gentle treatment she receives (2: 412). She is also, Strachey emphasizes, sincere. But most impor-tantly, she exemplifies the effort of human consciousness to outwit time.

"We have an interval," Pater writes in *The Renaissance,* "and then our place knows us no more." His answer was to expand the moment through the intensification of impres-sions. Victoria's response is more materialistic, but no less genuine; she and her consort spend their time building, planning, and acquiring *things,* material objects that some-how reflect and solidify their otherwise tenuous position in a world of flux. In doing so, they mirror the biogra-pher's task of resurrection and commemoration. And in their final failure, they offer a criticism of that task. The Crystal Palace—itself a kind of biography of the age—is dismantled; the Prince's frescoes fade. There is always, Strachey seems to be suggesting, something one fails to take into account. After Albert's death, the Queen pins his picture at the head of every bed she sleeps in. But all this

object-making presupposes the absence of what it pretends to convey. Dead pets are cast in bronze only because
they are dead. The commemorative impulse, finally, sig-
nals an absence, not a presence, a point that Strachey as
biographer refuses to ignore.

Just as the past cannot be re-presented, but only noted
as absent, history itself—the chain of events shaping future events—cannot be pinned down or controlled. Political power is fragmented, divided among Victoria, Albert,
the cabinet, and various prime ministers. Imperialism itself
seems simply an attempt to disguise the sense of increasing
confusion. Shadowy figures like Lehzen, Stockmar, and
Leopold drain off power from the central figures, while an
opaquely inexplicable Fate drains off power from them
(Johnstone 305). The Queen sits in the light of her simplicity surrounded by forces she cannot fathom, much like
those eighteenth-century French aristocrats Strachey describes so vividly in *Landmarks of French Literature*, dining
by candlelight while outside dark forces gather.

Victoria herself, Empress of India and symbol of an era,
seems more a passive expression of her time than its creator. She is, Strachey writes,

> the embodiment, the living apex of a new era in the genera-
> tions of mankind. The last vestige of the eighteenth century
> had disappeared; cynicism and subtlety were shrivelled into
> powder; and duty, industry, morality, and domesticity tri-
> umphed over them. Even the very chairs and tables had as-
> sumed, with a singular responsiveness, the forms of prim so-
> lidity. The Victorian Age was in full swing. (195)

Like Woolf's treatment of Victorian furniture in *Orlando*,
the passage, by personifying the inanimate, turns history
into a bewildering pageant that somehow happens. Victoria's will is fiercely imperious, but it spends itself without
affecting the essential political developments of her time.
During the first part of her reign she submits herself to Al-

bert; during the second, to her ministers. At her death, Strachey concludes, "the Crown was weaker than at any other time in English history" (411).

Her power grew less, Strachey writes, but "the prestige of the sovereign had immeasurably grown" (414). In order to become the "Victoria" after which her age was named, the Queen had embraced domesticity and allowed Albert to win the battle of wills that followed their marriage.[7] In a sense the symbolic Victoria exists at the expense of her individual existence. Central to *Queen Victoria* is this notion that everything exists at the expense of something else. There is an incessant exchange of power and energy: Albert wields the power, but his wife has the physical vitality that alone would make it effective. Because of this incessant exchange, it is impossible to fix the actual cause of events. It is also impossible to predict their outcome. Stockmar laboriously creates the perfect prince, and in doing so perhaps "accomplished not too little but too much" (284), for Albert kills himself with overwork. "How subtle and how dangerous are the snares which fate lays for the wariest of men!" Strachey exclaims (284).

One of those snares is time, which brings old age and death, the final confutations of human will. Strachey's dying subjects linger, increasingly shut out of the world they had hoped to dominate, before fading silently out. Melbourne's senility is chronicled in detail. And after Albert's death Victoria herself, according to Strachey, felt she had outlived her true role: "She herself felt that her true life had ceased with her husband's, that the remainder of her days upon earth was of a twilight nature—an epilogue to a drama that was done" (297).

Time, then, is a weapon against the meanings human beings affix to things and people. Victoria and her age respond by attributing these meanings more ferociously than ever, keeping diaries, building memorials, compiling photographic albums. As she grows older, the Queen grows more and more obsessed with her possessions, which seem to offer her "palpable barriers against the outrages of change and time" (298). She keeps scrupulous records of everything she owns and refuses to throw anything out: "There should be no changes and no losses! Nothing should ever move—neither the past nor the present—and she herself least of all! And so the tenacious woman, hoarding her valuables, decreed their immortality with all the resolution of her soul. She would not lose one memory or one pin" (399). Victoria's efforts are doomed because she has equated imaginative and literal reconstructions. The attempted fusion of object and meaning is impossible. Imaginative reconstruction can create but not represent or capture a past moment's significance. The biography and statue of Albert commissioned by Victoria both fail to convey the man himself.

Thematically, then, Strachey suggests that what actually happens is beyond the knowledge and control of individuals—that behind every master is another master. Underlying history's elusiveness is time itself, constant causer and reminder of loss. Through stylistic choices and through narrative technique, Strachey reinforces this sense of huge nonhuman forces shaping human lives. Most obviously there are references to fate, to a "wheel of fortune" (144). This linking of human destiny to larger, impersonal and uncontrollable forces surfaces imagistically in the use of meteorological and related metaphors. Describing the rise of liberal sentiment in the early nineteenth century, Strachey writes, "The mighty still sat proudly in their seats, dispensing their ancient tyranny; but a storm was gathering out of the darkness, and already there was lightning in the sky" (31). The movement seems to be removed from human agency, equated with the least controllable of natural phenomena.

The human life span is linked to the passage of seasons (Melbourne as an autumn rose) and especially to portions of a single day: Victoria's life after Albert's death is a twilight (297), and as it draws to a close, Strachey twice combines weather and time of day: "And so, after the toils and tempests of the day, a long evening followed—mild, serene, and lighted with a golden glory" (384). But at the start of the last chapter he contradicts himself. "The evening had been golden," he suggests, "but, after all, the day was to close in cloud and tempest" (420). One gains a sense of harmony, of continuity from this union of human and natural measurements, but much like that continuity posited by Pater, it is extremely prone to fluctuation, characterized, as Rachel Vinrace notices, by an utter disregard for human subjectivity.

Strachey's heavily modified sentences somehow conspire with the meteorological metaphors to suggest a universe where dimly understood mechanisms crush human effort. The examples are rife and oppressive:

> The tide of circumstance was flowing now with irresistible fullness towards a very different consummation. (193)

> The wheel of fortune turned with a sudden rapidity; and he found, in the arms of Victoria, the irrevocable assurance of his overwhelming fate. (144)

> An ambiguous, prepotent figure had come to disturb the ancient, subtle, and jealously guarded balance of the English Constitution. (250)

Each of these sentences seems a case of overkill, with several words making the same point: *tide, irresistible, fullness, consummation,* all suggest inevitability, as do *irrevocable, overwhelming,* and *fate* in the next sentence. The effect is similar to that Michael Riffaterre attributes to overdetermination: "The effect of over-determination," he writes, "is to transfer the meaning of one word to several, as if it were saturating the sentence with that meaning, so that the reader feels the sentence keeps on confirming overtly what he gathered from a single word" (Suleiman and Crossman 127n). Certainly the reader responds to such repetition with the sense that the figures depicted are trapped indeed by circumstances and attributes so effusively stated.

Yet Strachey's style is not always so overpowering. At times his language serves to dissolve rather than solidify, giving human consciousness a translucence with the potential to transform rather than be determined by circumstance. Here language has a tremendous advantage over more tangible materials—a point Strachey hints at when he asks ironically, "Words and books may be ambiguous memorials; but who can misinterpret the visible solidity of bronze and stone?" (318). Ambiguity at least has the virtue of stimulating thought, of triggering the imagination, unlike the "vast and elaborate mausoleum" built by Victoria (318).

When Herbert Read compared the famous last paragraph of *Queen Victoria* to a passage from Joyce's *Ulysses*, he castigated Strachey for his rhetoric. The passage, he argued, seems vivid, but in fact offers little concrete imagery and defeats all efforts at actual visualization (Heilbrun, *Androgyny* 187). Certainly Read is right in suggesting that Strachey's prose is hard to visualize, but the difficulty, I believe, is inseparable from Strachey's purpose in *Queen Victoria*: to deconstruct linguistically an age obsessed with solidity. His modifiers rarely add up to a picture, tending instead to repeat each other or occasionally contradict each other, or even undo themselves; like Conrad in *Heart of Darkness*, he has a fondness for adjectives with negative prefixes or suffixes—*ir*resistible, *ir*revocable, *un*familiar. There is no pretense of actually conveying a material image, when, for example, Strachey describes Napoleon III as an "unfamiliar, darkly glittering foreign object moving so meteorically before her" (271). The intangible language insists instead on the image's absence and on its own compensatory linguistic excess.

In unraveling Victoria's mind, Strachey is, in a sense, unwriting his own biography, insisting on the evanescence of his subject's life, the unavailability of its essence. Her own attempt to fix her experience in language is the source of the biography's unexpected poignance. For Strachey seems at once her coauthor and her critic when he describes, for example, her feelings about Scotland:

> Each hallowed moment stood out clear, beautiful, eternally significant. For, at the time, every experience there, sentimental or grave, or trivial, had come upon her with a peculiar vividness, like a flashing of marvellous lights. Albert's stalkings—an evening walk when she lost her way—Vicky sitting down on a wasps' nest—a torchlight dance—with what intensity such things, and ten thousand like them, impressed themselves upon her eager consciousness! (265)

The passage raises questions about narrative technique: is Strachey speaking as objective narrator in that first sentence, or from within his subject's mind? Clearly each "hallowed moment" did not stand out "clear, beautiful, eternally significant"; had it done so, there would be no need to memorialize the past, to make statues and biographies. That first sentence, then, is less objective assertion than an example of what the mind does to experience, how it turns the formless into a design, creating a "moment of make-believe," in Rachel Vinrace's words. But Strachey's task as biographer here resembles Victoria's own effort to clutch the past. As the syntax becomes fragmented, the names familiar, the passage moves more and more evidently into Victoria's consciousness, and the reader's sympathy becomes qualified by his sense of the intrinsic hopelessness of that effort.

Throughout *Queen Victoria*, Strachey employs that modulated narrative voice he developed in *Eminent Victorians*. Variations on the interior monologue are frequent; describing Victoria's feelings about leaving Scotland, for example, Strachey writes, "She could hardly bear it; she sat disconsolate in her room and watched the snow falling. The last day! Oh! If only she could be snowed up!" (268). The narrator impersonates others as well: Leopold, Albert, Stockmar, even a kind of generalized public opinion: "Deep in the darkness the Baron loomed. Another foreigner! Decidedly, there were elements in the situation which went far to justify the popular alarm" (251). The effect of all this narrative impersonation is to suggest that if history itself is an inevitable chain of events shaped only by an inscrutable fate, it is nonetheless transmuted by the particular imaginations experiencing it.

Edmund Wilson has pointed out that Victoria's attractiveness in the biography derives from the personal— rather than external, political—view we get of her:

> To Strachey's Victoria, the role of queen is a woman's personal experience, a matter of likes and dislikes, of living up to social obligations. This is the force of the famous deathbed scene, which has been imitated so often by people who have tried to reproduce the cadences without understanding the point: that Victoria has lived through the Victorian Age, has stood at the center of its forces, without knowing what it was all about. (552)

Victoria's *personal* experiencing of her role has, in a sense, been at the expense of her ability to dominate. She has chosen to lead, Wilson points out, the "woman's limited life." But along with that limited life goes a less limited imagination, and if Victoria has indeed failed to understand the Victorian Age, this has not kept her from incarnating it. Her most striking quality, according to Strachey, is a "peculiar sincerity" (416). If Victoria weakens the queenship by personalizing it, it is because for her there is no distinction between her political position and her personality. From her fusion of them into the single, transparently clear, crystal pebble of her personality come both her power to imagine and her powerlessness to affect.

In *Queen Victoria*, then, Strachey counterpoints the queen's making of herself with her unmaking by time, even as he himself seems at once to be constructing from without a clearly delineated figure, then dissolving it from within, as he inhabits its imagination. Victoria herself has a misplaced faith in an overliteralized view of the imagination that severely limits its power to transform. Jerome Buckley describes Victorian taste as obsessed by verisimilitude at the same time that it feared enchantment: "All successful ornament," he writes in *The Victorian Temper,* "was . . . expected not only to attain the appearance of actuality, but also to suggest that the illusion was merely illusion" (133). Victoria's collecting instinct, her journal-writing, her taste for such objects as the centerpiece designed by her husband "which arrayed upon ornate pedestals the Queen's favorite dogs, modeled from life, together with a dead hare, a caged rat, and the remains of a dead one" (Buckley 133), are wrongheaded responses to the elusiveness of time. What she has tried to solidify, Strachey, in that famous final paragraph, dissolves, redeeming her, in a sense, from her own literalism. Instead of a catalogue of her possessions, like the one she herself compiled, he describes a series of intangible visions: "Perhaps," he writes, "her fading mind called up once more the shadows of the past to float before it, and retraced, for the last time, the vanished visions of that long history—passing back and back, through the cloud of years, to older and ever older memories—" (423). She has spent her life doggedly weaving herself; here Strachey unweaves her. *Fading, shadows, float, vanished, cloud,* all suggest obscurity, intangibility, dissolution. The movement backward through time seems to unwind the plot of her life, as the perceptions become more and more fragmented and childlike.

In "Florence Nightingale," Strachey found a way of rejecting Victorian assumptions about plausibility and life-plots. Through Victoria he explores the effort of identity to assert itself against time. Using biography, the form traditionally used to assert the claims of identity, he instead suggests its limitations, its essential imaginative failure. For what Strachey writes of Victoria's collecting instinct could apply equally well to the biographical impulse:

> The collecting instinct has its roots in the very depths of human nature; and, in the case of Victoria, it seemed to owe its force to two of her dominating impulses—the intense sense, which had always been hers, of her own personality, and the craving which, growing with the years, had become in her old age almost an obsession, for fixity, for solidity, for the setting up of palpable barriers against the outrages of change and time. (398)

By aligning himself with his subject's point of view and revealing her emotions so sympathetically, he seems to accept her own self-valuation. In fact, though, he reveals its limitations; the actual mechanisms of history and the greatest intensity of experience escape her clumsy attempts to grasp them and hold them fast.

Pater's depiction of imagination interacting with flux, Rachel Vinrace's starker vision of momentary transcendence followed by blindly operating natural laws, and Strachey's tension between determinism and imaginative freedom are all, I am suggesting, related treatments of the thematic underlying novelistic biography. In reaction against the Victorian view of great men as willfully transforming history, the novelistic biographer is prone to dichotomizing history and imagination at the same time that he participates imaginatively in his own historical reconstruction. The paradox leads to an almost obsessive concern with these issues, as they operate thematically, in the subject's life (what role did imagination play in his life?); structurally, in his shaping of that life (to what extent does the biographer attempt to imitate the structure of his subject's life?); and narrationally, in his recounting of the life (does he use imagination to reconstruct the subject's own inner—imaginative—life?). Skeptical of historical objectivity, novelistic biographers take a "relativistic, anti-mimetic stance" (Monsman 2); with Forster, they are doubtful of the Aristotelian assumption that plot reveals character (*Aspects* 58). Yet they are equally skeptical of the romantic assumption that character can transcend plot.[8] Strachey deconstructs Victorian heroes, eager to show the causation behind apparently free will, but in the preface he argues against seeing people as mere "symptoms" of the past. The result is a return again and again to the interplay between a linear chain of inevitabilities and the potential of individual consciousnesses to re-imagine what happens.

Scott reveals a concern with similar issues as early as *The Architecture of Humanism*. Subtitled "A Study in the History of Taste," it is, in its way, as fierce a book as *Eminent Victorians*. Scott discusses and demolishes five "fallacies" supporting the Victorian preference for Gothic over Renaissance architecture: the romantic, the mechanical, the ethical, the biological, and the academic. His remarks about the biological or "evolutionary" fallacy indicate a resemblance between his concerns and Strachey's. The evolutionary approach, he suggests, because it explains rather than evaluates, was a necessary antidote to ethical criticism, but its emphasis on sequence—the detection of signs of future architectural developments in past styles—leads its adherents to undervalue those features that do not play a developmental role:

> Renaissance architecture is a very unfortunate field for the exercise of this kind of criticism, for the reason, already established, that it was an architecture of taste; an architecture, that is to say, which was not left to develope [sic] itself at the blind suasion of an evolutionary law. It cast off its immediate past and, by an act of will, chose—and chose rightly—its own parentage. It scorned heredity; and, if it sometimes reflected its environment, it also did much to create it. It could change its course in mid-career; it was summoned hither and thither at the bidding of individual wills. . . . *Here was no procession of*

ordered causes, but a pageant of adventures, a fantastic masque of taste. [my emphasis] (130–31)

Scott, then, no less than Strachey, is concerned with the potential disruption of impersonal laws by the creative imagination. As a biographer, he is at once an ally and a critic of that disruption.

According to Iris Origo, Scott's next project after *The Architecture of Humanism* was to be *A History of Taste*. She describes the page that lay, unfinished, on his desk, bearing the words

A HISTORY OF TASTE
    Volume I
    Chapter I
        It is very difficult

and nothing else (*Images* 104). Instead he began a work on a smaller scale, the biography of Mme de Charrière, *Portrait of Zélide*. Like Strachey, he is interested in the act of self-making; what most stands out about Zélide is the patterned quality her life takes on—a life that seems on the one hand artfully shaped, a triumph of taste, and on the other, tragically limiting, a failure of the imagination. For like Victoria, Zélide does not recognize her own imaginative complicity in the life she leads; she believes she is simply facing the facts and in so believing, forfeits her power to alter them.

The author of *The Architecture of Humanism* (1914) and *The Portrait of Zélide* (1925) and editor of six volumes of *Boswell's Private Papers from Malahide Castle* (1928–1932), Geoffrey Scott appears in no British reference book.[9] Yet both his books were quite successful, and with *Zélide* he became known as an innovative biographer, one of the best of Strachey's followers.

"He was tall, & dark & had the distinguished face of a

failure," Virginia Woolf writes of him in her diary (3: 244). He surfaces in the memoirs of Nicky Mariano, Nigel Nicolson, and Iris Origo, and in biographies of Harold Nicolson, Vita Sackville-West, and Edith Wharton as a charming, often depressed egotist whose life was oddly entwined with other biographers. As a friend and neighbor of the Berensons in Italy, he met numerous literary figures, including Woolf, Strachey, and Percy Lubbock. In 1918 he married Lady Sybil Cutting, whose daughter Iris became a biographer and published her first book, *Allegra*, with the Hogarth Press in the 1930s. The marriage was not a success except, according to Origo in *Images and Shadows*, during the time they worked together on *Zélide*, which Scott dedicated to his wife (105). But almost simultaneously Scott fell in love with Vita Sackville-West, another future biographer, and during their brief affair in 1923 they exchanged manuscripts. He commented on her poem *The Land*, while she responded to Zélide, which he, in a letter to her, even called "our book" (Nicolson, *Portrait* 197). In 1927,[10] he and Sybil were divorced; she later married Percy Lubbock, yet another biographer. Scott died in 1929 in New York, where he was working with Colonel Ralph Isham on the Boswell papers.

Scott's only theoretical discussion of biography is his commentary on the Boswell papers, of which he lived to edit six volumes. This commentary emphasizes the immense labor and vast ambition of Boswell's effort to endow so much detail with so much life. It is ground-breaking in its emphasis on Boswell's artfulness, his self-consciousness as a biographer.[11] Other biographers, Scott writes, "did not even know that biography is impossible," while Boswell at least had the sense to complain, for example, "I cannot pourtray commissioner Cochrane as he exists in my mind" (6: 16, 17). The implication, of course, is that Scott had himself concluded that biography was impossible; he began his work with Boswell's papers three years after his biography of Zélide was published. In a letter to Nicky Mariano he writes, "It is curious how intimately one gets to know the people one writes about. Mme de Charrière is as real to me as almost anyone in real life" (Mariano 26). The transmutation into language of so vivid a mental image could be a difficult task, realized either clumsily or too revealingly; in the same letter, in fact, he worries that Mary Berenson will note a parallel to her relationship with Scott in Scott's depiction of Zélide's relationship with Benjamin Constant.

In his concluding note to the biography, however, Scott takes a more detached stand: "All I have here done is to catch an image of her in a single light, and to make from a single angle the best drawing I can of Zélide, as I believe her to have been; I have sought to give her the reality of a fiction; but my material is fact" (215–16). "To give her the reality of a fiction": the aim is one he shares with Strachey and Cecil. The pictorial imagery, however, with its emphasis on narrative perspective, seems to suggest a more mediated approach, one where the narrator's relation to his subject, his angle of vision, is itself the drama portrayed. Edel places *Zélide* in a category distinct from Strachey's, which he calls "pictorial" (*Literary Biography* 85), stressing the work's lack of chronological development. In fact, though, Scott has a great deal in common with Strachey. He allows himself fairly free access to his subject's inner life, while retaining his omniscience, and he stresses the ironic fixity of fate, in contrast to his subject's self-deception. And like Strachey he is fascinated by the human impulse—most evident in those for whom direct action is problematic—to weave a self.

Scott defines Zélide from the start as a duality: La Tour paints her as passionate and impulsive; Houdon sculpts her as "sceptical and aloof" (1). Warm and cold, feminine and masculine, imaginative and rationalistic: the paired contrasts appear again and again in shifting terms, echoed in the book's closing words: "The mind has drawn its pattern," Scott concludes, "The Portrait of Zélide: a frond of flame; a frond of frost" (210). This duality leads to her failure in several ways, according to Scott. She fails to harmonize qualities that could have been complementary but instead produced only contradictory, mutually destructive impulses. She herself insists on her rationality, blinding herself to a substantial portion of her own personality, and thus barring herself from fulfillment. Finally, the self-deception facilitates repetition; she does not learn from experience, for she can see only half of it. The precocious girl of the book's opening pages is virtually identical to the dying woman of its conclusion. Each man in her life plays a similar role as well. Bellegarde is succeeded by Boswell who is succeeded by DeCharrière, Hermenches by Constant, and in relation to each, she is blinded by the same insistence on her own rationality.

Cooperating with this apparently innate duality to doom Zélide is fate, Scott's term for those circumstances, such as her social and historical position, which keep her from self-fulfillment. When she loses Constant to Mme de Staël, for example, she is a child of the eighteenth century defeated by the nineteenth. Her placement in history reinforces or echoes her own rejection of emotion. Like both Strachey's Melbourne (in *Elizabeth and Essex*) and Cecil's, she is simultaneously and identically doomed by internal duality and external displacement in time.

This determination by circumstance and character is reflected in the biography's structure: as early as page two, Scott describes Zélide's death in "that desolate Swiss manor, her chosen exile," feeling herself a failure (2). At the time of her death, according to Scott, an autopsy revealed that from childhood she had suffered from an "internal malady," a rather grotesque literalization of the irony implicit in any biography—that its seminal moment is not the birth but the death of its subject—but also an image for Zélide's particular fixity of character.

To such a predetermined personality, the passage of

time has little meaning, as suggested by the opening of Scott's penultimate chapter: "One day is like another at Colombier. Older grows Mademoiselle Louise in the vegetable garden, older Mademoiselle Henriette at the card table, older Monsieur de Charrière by the fire" (204). The subject-verb inversion, the repeated adverbial phrases, the commonplace domestic occupations (invoked not as activities but as locations) suggest the lackadaisical adding of day to day, a sense of time devoid of dynamism or change. Strachey gains a similar effect by treating the passage of time as a succession of dramatic scenes: "Lord Palmerston's laugh—a queer metallic 'ha! ha! ha!' . . . was heard no more in Piccadilly; Lord John Russell dwindled into senility; Lord Derby tottered from the stage. A new scene opened; and new protagonists . . . struggled together in the limelight" (327).

For both Strachey and Scott, there is a tremendous contrast between time as experienced by a particular consciousness (which is scarcely time at all since it seems to stop entirely) and time as it measurably elapses and manifests itself in old age and death (which is also scarcely time at all since the process itself eludes human awareness). Both versions of time, the slow and the fast, leave human consciousness helplessly agog on the sidelines.

Queen Victoria gains much of its impact from the narrator's partial alignment with individual viewpoints; Scott's *Portrait of Zélide* is less balanced in this respect. The book's very form seems complicitous with Zélide's doom, its tightly knit feeling of inevitability derived from her trapped personality tracing again and again the same unhappy pattern. Repeated imagery and events structure the biography, and the imagery is itself hackneyed: the ego is a cage offering no escape; Zélide's relation to Constant is a castle gradually subsiding into ruins; life is a badly written play. Zélide is trapped not only by the patterning of her own self but by past formulations of how that patterning works.

Yet Scott, like Strachey, is concerned with his subject's potential for transcendence. She is not a mere passive victim at the hands of fate, but a co-conspirator in that fate, who, had she recognized her constitutive role, could have freed herself. Zélide does not acknowledge the imaginative element in her own analyses, the fictive element in the facts she prides herself on facing. The apparent induction of consequences from causes may be more creative than analytical. Scott writes of Constant and Zélide: "Bruised by the past, they sought to protect themselves against the future by a vivid forecast of its perils; thus they created and gave rein to their own nightmare. Like children playing at ghosts, they found themselves overtaken by the shadow of fear; and even before the spectre had taken shape they were in flight" (150).

Similarly, reports may be merely rumors, such as those that alienate the two while Constant is at the German court, while the recording of experience may be in fact the invention of another self, "something apart and often ironically diverse from that other personality of act and speech" (152). "Patterns in the mind: all her life she had been drawing them," Scott writes (208). The word *draw* takes on a crucial ambiguity here (and the word recurs in the book's last sentence): it suggests the relatively passive acts of pulling from behind or getting by chance, but also the clearly creative act of portraying or composing. It is this latter meaning that Zélide fails to recognize.

As biographer, Scott, on the other hand, does recognize the extent to which *his* version of reality is a pattern he draws. "To dip the quill in ink is a magical gesture," he writes of Zélide's letter-writing, but the same could be said of biography-writing and, unlike his subject, he makes the most of it. He frequently, for example, describes scenes as paintings—a Cuyp landscape, a Longhi scene, or this "Dutch interior" he inserts, emphasizing its artificially posed quality by switching to the present tense:

A Dutch picture. Madame de Charrière is seated in her upper room working with her maid in the stillness. A broad band of sunlight slants from the half-shuttered window in the corner and falls upon Henriette Monachan pondering, pen in hand, at the table; her mistress looks up, watching her from the shadow. Madam [sic] de Charrière has narrowed her life until the company of Henriette is all she asks. (197)

The moment may well have occurred, but its presentation by a witness in the present tense announces its fictiveness, as does its echo of Boswell, who referred to his life of Johnson as a "Flemish Picture" (869).

Like Strachey, Scott does not hesitate to enter his subjects' minds, moving freely from narration to rumination. Occasionally a change in tense accents the shift, as when Zélide contrasts Constant's wit with her husband's slowness. At night, Scott writes in the past tense, she and Constant talked: "To talk! the joy of it. Benjamin's talk is unforeseen, swift like summer lightning. . . . Poor Monsieur de Charrière, ankle deep in a bog, with him you move a yard at a time to a fearfully foregone conclusion. After fourteen years at that pace, here, indeed, is something like motion!" (100). But even as the scene moves out of Zélide's mind, the present tense dominates, turning the biography for a few pages, at least, into something very like a play.

Scott eagerly acknowledges the resemblance of his portrait to a play, suggesting that the prologue of Zélide's marriage was epic, "but the climax was comedy; and the end, tragedy" (13). He uses theatrical language to achieve a dramatic effect, to create expectation:

Zélide is right; the play is never finished. The lowered curtain will rise on another act. Another actor is waiting in the wings.
Enter Madame de Staël. (172)

All these narrative techniques, then—the composing of pictures and scenes, the inner speech, the use of the present tense—emphasize the biographer's artifice, his free use of factual material on his palette. Virginia Woolf compared biography to painting with photographs instead of oils (*Letters* 6: 285); Scott freely dissolves those photographs into a more manageable material. The work of art that results is very much his rather than his subject's; his framing of the Dutch picture only accentuates Zélide's confined life; his dramatizing of Mme de Staël's arrival points up the dramatic irony at Zélide's expense. For Zélide's skepticism excludes her as definitively as Victoria's literal-minded sentimentality from participation in the act of self-creation.

Perhaps it is inevitable that many biographies written between the wars conclude with the hypothesized memories of their subjects. Certainly the echo of Strachey's conclusion to Queen Victoria has been potent, and it is detectable in Scott's closing paragraphs.[12] Forster points out in *Aspects of the Novel* that, along with marriage, death is the only point at which plot and character can truly be said to coincide, suggesting one reason why these events serve as the biographer's linchpins. André Maurois argues that death turns every life into a work of art by providing it with a feeling of completion.[13] This summing up from within at the final moment provides, seamlessly, a closure for both book and life. When most effective, in *Queen Victoria* and in *Zélide*, it serves also to erase the solidity lent by the bulk of the biography to its subject, to reassert the momentarily woven, fictive quality of the biographical image. The apparently objective facts and laws to which Zélide has devoted her life and to which the biographer has apparently made his obeisance are revealed finally to be fantasms: "Facts: fate: mere images, bold as the ripple on the moat at Zuylen, brief as the wind there; images—Zélide with Hermenches in her thoughts, her brother home from the sea, Benjamin and again Benjamin and a blankness— the dark before her no emptier than that void" (210). To the dying Zélide, future and past are equally void of substance, as they are in Pater's depiction in *The Renaissance* of time as a stream, with self reduced to a "strange, perpetual weaving and unweaving. . . ."

When David Cecil wrote of Pater in 1956, he ridiculed the dualistic scholar/aesthete as an Oxford don incongruously wearing an "apple-green silk neckcloth" (*Fine Art* 259). His personality (timid) and his purpose (daring) did not mesh, according to Cecil, nor did he have the imagination to understand and transcend his duality (274). The complaint, of course, is paradigmatically that of the novelistic biographer, but it also reflects a rejection of Pater's romanticism, a shift away from imagination's transformative potential toward an ever more predetermined, more impersonal sense of the self.

At the end of his biography of Cowper, Cecil describes the irony by which the poet's greatest poem grew out of his profoundest desperation: "By the last and most baffling caprice of that destiny whose plaything he was, those afflictions against which he had exhausted his life in struggling, now, in the very moment of his defeat, revealed themselves as the instrument of his greatest achievement" (298). The echo of Hardy's tendency to portray man as sport for the gods is significant. Cecil's *Stricken Deer* is a strikingly Hardyesque biography, its central concerns ably—if unknowingly—depicted by Cecil himself in his 1943 *Hardy the Novelist.*

Hardy, according to Cecil, portrays man in conflict with Fate, as it is embodied in weather, in innate character flaws, in chance, and in love (40). Often a character's fate is shaped by circumstances unknown to him, much as Oedipus's end was implicit in the origin he did not know of. And all this, according to Cecil, takes place on a huge scale, against a natural backdrop whose permutations are portrayed panoramically, as if from a great distance (41–46).

Except for the importance of love, all these characteristics detected by Cecil in Hardy are present in Cecil's *The Stricken Deer* and, to a lesser extent, in his *The Young Melbourne* (1939).

Published in 1929, Cecil's *The Stricken Deer* was the first of several biographies and many works of literary criticism. Like *The Young Melbourne*, it bears the Strachey imprint: fascination with the relation of fate to imagination. But more than in *Queen Victoria*, fate has the upper hand. Cecil has also been compared to Strachey on the basis of his style; certainly all the novelistic biographers bring a new stylistic self-consciousness to the writing of biography, an innovation many regard as obtrusive. Humphrey House attacks Cecil for his "post-Stracheyan" sentences, while defending Strachey himself, whose detachment, he argues, has been ignored by his followers' call for expressivist biography. House attacks Cecil for his advocacy of biographical self-expression, his attention-getting style, and his tendency to pity his subject, as well as a tendency to slide, unobtrusively and dishonestly, from the ironically poetical to authorially endorsed poeticizing (260–64). But Strachey himself is as guilty of that slide as Cecil; in fact House has aptly described that modulated, ventriloquistic quality I have argued is characteristic of Strachey's narration, which refuses to act as a stable commentary authoritatively integrating the subject into the reader's and biographer's shared context.

Cecil himself told James Clifford that he never wrote a biography without an "emotional or intellectual tie" to the subject. This does not mean, though, that the biographer takes over center stage from his subject, but that he gains access to the subject through himself. As early as 1918, in *The Eton Review*, Cecil wrote of the modern novelist's interest in man's emotions, rather than his situation, an interest that gives him freer access, through his own identification with the subject, to his inner life. "The parts of man with which [the modern novelist] is occupied are those which are common to the race and not peculiar to the individual. I mean the emotions," he writes, describing an approach which takes the narrator away from the sidelines and into the fray itself, aligned with his own characters, since "only we ourselves are conscious of our own emotional experiences" (47).

The Trollopean novel of situation, Cecil argued in *The Eton Review,* had been replaced by a less particularized approach, a transition enacted by Cowper himself as he sinks from peace into madness: "The homely serenity of normal every day had failed him; the story of his life had changed from a Trollopean comedy of domestic manners to the soul tragedy of a Dostoyefsky. And he was to rise from hell borne on the sublime ecstasies of an Alyosha Karamazof" (*Stricken Deer* 75–76). The shift from Trollope to Dostoievski, from surface specificity to deep, impersonal passions reflects what James Hafley calls a characteristically Georgian sense of an "under-life" (13). Pater's web-like self, whose actual threads stretch out far beyond its imagined boundaries, already suggested that much of each individual's substance is shared with other individuals. But later writers took the idea further, supported in particular by Freud's formulation of an unconscious. Forster argues in *Anonymity* for two personalities, an upper and a lower, nameless, with "something general about it," in common with everyone else's lower personalities (16); Virginia Woolf comments on *Orlando,* "the theory being that character goes on underground before we are born; & leaves something afterward also" (Moore 308). And earlier than either, in 1914, D. H. Lawrence writes Edward Garnett about *The Rainbow:*

> You mustn't look in my novel for the old stable *ego* of the character. There is another *ego,* according to whose action the individual is unrecognizable, and passes through, as it were, al-

85

lotropic states which it needs a deeper sense than any we've been used to exercise, to discover are states of the same single radically unchanged element.(75)

This under-life means that the delineation of a self is a creative, not critical act, for it means imposing invented boundaries on a continuity, and in this sense might seem to make biography more difficult, but on the other hand it means the biographer can look inside himself for insights into his subject. This, I would argue, is the assumption underlying Cecil's "expressivist" biography. It also pushes Cecil towards a more deterministic view of the self, since the impersonal self is less accessible to deliberate shaping or reimagining by the subject. "The past," Cecil writes at the start of *The Stricken Deer,* is "a great river ever fed by new streams . . . carrying on its mysterious surface fragments of wreckage, survivals of an earlier day not yet dissolved into oblivion" (4–5). Indescribable because incomplete, the past is also accessible because incomplete, and for the same reason it is beyond the control of those who lived in it. Present in Strachey and Scott, the paradox takes its extremest form in *The Stricken Deer,* where Cecil depicts the painful gap between myth and logos, in Hernadi's terms, between events viewed from within, as incomplete intentions, and from without, as completed causal chains.

According to Cecil's portrait, Cowper's life was rigidly predetermined. His relationship to his mother was extraordinarily close and painfully interrupted by her early death. His early schooling destroyed his nervous system. He may have suffered from "an intimate deformity," and he was, besides, "despondent by nature" (21). He was, in addition, the "epitome of his environment" (16), so that the very times in which he lived reinforced his own propensities. Nor was change or development available to him, according to Cecil: "It is a great mistake to think that people's characters alter as they grow older; though different circumstances may bring different sides of them into prominence. Cowper the child was like Cowper the man" (18).

Given so many causes tending towards one effect, Cowper's life-course takes on the inevitability of a "drama whose action is as simple, as strange, and as terrible, as that of a classical tragedy" (15). Such a coinciding of life and tragedy was the ideal sought by novelistic biographers. Nicolson's highest praise, applied in *The Development of English Biography* to Gosse's *Father and Son,* was that it resembled such a tragedy (146). Maurois argued that every life had the potential for aesthetic coherence because of its naturally tragic shape. "The creature, not the creator, of his destiny" (18), Cowper lends himself, like Oedipus, to two conflicting plots—that of fate, which will win, aligned as it is with the "facts," with the logic of causality and the demands of aesthetic coherence; and that of the individual man seeking to shape his own destiny. Cecil, like Scott, is obsessed with pattern: it serves him as an image for human intentionality and for human doom. There is the pattern, the sense of order Cowper can sometimes establish through his own powers or the mother-figures upon whom he leans, a pattern imposed by his imagination; and then there is the pattern underlying the life as *Life:* the one dictating that birth be followed by death, just as, in the book's American edition, the chapter headed "morning" is followed by "night."

Cowper's love of domesticity, his evangelicalism, and his poems are all efforts to impose his order on the world. For stretches of time, with Mrs. Unwin, for example, the "wretched tangle of his life-history fell into a simple beneficent order" (86). His pet hares, his household chores, and his poetry-writing give shape to his life: "By 1780," Cecil writes, "he had managed to weld the shattered, scattered fragments of his life and thought into some sort of permanent pattern" (154–55). That pattern, though, the human one, is never quite permanent, for it is tenuously superimposed, the moment of make-believe. And in fact in describing one such moment, Cecil echoes a characteristically Woolfian depiction of consciousness freed from then abruptly returned to external constraints: [14]

> Sometimes as he sat there in the gathering dusk, . . . he would sink into a drowsy reverie. Idly he fancied castles and forests in the crumbling coals. . . . And then his attention would wander, and he would sit gazing with fixed, absent eyes, lost for a short moment perhaps in some country of his desire—green blossoming woods of spring, or by the glittering sea. Suddenly a noise would penetrate his consciousness—the wind rattling the window, or the maid coming in with the tea. Blinking his eyes in the unaccustomed brightness of the candlelight, he would shift his position and return to earth. (157)

The vividness with which the imagination is portrayed, the irresistible detail in which Cecil paints the domestic life of Cowper and Mrs. Unwin as a kind of cozy nook in a furiously dangerous, disordered world, create a gripping tension between the reader's identification and his omniscience.

Cecil's portrayal of time as independent of human experience and outside human control suggests from the start that the pattern of logos will triumph over myth. The seeds of Cowper's destruction are within him from the start; inexorably, they unfold, as the tragedy moves from act to act. People do not change, according to Cecil, but time does pass; as in Strachey and Scott, chronology is visible only as it acts physically on one's surroundings and remains unintegratable into any meaningful process of development. "Little lines of laughter had drawn themselves at the corner of mouth and eyes," Cecil writes of Cowper. "But otherwise he and his situation had altered little" (43). What changes there are, are portrayed as a vast panorama of movement devoid of purpose. "Surging and swirling, flowed on the vari-coloured stream of eighteenth-century life," Cecil writes (83). And "All around him surged and roared the palpitating, many-coloured London of 1741"

(23). The subject-verb inversion recalls Scott's similar constructions for a similar effect: preceding any agent, the action appears unmotivated, beyond human control.

The novelistic biographers have all been accused of over-
writing, and certainly all are stylistically self-indulgent. One
unavoidably striking characteristic of *The Stricken Deer* is its
extravagant diction. Cecil has a predilection for the word
lurid (matched only by Nicolson's for *morbid* in his *Tennyson*),
and in describing Cowper's madness, no word seems vivid
enough, no trick of melodrama too exaggerated. When
Cowper, desperately wanting to avoid being examined for
a legal position, goes mad and as a result does indeed avoid
the examination, Cecil writes, "His wish of ten months
back was terribly fulfilled. He was a gibbering, raving ma-
niac" (71). The insane Cowper is somewhat inaccessible to
historical records; of another bout with madness Cecil
writes: "But as he descends to his inferno, once more the
smouldering clouds rise and hide him from our sight. . . .
Now and again the clouds lift, and we catch a glimpse of
his face; but it is distorted beyond recognition by the
flames of misery and madness that leap around it" (139).
And the last act of his tragedy ends "in the Elizabethan
manner, amid shriek and blood-boltered spectre and wild
infernal darkness" (263).

The redundancy, the hellish imagery, the reference to
Elizabethan extravagance all suggest a reality beyond our
daily experience, a mythic reality of infernal descents and
resurrections. This reality is *fact,* he insists: "The nervous,
scholarly barrister of the Temple was to die in a lurid agony of despair and madness, and be born anew in another
place. . . . This is the fact, the astounding, terrific fact"
(53). The suggestion is that the laws of causality have been
extraordinarily, inexplicably violated: "In vain we scan the
imperfect records left to us in an effort to understand the
real origin of Cowper's catastrophe" (53). The doom, in
other words, that seemed so clearly dictated by circumstances, so clearly attributable to several causes, remains

also a re-enactment of mythic rites, an outgrowth of prior texts as much as of prior events (see Culler 29). The lost origin of catastrophe, whose inaccessibility forces Cowper to act out his tragedy, also moves that tragedy beyond personal circumstance into the realm of communal myth. This, perhaps, is the final irony that allows Cowper to write "The Cast-away." It is the same irony that leaves Tess a sacrificial victim at Stonehenge and Oedipus a ritual scapegoat.

In summary, novelistic biographers immerse themselves in their subjects' inner lives while retaining their retrospective omniscience. Acutely aware of their dual perspective, they portray their subjects, too, as split between predetermined fate and transforming imagination. Part of that fate is to be torn asunder by contradictory characteristics or drives. In contrast, then, biographers suggest a hypothetically unitary self which they create out of their subjects' failure to harness fully their own imaginations. For unless the imaginative nature of selfhood is acknowledged, personality becomes a prison, isolating the self from others' versions of reality, facilitating self-deception and ineffectuality. But self-deception is very close to self-invention. Recognizing that the self is an imaginative creation would have allowed the biographical subjects to unify without imprisoning themselves; as they are portrayed by the novelistic biographers, however, the recognition escapes them. Thus Cecil in *The Young Melbourne* lingers over the statesman's relation to his wife because he can portray her as so utterly and so dramatically self-created and self-deceived. In *The Last Journey* Nicolson, writing on Byron, chooses as his focus his subject's final months in Greece, where he sought to lead a revolution and instead died amid chaos. But the biographers themselves do acknowledge the role of imagination in creating a self, and unify their books by positing the self-that-might-have-been, an imagined self which would itself have understood its imagined-ness. Believing, then, that action does not reveal character, which is formed and experienced internally, they nonetheless borrow dramatistic structures, suggesting that the life does have its own unity, though it is one of personality, not action, hypothetical and not actual. And in writing of that life, the novelistic biographers combine an elegiac with an ironic tone, suggesting, in yet another way, the interplay between identification and distance, between imagination and fate.

Between 1918 and 1939, a great number of novelistic biographies were published. In all of them, the influence of Strachey is evident; Woolf's 1927 letter to Strachey on the subject is scarcely exaggerated: "If only every good spectacled Don and schoolgirl did not think themselves LS & proceed to put it into practice!" (Woolf and Strachey 160). She is referring specifically to D. E. Enfield's extraordinary biography of Letitia Landon, the Victorian poet, which Hogarth Press was about to publish. Enfield's earlier biography of Louise Colet fits into the same novelistic category, as do Bosanquet's 1927 *Harriet Martineau*, Edith Sitwell's 1936 life of Queen Victoria, Hugh Kingsmill's 1928 *Matthew Arnold* and his 1938 *D. H. Lawrence;* Malcolm Muggeridge's *The Earnest Atheist* (1936), a life of Samuel Butler, and Harold Nicolson's *Tennyson* (1923), *Byron* (1924), and *Swinburne* (1926). Aldous Huxley's 1941 biography of Cardinal Richelieu, *Grey Eminence,* is another example of novelistic biography, but outside the scope of this study. In all these works, the subject's self-image is revealed as deluded and self-limiting. The biographers tend to use the subject's own writing as a way of getting at thoughts and emotions. Kingsmill, in particular, is shameless in using Lawrence's novels to fill in what he does not know about Lawrence's life, producing, as a result, an unappealing pastiche. The method works best, it seems to me, when the tone is not so judgmental and the analysis more tentative. Strachey's *Queen Victoria,* for example, reveals what a complex mixture of irony, sympathy, and linguistic play novelistic biography can be.

An exhaustive discussion of the many novelistic biographies would be impossible. A few that move in more experimental directions, though, are worth talking about. Doris Enfield's 1928 *L. E. L.: A Mystery of the Thirties*, for example, which borders on novelized biography and is not, finally, convincing, does incorporate innovative techniques: Enfield structures the biography around a series of traumatic childhood experiences; her narrative is fragmented, some sentences incomplete and some in the present tense; and she quotes extensively from other texts, placing L. E. L. in relation to a particular historical moment and the texts that produced her. The result is a novelized psychobiography that has much in common with Strachey's *Elizabeth and Essex*.

The definitive childhood experiences are presented in five scenes: (1) Letitia realizes that her Nanny, who promised to stay with her, is actually leaving to get married; (2) Nanny responds coldly to her grief, telling her, "What a tiresome girl it is"; (3) Letitia overhears, as she prepares for a party, "Did you ever see such a plain little thing?" (4) she discovers fantasy as she reads about Sylvester Tramper's African wanderings; and (5) she is noticed by Mr. Jerdan, the editor who will "discover" her.

Landon's entire story is in these scenes: initial rejection turned to fantasy turned to popular success. Though she dreamed initially not of marriage but of adventure, the original dream becomes transposed in her poetry into a single theme, sentimental love: "blighted feelings, hopes destroyed, a broken heart, a slow decline, an early grave" (61). These poems become vastly popular and L. E. L. socializes with the London literati—though scandals arise about her relationships with men, which in fact were perfectly innocent, Enfield suggests, the rumors perhaps deliberately fueled by Landon herself. Finally Landon marries Captain Maclean of West Africa after reading his account of his experiences there, an account recalling Sylvester Tramper and her earliest fantasies. But both adventure and romance fail her, her husband treats her coldly, and she dies mysteriously in Africa, a possible suicide.

The emphasis on a single psyche's self-deception—particularly a woman's effort to divert ambitious goals into erotic ones—L. E. L. shares with the earlier *Lady of the Salons,* about Colet. It differs, however, in its heavy use of dramatic conventions and its utter neglect of narrative continuity. Each scene is presented with virtual stage directions and set designs, often in sentence fragments or in the present tense. "Friday morning, Letitia's bedroom," begins one such scene (30). Or, "A silvery mist turns to grey in the park outside" (25).

At the heart of *L. E. L.* is, as in *Elizabeth and Essex,* an absence: the absence of a strong poetic voice from English literature and the absence of Letitia Landon from her real life. Surrounding the absence are texts: accounts of Byron's funeral and Victoria's coronation, Landon's poems and her inquest. The narrator's first words appear on page nineteen, preceded by juxtaposed newspaper reports of Byron's funeral. Landon herself is not mentioned until six pages later. Enfield is interested in the parallel between the psyche of a popular poet and the era that embraced her.

Landon's popularity comes during the "long eclipse of English taste" following Byron's death (68). At twenty-five, she was commonly regarded as a genius. But with the coronation of Victoria, the end is near; there are "cheers welcoming in a new era in which she has no part" (150). In between, there was merely her empty verse and her empty literary hobnobbing, matching the overall literary void.

More interesting than the story itself, then, is the way in which it is shaped by texts, all as emphatically fragmentary as the scenes through which Enfield depicts Landon's childhood. The biography is framed by quoted excerpts; the accounts of Byron's funeral are matched by an entire chapter of depositions from the inquest following Landon's death. *Sylvester Tramper* and her poems provide fantasized escapes, while her reading of Maclean's report on Africa returns her to "the lost paradise of her childhood" (130). Most mysteriously, anonymous letters and rumors bring an end to her engagement to John Forster. Did Landon herself send the letters, Enfield wonders, "prompted by some pathological cleavage in her personality to destroy with one hand the happiness she tried to grasp with the other?" (93–94). Certainly anonymous letters—like legal sentences—are one way of bringing fantasy into contact with reality; whether true or false, the words they contain affect the life they describe.

L. E. L. is not a biographical masterpiece. But it reflects quite clearly the experimental mood among biographers in its rejection of narrative continuity, its conception of a life turned by trauma and repression into a fantasy-machine, an elaborator of texts aiming to hide the essential absence at its core. It demonstrates how the biographer writing under Strachey's influence might begin by recognizing the vital role played by self-deception in life and, in a novelistic biography, expose the disjunction between image and fate; then move toward a more radical (and in Strachey's case less judgmental) position whereby there is no disjunction and no delusion, and reality itself becomes the product of the imagination.

Like Enfield, Harold Nicolson began by being heavily influenced by Lytton Strachey, then gradually moved in new directions. His *Tennyson* employs a modulated narrative voice that seeps into the subject's mind, and even the prose rhythms are Stracheyan at times. When Tennyson remembers and mourns Hallam, he sounds much like Victoria on her deathbed. The memories pile up in parallel constructions until the sentence climaxes: "and oh! the way he would take one's arm, on summer evenings, under the limes!" (88). Tennyson's "strangely dual nature" is typical of the novelistic subject (60). Here, and in *Swinburne*, Nicolson uses psychological terminology, diagnosing neurotic

94

crises and pathological fixations so that the subject seems trapped and static, overshadowed by the narrator's greater insight.

Five years after *Tennyson*, Nicolson published his openly fictionalized *Some People*. The ironic tone, the use of telling physical details, the brevity of its portraits, and its impudently casual treatment of the powerful are reminiscent of *Eminent Victorians*. To some extent, then, Nicolson seems merely a more prolific Strachey. But when *Some People* is read alongside the 1928 *Helen's Tower*, another element emerges: the dramatization of memory. In his 1928 *Development of English Biography*, Nicolson predicted a growing split between scientific and literary biography (155); *Some People* announces his movement away from the clinical; he seems less interested in psychological motivation than in sensual immediacy and the oddly arbitrary juxtapositions produced by his own memories.

In 1932, Nicolson considered writing a sequel to *Some People*, but hesitated, feeling the appropriate mood had passed (*Diaries* 117). Two years later, influenced by his reading of Proust, he wrote, "I shall . . . write an autobiography in six volumes. It will be called F. A. or Fictional Autobiography"; it is to be a "study in mutations" (168). Two weeks later, he wondered whether it should be autobiography or biography—i. e., written in the first person or third (170). Then he abandons his "magnum opus" (169), though commenting that rather than return to politics, "obviously I should rather be the Proust of England" (206). In 1936 he finally began *Helen's Tower*, complaining to his wife as he researched his uncle's Irish roots, "This *à la recherche* business is not really much fun when the *temps* is as *perdu* as all that" (270).

Nicolson was attempting a deliberately Proustian biography. Woolf in *Orlando* used Proustian chronology and phenomenology to ridicule the traditional biographer's helplessness before life as it is actually experienced. Nicolson does something different: the narrator's memory becomes the book's true subject, while his uncle is seen only in flashes of memory. As Enfield's *L. E. L.* leans toward psychobiography, Nicolson's *Helen's Tower* verges on mediated biography, showing again the drive toward experimentation of the novelistic biographers.

Some People is about how people's distorted ideas of themselves and each other generate fictions in which they wholeheartedly believe. Miss Plimsoll's admiration for the Navy, Marstock's image as the perfect schoolboy, the Marquis de Chaumont's incredibly snobbish mother, Jeanne de Hénaut's superiority as teacher and Frenchwoman: all are fictive creations—as much so as if they had been novelists writing stories about themselves. Yet they are committed to these fictions, convince others of them, and attempt to live them out, with varying degrees of success. Given the inventiveness with which most people perceive their own experiences, why not, Nicolson seems to be suggesting, use made-up names and alter events?

If perception is unreliable, memory is even more uncertain. Only certain objects, it seems, can bring back the past with any immediacy. If once associated with intense emotion, objects retain a magically evocative power resembling Proust's involuntary memory. By structuring *Some People* and *Helen's Tower* primarily around such objects and associations, Nicolson grants private emotion primacy over public event; and the apparently trivial, primacy over the consequential.

In the first sketch of *Some People*, for example, Nicolson begins with object and sense impression from which, unemphatically, the event emerges: "Miss Plimsoll wore dogskin gloves which smelt faintly of ammonia. It was these gloves which she clapped across my face when the Greek lady committed suicide on the Acropolis" (6–7). In the same sketch, Nicolson feels remorse because he and his brother have made Miss Plimsoll cry as they worked at building a hut. Charged with the child's emotion, the hut endures—in memory and, it turns out, in reality—triggering the same emotion when it is visited twenty years later, when the Embassy, symbol of public affairs, has left only "charred remains" (11). Like Arketall, Lord Curzon's valet, who almost disrupts affairs of state by placing his master's trousers under his bedspread, Nicolson buries diplomatic history in domesticity and personal emotion.

In *Helen's Tower*, Nicolson again juxtaposes hut and Embassy, viewing (in figurative terms) the Embassy from the hut, while contemplating the oddities of memory. Helen's Tower was built by Lord Dufferin to honor the memory of his mother, Helen. Nicolson calls it a "sad symbol of transition, that poignant emblem of memory" (247). The title displaces Dufferin from the center of his own biography. Emphasized instead is Dufferin's attempt to memorialize his mother, suggesting that the true portrait of a man is a depiction not of his career, but of how and what he remembers. This is perhaps what Nicolson means when he writes, "This book is a study in transitions; it is not the history of a great public servant . . . I am not primarily concerned with that career. I am concerned only with a complex personality" (126).

The word *transition* echoes Nicolson's earlier comment in his diary that he would write a "study in mutations." The concern is clearly with how the past enters and transforms the present. Biography itself is a transformation of past into present, a "Helen's Tower." By portraying himself remembering his uncle, he turns it into a disturbingly circular and very Proust-like portrait of himself observing his uncle, but also of himself creating the childhood self who observed his uncle.

Historical distance and chronology are disrupted from the first sentence, which implies a preceding context: "At breakfast, the next morning, each of the three footmen wore powdered hair" (1). That "next morning" insists on the inviolable continuity of events into which we seem to have been suddenly inserted. It also reinforces the book's circular structure, for after backtracking and describing his uncle's early life, Nicolson writes—235 pages later—"On reaching the Embassy, he hurried upstairs to the breakfast room, since he was a trifle late. He greeted his young sister-in-law affectionately. And upon the curls of her youngest son, he placed his large brown hand" (235). On page 235, we finally absorb the background necessary to understand the book's opening sentence. In a sense Nicolson has duplicated the process by which he himself grew from a small child experiencing without understanding to the adult able to place his uncle in context, to piece things together.

The past enters the present, then, in ways that have nothing to do with orderly sequence. Nor is intellectual reconstruction relevant; as in *Some People*, emotional intensity is the measure by which an event's memorability is determined. "How intermittent and how relative are our childhood memories!" Nicolson writes (8). The various incongruous objects retained in the mind are linked, he says, only by the moments of fear that impressed them on his consciousness and possess no intrinsic importance: "Some object (it may be a birthday present or no more than a door handle) remains vividly in our minds and we suppose that this object did in fact represent a centre of excited experience lasting over several months" (9). Chance juxtapositions can also determine associations: the lights of Paris, Nicolson associates not with Paris itself, but with "the smell of camphor and the feel of my mother's puffed brocaded sleeve against my cheek" (8). The logically central experience is displaced by an illogically related sense impression. Smell and touch are for Nicolson the most potent evokers of the past (72–73), he says in an explicitly Proustian discussion of involuntary memory.

The "complex personality" which Nicolson said he was portraying remains, finally, a bit vague, his complexities unexplored. The tower, with its jumble of objects collected on his travels and its inscriptions honoring his mother, some effaced, is an apt but unrevealing image. But as Duf-

ferin fails to emerge, so, too, does the narrator, who remains a stereotypically bumbling child. The disconcertingly
childlike angle of vision from which the biography is written proves no threat to the world it depicts. Just as Lord
Curzon could say of his drunken valet Arketall, "I liked
that man," and thus both enjoy and expel disruptive humor, Nicolson can playfully assert the primacy of irrational
memory without ever entirely subjecting himself to it.
That an established biographer would sit down to write a
Proustian biography is reason enough for examining it,
but one is left with some understanding of Virginia Woolf's
"profound distaste for Harolds Dufferin, its falseness"
(*Diary* 5: 119).

IV

Omniscience Rejected: Mediated Biography

"The question of the relation in which the writer stands to the story": so Percy Lubbock describes "point of view," recognized since Henry James as one of the critical issues of novel-writing and novel-reading (*Craft* 251). One could narrate omnisciently, using the sweeping narrative overview Lubbock calls "panorama" as the predominant mode of presentation, or one could narrate from behind a center of consciousness, aligned with a particular character's viewpoint.[1] Formulating the distinction in his 1921 *The Craft of Fiction*, based heavily on the critical writing of his mentor Henry James, Lubbock came down firmly in favor of the latter alternative, what Genette in *Narrative Discourse* calls internal focalization using mimesis.

Six years later Forster, in his *Aspects of the Novel*, suggested Lubbock had been too doctrinaire in rejecting those writers who shift narrative viewpoints, but the trend toward theoretical self-consciousness was irreversible. Robert Scholes has argued that the falling out of favor, in the late nineteenth century, of narrative omniscience was part of a broad cultural movement away from authority toward relativism (276). Certainly with James, the question of narrative viewpoint becomes irrevocably problematized, the subject of critical debate and even fictional thematization.

For what are the efforts of Strether, Marlow, and Dowell (in Ford's *The Good Soldier*) to understand, if not the dramatization of perspectival perception?

It is curious that so little of this narrative controversy has spilled over into the discussion of nonfiction. Genette suggests that the externality of referents to a work like Michelet's *Histoire de France* makes a relevant theory of narrative less important than in the study of fiction (27).[2] While Scholes includes the historical writing of Herodotus and Tacitus in his discussion, he follows only fiction through its development over time. Yet when James wrote his biography of William Wetmore Story and Lubbock his works on George Calderon, Mary Cholmondeley, and Edith Wharton, they did not forget that in their fiction and criticism they had made the acts of perception and narration their central concern. Nor did A. J. A. Symons forget, when he wrote his *Quest for Corvo*, a life of Frederick Rolfe, that a few years earlier he had urged biographical innovation on his audience in a talk entitled "Tradition and Biography." They could scarcely, when they turned from fiction or theory to "truth," take their own narrative position for granted. Writing in a genre that offered them authorial omniscience as an unquestioned prerogative, they insisted on writing instead from a limited point of view.

James and Lubbock in particular make an idiosyncratic contribution to the hitherto limited range of biographical narrative personae, creating a narrating "I" that serves as its own center of consciousness, portraying mimetically their own biographical perceptions. This first-person biography may sound a lot like memoir or even Boswell's *Life of Johnson,* but there are some important differences. Both the memoirist and Boswell portray themselves in relation to a living subject. They write, in other words, of an historical past in which they and the subject shared experiences. They also use their situation as witnesses to reinforce claims of accuracy and insight. For James, Lubbock, and Symons, on the other hand, the relation to the subject is primarily in the present tense. Whether or not they had been acquaintances, the dead-person/biographer relationship dominates. And their position as witness, their personal involvement in the story they tell, does not enhance but mitigates their claim to knowledge. Johnson told Boswell that no one should write a biography except of a subject with whom he had eaten and drunk; these modern first-person biographers suggest that the act of writing of another is itself a kind of cohabitation, and the result is a dramatic but sharply limited, individualized view of the subject—a view that repeatedly insists on its own partiality, that is more a dramatization of biographical perception than a biography.

The mediated biographer need not have been personally acquainted with his subject. What matters is the posthumous relationship—its intensity and its role in the biography. Simply because an author knew his subject, as Forster, for example knew Dickinson, does not mean that he will choose to make this relationship the single viewpoint from which to write his biography. Nor does mention of the biographical process itself make the work mediated. Woolf, in *Roger Fry*, depicts herself before a box of Fry's letters and notes, trying to make sense of them. But while the image is evocative, it is not central: we have not, from the book's start, been looking over Woolf's shoulder, drawn into the biographical quest itself. The definition, finally, comes down to a question of emphasis, but where biographical perception entirely supercedes biographical subject, the work's distinctiveness is quite clear.

Philippe Lejeune has pointed out that whereas in autobiography, the relation of main character to extratextual model is, by definition, one of identity, in biography, a relation of resemblance is precisely what must be created, while identity is an "impossible horizon" (157). The traditional first-person biographer, I would suggest, sticks to the biographical goal of resemblance. James and Lubbock, however, lean towards the autobiographical model, which substantially loosens their bond to external referents. Their identity to themselves is a given; their depiction of another—as a depiction of their own perceptions—is almost equally immune to verification. (Symons is different; he attains a similar effect, but by juxtaposing varying viewpoints, not just interposing his own.) These modern first-person biographers, then, use their relation to the subject to undermine the possibility of an empirical, objective history, pushing historical discourse, in fact, startlingly close to nonreferentiality.

Because these biographers insist on the presence of a perceiver between the subject and the narrative, I have called their works *mediated* biography. All biography is, of course, mediated, in that a single mind must meld and interpret the material, but these biographers portray the mediation itself as subject matter. In that these biographies dramatize perception, making their narrator's mental activities immediately accessible to the reader, they may seem the very opposite of mediated, but their immediacy results from their displaced focus. It is as if the narrators were standing in front of a slide projector: they are themselves immediately present to the viewer, and thus experienced dramatically, unmediatedly, but the slides themselves are now visible only in relation to them, as patches of color strewn about their figures. By dramatizing the mediated element of biography, then, James, Lubbock, and Symons do in a sense dispel it, but in doing so they call into question the story itself—that drama on the screen before them, made scarcely discernible by their obstructive presence. The dramatization of perception, of experience as mediated by consciousness, is the paradoxical fusion initially performed by James himself in his novels. Transposed to biography, though, its initial effect is less to dramatize than to disrupt the storytelling, for the obstruction of the expected show is noticed well before the reader can pick out the displaced show enacted with such immediacy on the narrator's own form. The main effect of these biographies is thus to thrust before the reader a perceiving/ narrating presence serving as a necessary but obstructing intermediary. Where the novelistic biographers achieve immediacy by placing the reader in contact with the subject's mind, the mediated biographers place the reader in contact with their own.

Besides their problematized narration, these biographers have other unconventional features. They tend, for example, to be anti-Aristotelian in their assumptions about character and action. Their subjects are neither shaped by circumstances nor expressed by action. The focus is on personality itself, in isolation from—or even in contradistinction to—particular achievements. James, perhaps, could not help himself, for he was commissioned to write a biography about a man he regarded as a failure, but Lubbock, faced with a man of action in George Calderon and a woman of action in Edith Wharton, directs his attention to precisely those points where action did not provide a smooth and revealing outlet for character. Symons carefully selects only those subjects who notably failed to do what their potential indicated they might, whose deeds, far from revealing an inner self, serve to disguise it.

In their rejection of action as character-revealing, mediated and novelistic biographers resemble each other. They share with Forster the belief that Aristotle was wrong when he suggested that, in Forster's words, "All human happiness and misery take the form of action" (*Aspects* 58). But while the novelistic biographer's response is to plunge into his subject's inner life, using a nonfocalized narration whose problematization surfaces as part of the subject's psychic drama, the mediated biographer is more restrained, revealing his own psyche, dramatizing his own narrative situation, but allowing his subject a quite separate integrity.

For both, then, personality exists apart from action, but only the mediated biographers portray its unity as the product of their subjects', not their own, imagination. The self, in fact, has an integrity so great as to become, increasingly as the twentieth century progresses, an aesthetic artifact in its own right. Johnson's *An Account of the Life of Mr. Richard Savage* and Carlyle's *Life of Sterling* portray similar disjunctions between ability and achievement, but in both cases the biographer characterizes the disjunction unambiguously as failure and attributes it to circumstance—Savage's mother and his poverty; Sterling's bad health. James, too, sorrows for his subject's artistic mediocrity, but he also views Story's life as almost redeemed by the grace with which it was lived. Even more clearly, Lubbock and Symons are utterly unconcerned with visible accomplishment, finding in the failures of the work, even the perversities of the spirit, just those dark places necessary to enhance the portrait as a whole. For those earlier biographers who, according to Cockshut, saw the life as a work of art by God, failure was a botching of His work, a violation of His intention. For the mediated biographers, in contrast, the life is a work of art created by the subject and appreciated by the biographer. Apparent failure, which suggests an inability to adapt to circumstance, may well produce a more aesthetically pleasing life than great success. The personality that can't adapt is also the personality that coheres; nothing is so neatly patterned as neurotic compulsion. From Froude's Carlyle, who carries his shadow wherever he goes, to Symons's Corvo, with his recurrent paranoia, the neurotic subject has made a magnificently compelling, coherent subject.

But where Carlyle's shadow is depicted on the same titanic level as his genius, a romantic flaw inseparable from his achievement, Frederick Rolfe's delusions are portrayed as paralyzing. Far from being the side effects of genius, they turn a potentially brilliant writer into a triumphantly bizarre personality, whose value lies in its opacity, its autonomy, its artistic unity. For Lubbock, too, though rather differently, life becomes art in the hands of the "liberated personality" (Brown 22), whose relations to others are comparable to a piece of lace, perhaps, or an intricate ballet. Even in his first book, his 1906 *Elizabeth Barrett Browning in Her Letters,* as Ashley Brown points out, Lubbock begins on the premise that "She was not finally and instinctively an artist," choosing her not for her accomplishment, but for her personality (25).

The work that results is a mis-en-abîme: the biographer creates a self creating itself. This mirrored self-construction is dramatized as a subtextual interplay between discourse and story, between narrational act and subject. James evoking ghosts from the past he shared with Story, Lubbock painting portraits, and Symons digging up layers of psyche mimic their subjects' own activity. And they do so in strikingly atemporal terms.

"A novel," writes Lubbock in *The Craft of Fiction,* "is a picture, a portrait . . . ," and like a portrait it must have "form, design, composition" (9). It must, in other words, have formal qualities unrelated to its storytelling, formal qualities that transcend and counteract its temporality. (To analyze a novel, he argues, is one way to remember it longer.) Lubbock subtitles his biographies "sketch" and "portrait" to indicate that they, too, have these qualities and thus exist outside of time. This atemporality is particularly characteristic of mediated biography. Symons's handling of time is unconventional, the sequence of his quest periodically usurping the different sequence of his subject's life. James's tendency to turn history into ghost story similarly anachronizes the past.[3] In his biography of Story, the narrative is fueled not by a sequence of events, but by a series of ghostly visitations, eruptions of the past into the present. James's *Story,* in fact, is one of Honan's prime examples of effectively innovative biography. Honan's advocacy of narrative complexity, of a vividly present narrative persona and of the reader's involvement in construing the subject makes his essay almost a manifesto of mediated biography—a term which, of course, he does not use.

The reader's participation is so necessary because mediated biography subsists on gaps. Its internalized focalization is premised on omissions, for no single perceiver can see everything. But the more intense gap is between biographer and subject. These biographers face openly the fact that their subjects are dead and the past distant, yet at the same time they insist on achieving the utmost immediacy in relation to both. In *Narrative Discourse* Genette, discussing Proust, describes a similar phenomenon, which he calls "mediated intensity," at the extreme of both showing and telling, reflecting "extreme mediation, and at the same time utmost immediacy" (168). The first-person narrator meditating his past accentuates its distance, enacting—through his split into subject and narrator—the gap between past and present. But if that past then erupts mimetically, as scene, rather than diegetically, as narration, this distance is joined to an immediacy that makes the gap all the more poignant, even magnetically attractive. Genette's analysis applies perfectly to James's ghosts— apparitions of the past as present—and the strange power they lend to *William Wetmore Story*.

Lubbock and Symons, too, have a paradoxical relation to gaps. Lubbock exaggerates his own insignificance, inexperience, and inarticulateness in comparison to his subjects, yet at the same time he is their delineator, and they seem to sit before him as he sketches. Just as James emphasizes the absence and inaccessibility of the bygone era he chronicles, Symons accentuates his initial ignorance and the huge gaps in his knowledge of Rolfe. These discrepancies generate a strange passion linking writer and reader. James's reminiscences "lively almost to indiscretion," Lubbock's intent gaze, and Symons's almost morbidly intense curiosity all grow out of these gaps and invite the reader's complicity in filling them.

All these narrative oddities have implications for traditional notions of causation, also. *Post hoc, ergo propter hoc* may be logically fallacious, but since the birth of empiricism, the assumption has been that a person's early impressions shape him, influencing his future decisions, which in turn shape the circumstances that determine his life. Character, in this view, to borrow Karl Weintraub's terms, *develops* through various collisions with circumstance (830). In mediated biography, however, the subjects don't develop but *unfold*. Ordinary causes are without ordinary effects, for the inherent personality pattern seems set and will simply be more and more manifest as it is repeated in a variety of situations. All three biographers portray this repetitive process as virtually willed, dictated by a perhaps unconscious desire to make the self coherent, even at the expense of achievement and happiness. Symons puts the problem in plainly Freudian terms; Rolfe's repression, initially unwilled, is predetermined by psychic mechanisms whose unconscious origin must be disguised by deliberate and increasingly complex embroideries, each layer an only slightly differing response to the same initial stimulus.[4]

The overall effect of mediated biography, then, is to subvert the narrative authority of the biographer by dramatizing the impact of subject on narrator. This dramatization calls the entire act of narration into question and at the same time radically alters the standard chronological sequence long typical of biography. The self most suited to such treatment (and in any case the self that tends to result from it) is quite separate from visible manifestations; its virtues lie in the aesthetic effect it has on others, not on what it does in the world. Even its growth is ahistorical, consisting of a series of repetitions rather than in interaction with circumstance.

To a large extent, this compromising of historical narration emerges from the critical theory of Henry James. When narrative viewpoint is problematized and omniscience rejected, the authoritative, synthesizing "histor" described by Scholes and Kellogg becomes obsolete (266). History—at least in the hand of self-consciously modern literary figures—becomes fragmented and sharply angled by its particular narrative perspective.

Henry James published his two-volume biography of the American sculptor and writer William Wetmore Story in 1903, the year of *The Ambassadors* and "The Beast in the Jungle." He had known Story, and especially he had known many of Story's friends, for as Americans in Europe their social circles overlapped. A native Bostonian, Story lived much of his life in Rome, where he sculpted huge, rather sentimental figures and wrote poetry. James, not impressed by his subject's artistic achievements, undertook the biography reluctantly, at the urging of Story's family (Edel, *James* 157).

James did not find biography an amenable genre, but the work he produced is all the more interesting for that reason. In an 1867 essay on historical novels, James distinguishes between the historian and the storyteller, speaking with awe of the oppressive, "impenetrable fact" faced by the former, who "works in the dark, with a contracted forehead and downcast eyes, on his hands and knees, as men work in coal-mines" (*Literary Reviews* 279). When, some time later, he himself became such a coalminer, he limited his labor to two months' dictation and let it reflect his tense yearning for the novelist's freedom: "His own creative and organizing imagination," Edel writes in *Henry James: The Master*, "played around the impersonal and inanimate documents and sought constantly to 'novelize' them" (157). This tension, combined with the "mediated intensity" of his relation to the past, actually adds to the biography's impact.

But if James felt the urge to novelize his subject, he also felt impelled not to. For while the novelist can know as much as he chooses about his own created characters, owing no deference to an externally existent human being, the biographer cannot. In quest of omniscience, *The Aspern Papers* suggests, the biographer runs the risk of dehumanizing himself, and—as his 1900 story "The Real Right Thing" makes clear—of cannibalizing his subject. For James, who insisted on the complexity and inviolability of human personality, a truly novelistic biography would be unthinkable.

But like Woolf, Forster, and countless other modern novelists, James believed it was the inner life that counted. "What a man thinks and what he feels are the history and character of what he does," he writes in his preface to *The Princess Cassamassima;* "The interest of the attitude and the act would be the actor's imagination and vision of them, together with the nature and degree of their felt return upon him" (viii). Action, in other words, is of interest only as perceived and reacted to by a sensitive if bewildered observer, the famous "vessel of consciousness" (ix). The chronicles of a man's deeds, a description of his attributes and belongings are, by themselves, of no more interest to him than Bennett's characterization-by-house-property (attacked in "Mr. Bennett and Mrs. Brown") was to Woolf. "There is," James writes of *The Ambassadors,* "the story of one's hero, and then, thanks to the intimate connexion of things, the story of one's story itself" (*Ambassadors* 1:x). The story of the story is for James the more dramatic alternative by far.

In accepting his commission, then, James faced a collision between his theory of fiction and the demands of biography. He could scarcely appropriate William Wetmore Story's consciousness as he had Lambert Strether's, yet to describe a person at all, he felt, meant to describe him from the inside; "To live over people's lives is nothing," he writes in *William Wetmore Story and his Friends,* "unless we live over their perceptions, live over the growth, the change, the varying intensity of the same—since it was *by* these things they themselves lived" (*Story* 1:125). Yet these things are precisely what escape the biographer, as James complains in a letter to Henry Adams:

> *Any* retraced story of bourgeois lives (lives other than great lives of "action"—*et encore!*) throws a chill upon the scene, the time, the subject, the small mapped-out facts, and if you find "great men thin" it isn't really so much their fault . . . as that the art of the biographer—devilish art!—is somehow practically thinning. It simplifies even while seeking to enrich— and even the immortals are so helpless and passive in death. (*Letters* 439)

It was perhaps in response to this problem, Edel suggests, that James in 1900 wrote "The Real Right Thing," in which the subject's ghost discourages his biographer (*James* 143): "He's there to *save* his Life. He's there to be let alone," the chronicler, George Withermore, tells the great man's widow. In attempting to penetrate his subject's mind— working in his study, reading his letters—"We lay him bare," Withermore complains. "We serve him up. What is it called? We give him to the world" (James, *Altar* 427). The story merely of the biographical subject is "thin," but the story of the subject's story—i.e., of his perceptions and responses—means appropriation and betrayal to the extent it is possible at all. The only alternative is the one dramatized by "The Real Right Thing": the story of the biographer's story.

Laboriously piecing together the past, George Withermore finds himself in direct communication with it. History is usurped by perception as the scene of research becomes instead the scene of communion:

> There were moments for instance when, while he bent over his papers, the light breath of his dead host was as distinctly in his hair as his own elbows were on the table before him. There were moments when, had he been able to look up, the other

side of the table would have shown him this companion as vividly as the shaded lamplight showed him his page. (420–21)

In the story, these circumstances suggest that the "real right thing" is to stop writing the biography. But James himself did not stop, with results that Edel in his biography calls "out of character," suggesting that only financial temptation drove him to complete the work (551). Certainly James's commentators have tended to ignore the work or regard it as unsuccessful. Elsa Nettels argues that if James focused on the biographical *process* more than on his subject, it was simply because his subject was so insignificant (117); in his 1879 *Hawthorne,* he had been far more interested in explanations than impressions. But *William Wetmore Story and His Friends* is, in fact, a wonderfully innovative work—one which reveals the first of the modern English novelists coming to grips with problems posed for biography by modern fictional theory. It grows directly out of "The Real Right Thing," providing a striking example of the biography-as-ghost-story. As ghost story, as the depiction of past circumstances erupting into the present, it provides just that quality of "present-ness" so prized by Park Honan.

"Everything," James writes, "depends on the composition" (*Story* 1 : 16). The painterly term occurs to James, as to Lubbock, because it suggests formal relationships, perspective—anything but mere data. The historical fact per se he finds without interest; in *William Wetmore Story,* he ridicules the characteristically English taste for "facts, facts, and again facts" in the person of poor Mr. Hayword, praised for his conversation, yet ignorant of a subtler school of talk:

A school handling the fact rather as the point of departure than as the point of arrival, the horse-block for mounting the winged steed of talk rather than as the stable for constantly riding him back to. The "story," in fine, in this other order—

and surely so more worthy of the name—would have been the intellectual reaction from the circumstance presented, an exhibition interesting, amusing, vivid, dramatic, in proportion to the agility, or to the sincerity, of the intellect engaged. (2:205)

Once again, James is insisting that more dramatic than the biographical account, is the story of the biographical account: Story's life perceived from a particular perspective and composed in relation to his friends, his era, and his psychological type.

The book is called *William Wetmore Story and His Friends* because the web of social relations and historical environment is essential to its composition and authorial viewpoint (James's own closest connection to Story is, after all, through their mutual friends); the period as a whole, James writes, "holds the elements together, rounds them off, makes them right. They partake of it, they preserve it, in return; they justify it, and it justifies the fond chronicler" (1:16).

Relations can be conceptual as well as social: the particularities of Story's "case" are put in relation to the larger phenomenon of Americans in Europe. Once again it is the act of relating that enhances James's connection to his subject, for the larger phenomenon is easily recognizable as James's own favorite novelistic stomping ground, Story's case resembling somewhat Christopher Newman's, Roderick Hudson's, Lambert Strether's. But the overriding relation is of course that between Story and his historian, who portrays himself quite frankly, seated before "a boxful of old papers, personal records, and relics all" (1:7). Each relic, "besides being delightful in itself, [is] delightful also in proportion to any old memories, impressions, visions of one's own, that one may read into it" (1:245). So intense are these "visions of one's own" that James, with his remembrance "lively almost to indiscretion," becomes, like George Withermore, an evoker of ghosts.

By insisting on his personal relation to his subject, James first turns history into memory, then literalizes memory as a succession of dramatic apparitions from the past. Words like *ghost* and *shade* appear frequently. Each name in Story's life becomes a beckoning wraith, soliciting James's attention—much as the dead crowd around Ulysses in *The Odyssey*. So pressing are these many invitations to elaborate that they form a kind of ghostly subtext in which James is solicited to death by his own oppressively vivid memory— oppressive not because the memories are sad, but because they offer so many good stories, each tiny fact radiating a multitude of possible ideas.[5] Constantly he is tempted to stray, to follow yet another ghost, to speculate on yet another case. When he forces himself not to stray he suffers, feeling his summary treatment of any name "both a breach of manners and a loss of opportunity." Finally, seeming on the brink of suffocation, he cries out for "a free hand and a clean slate altogether": "All of which simply means, I think, that the prose-painter of life, character, manners, licensed to render his experience in his own terms, might do more justice to such a subject than the mere enumerator, to whom liberties, as they are called, are forbidden" (2 : 197).

That James finds Story's life so overwhelmingly full of artistic stimuli makes an ironic counterpoint to his account of Story's artistic failure. Story's life, so free, so eventful, so happy, was, in James's view, a "beautiful sacrifice to a noble mistake," that of having too few indifferences. Flexible, easygoing, universally enthusiastic, Story lacked the obsessive commitment necessary to the artist. He was, according to James, essentially unresponsive, with the result that "Nothing really happened to him but to be his remarkably animated and various, his exuberant, sympathetic, intensely natural self" (1 : 34). Like Marcher, who made his appearance in print the same year in "The Beast in the Jungle," Story is a man to whom nothing happens. He is also, of course, a man to whom everything happens; unlike

Marcher, unlike James, he has a fully, happy, busy life, including wife, children, friends, even—briefly—fame.

The success of *William Wetmore Story* lies in this interplay of lived and unlived lives—Story's, Marcher's, Strether's (*The Ambassadors* was also published in 1903), and James's own. At the same time that he chronicles Story's eventful outer life, James illustrates the nullity of his artistic achievement, while portraying simultaneously the suffocating intensity of his own responsiveness—at the expense, one infers (and Marcher implies), of his own outer life. Taken to its extreme, this gap between inner responsiveness and outer stimulus becomes Marcher's solipsistic delusion. Inbetween Marcher's madness and Story's utter sanity is James the biographer, creating in *William Wetmore Story* a ghostly overlay that unwrites Story's story, replacing it with James's own imaginative life.

The biography ends with James's visit to the convent at Vallambrosa, a convent visited and described by Story. "It was all so beautiful that it was sad—" James writes, "with a distinction the sense of which weighed like an anxiety":

> Something of that sort, something supreme in the solemn sweetness with which the whole place surrounded him, I can imagine our friend to have felt as he sat, with the last patience, in the September days, listening to its voices. They might have been saying to him how far he had come from the primary scene and how much he had left by the way, as well as, indeed, how much he had found and laboured and achieved. They might, above all, have seemed to breathe upon him the very essence of the benediction of the old Italy he had chosen and loved and who thus closed soft arms about him. (2:338)

This mingling of biographical narration with subjective perception James permits himself, clearly, because he himself has visited the spot. It is his imagination that dominates this final vision, as the subject definitively shifts from William Wetmore Story and *his* friends, to William Wetmore

Story, *our* friend. Story suffocated by a ghostly vision of an Italy past is very much James's Story, dying amid an environment animated by James's imagination. This final paragraph anticipates the end of Strachey's *Queen Victoria* in its speculative use of memory to sum up both book and life, its lyrical fusion of narrator and subject. Like Strachey's conclusion it suggests that whether the true story of Story was what did happen to him or what didn't, the only possible biography of Story is the story of Story's story as it unfolds in the interplay between his own imagination and his chronicler's.

Since James's idiosyncratic approach to biography was dictated by his own theories about characterization and narration, the man who systematized and popularized that theory, Percy Lubbock, was bound to take a similar approach. Lubbock's 1921 *The Craft of Fiction* borrows its terminology and treatment of point of view from James's prefaces and essays. His formulations will be recognized as underlying much of what I have said about *William Wetmore Story and His Friends*. They also underlie, though somewhat differently, Lubbock's own biographical writing—on George Calderon, Mary Cholmondeley, and Edith Wharton.[6] Most striking is Lubbock's treatment of the novel in pictorial terms. (The pictorial analogy is evident in his biographies, too, in the recurring subtitle "A Sketch . . .") History and biography, long the structural models for novel-writers, are displaced by the painterly notion of narrative perspective.[7] Key concepts are expressed in visual and theatrical terms: scenic versus panoramic, for example, or dramatic versus pictorial. Time is for him, as plot will be in Forster's 1927 *Aspects of the Novel*, the Enemy, sweeping the novel on a kind of conveyor belt into obscurity. If the novelist is an artist, Lubbock argues in *The Craft of Fiction*, it is not because we remember a sequence of chronicled events, but because we retain an atemporal vision of form and design (9).

Linked to this rejection of time is a rejection of narrative omniscience. Lubbock's insistence on invisible narration and consistent perspective has been modified and demolished many times since. What interests me are the implications such a doctrine has for biographical writing. The author's task, Lubbock argues, is to *dramatize* his story, so that it appears unmediated by a narrating consciousness. The problem then becomes, of course, how we gain access to the characters' inner lives without the insight of an omniscient narrator. Lubbock's solution is the Jamesian—and Dostoievskian—dramatization of the inner life, as perception itself becomes the stuff of the plot. This he calls the "indirect method" (149), of which Strether is the leading representative. The "impulses and reactions of his mood," Lubbock writes, "are the players upon the new scene" (157). The point is similar to James's preference for the story of the story. "A distinction is made," Lubbock writes, "between the scene which the man surveys, and the energy within him which converts it all into the stuff of his own being" (143).

Like James, Lubbock displaces the center of his biographies from the subject to his perception of the subject. The result, though, instead of a Jamesian ghost story, is a portrait or "sketch from memory," as he calls it, in which he seeks above all the characteristic gesture, the generalized trait that transcends time and circumstance.

The same year as *The Craft of Fiction*, 1921, Lubbock published *George Calderon: A Sketch from Memory*. Calderon, oddly enough Story's nephew, bears a certain resemblance to his uncle. He, too, refuses to sacrifice life for art; he, too, makes his way through varied experiences without seeming deeply affected by them. His childhood is unimportant to him, and he never grows old (Lubbock 32). Even more than Story he is a man to whom nothing happens—until his enlistment in World War I, which brings him, simultaneously, apotheosis and death.

But Lubbock refuses to see Calderon's life as unfinished or botched. Unlike James, who sees Story's mediocre art as a sign of failure, Lubbock gathers together the unfinished books, the undistinguished plays, and the abruptly ended life into a single whole. This complicity of biographer and subject in turning the life into aesthetic artifact is characteristically modern—more modern than James's sadness at a man's failure to realize his full potential. "It was himself that was complete," Lubbock writes of Calderon, "rather than his work" (71).

In his 1947 biography of Edith Wharton, Lubbock writes, "Not what she did but how she did it is my concern" (120). His aim in writing about Calderon is similar: "to show what he was and how he died"—not what he did. While insisting that Calderon was a man of action, an anti-Hamlet (125) with the "soul of a paladin," Lubbock describes not his deeds but his personality, his characteristic way of affecting others.

The biography's opening words define his effort: "To me, as I try to describe the quality of George Calderon's rare nature, and to number his many gifts, and to define the character of his achievement, it is his own figure that appears, vivid as life, with a well-known look which checks and deflects any undertaking of that kind" (11). "To me," the opening words, indicate to what extent Calderon will be viewed only as he affects Lubbock, and, more importantly, as he appears to Lubbock in the present, not as pieced together out of the past. *Describe, number, define,* verbs insistently suggesting referentiality, objectivity, fact, are abruptly vanquished by Calderon's own figure, which, ghostlike, stops his attempt at historical explanation. Like George Withermore, Lubbock is interrupted by his subject's apparition and forced to abandon the panoramic narration of actions for the densely nuanced dramatization of his own mind in relation to Calderon. As in *William*

Wetmore Story, the biographer himself becomes a Strether-like figure, whose tense attempts to see clearly and precisely provide the drama.

Despite the fact that his friend was the quintessential man of action, then, Lubbock is not interested in action. He buries exciting events in syntactical obscurity while focusing instead on the immediately visible impression made by those events—as when he notes Calderon's "whimsical interested face as he describes the delight of searching a ruinous farmhouse in the dark, where a German sniper is known to be concealed" (148). What we have here is the narrator's remembered perception of the subject's remembered reaction to the search. It is an odd way to treat a man of action, but Lubbock prefers the atemporal essence to an epic narration of deeds: "sooner than dwelling on his bravery and devotion, I like to think of his perpetual, inimitable, familiar self; in which his great qualities had always shone needing no emergency to kindle them . . . in which, the whole alert and amusing and splendid nature, we recognize our friend (149–50).

The book's imagery reinforces this sense of temporal and even geographical transcendence, for Calderon as pilgrim, as paladin, as fighter of paynim is a man from another era and place—a medieval knight gone east to fight in the Crusades. But for all his temporal transcendence, Calderon is displaced; he may have the qualities of a knight, but his era offers him no outlet for them—until World War I. In going to war, Lubbock writes, Calderon seems to come into an inheritance, but he also walks off-stage, beyond the ken of his biographer. He dies in even greater obscurity, missing in action at Gallipoli. In place of an epitaph (his body was never found), Lubbock supplies a biography.

The earliest biographies are said to have been accounts of heroism inscribed on burial mounds and cenotaphs. Lubbock's biography at once falls into this tradition and works ironically against it, for it does not supplement but replaces burial. Books, in fact, are a crucial recurring image that depict as well as commemorate. "His path was strewn with books half-written," Lubbock writes, both literally and metaphorically. But rather than regret its fragmentation, one can see Calderon's life as a whole, each action manifesting a different side of a coherent person, his genius being "independent of any single vehicle": "Each of the many things he put his hand to is thus a chapter of a single, completed work—a work that was his life. And it is because the chapters are so scattered and apparently disconnected that we wish to bring them together, so far as one friend may, and to show how closely they were harmonised in his own imagination" (23). When Calderon enlists, he leaves behind a huge, unfinished work on Slavonic folklore. Once in the army, he rejects his job as unarmed interpreter, preferring to be an armed soldier. "In George Calderon's book . . . the chapters were by no means all written with ink on paper; many of them were created in other material altogether" (99). But the man who consistently preferred action to words is ironically dependent on his biographer for his existence. Even his death at Gallipoli is transmuted into literary terms, making "a final page in which the whole character of his work was summed up" (26).

While the book covers Calderon's life between the ages of about thirty and forty-seven, it virtually ignores chronology as a structuring principle and as a factor in its subject's development. The passage of time has little to do with the formation of Calderon's character, and the plot of his life is without clarity, suspense, or climax. Change appears agentless, an almost random succession of images. "As these visions succeeded one another," Lubbock writes, "the years slip by, the company changes, the groups of children grow up, I approach the end of the story" (144). The biography comes close to abandoning narrative for character study, approaching the point described by Nelson Goodman, when chronological ordering is superseded by conceptual categories. It does not do so, however, since Calderon's life course does hover in the background, Lubbock's present-tense evocation superimposed on, not replacing, its intermittently temporal order.

Lubbock's biographies of Mary Cholmondeley (1928) and Edith Wharton (1947) are more extreme in their disregard for childhood and for development. With their overriding emphasis on a present-tense relation between biographer and remembered subject, both could arguably be described as character studies rather than biographies. In both, the subject's personality defines itself through social relations rather than accomplishments. Lubbock devotes an entire chapter apiece, in *Cholmondeley*, to Rhoda Broughton and Howard Sturgis, and in *Wharton*, friends give lengthy accounts of their own perceptions of the subject. In both, as in *Calderon*, the biographical focus is deliberately displaced from the subject's achievements, so that personality is presented as a work of art in its own right, which, with the biographer's cooperation, forms a new kind of aesthetic artifact.[8]

Neither James nor Lubbock provides any theoretical discussion of biography. Primarily novelists, they theorize only about fiction. But discussion of fictional technique involves discussion of narrative technique, and narrative technique, whether explicitly acknowledged as such or not, is the common ground shared by fiction, biography, and history. James and Lubbock as biographers are very much the James of the prefaces and the Lubbock of *The Craft of Fiction*.

A. J. A. Symons differs from James and Lubbock in many ways, the most obvious being that he published no fiction and did write theoretically about biography. He looked not to James but to Lytton Strachey as his precursor. I include him among the mediated biographers because, like James and Lubbock and unlike Strachey, he chooses to dramatize, in his writing, his own role as biographer, but it is unlikely that he was in any deliberate way following their lead.

Strachey's emphasis on interpretation does have something in common with James's narrative perspectivism, in that both are acutely aware of the narrative act itself. James's critical theory was very much in the air. In a letter to Eddie Marsh, Symons defends LeFanu's *Wylder's Hand* as having no loose ends "beyond the first person confusion, which is after all allowed by convention in pre-Jamesian authors,"[9] indicating just how aware *post*-Jamesian authors—Symons in particular—inevitably were of their narrative options. *The Quest for Corvo,* Symons's most famous work and only full-length biography, was published in 1934, with the subtitle *An Experiment in Biography.* It was written, he says in a prefatory note, to test the innovations he had called for in his 1929 lecture. Written very much as a detective story, with chapters called "The Problem" and "The Clues," *Quest* portrays the biographer as a hunter-down of witnesses and manuscripts.

Symons was, in fact, a bibliographer and a bibliophile. A founder of England's First Edition Club, he compiled an unfinished bibliography of writers of the nineties, and *Quest for Corvo* can be read as a bibliographic, rather than biographic, drama. The book opens with Symons's first sight of a Rolfe manuscript and ends when he has seen the last of the long-lost material. There is a hint, even, of bibliographic megalomania in his concluding paragraph: "alone of living men, I had read every line of every [manuscript]" (290).

This interplay of bibliographic and biographic plots serves the same purpose as James's ghosts and Lubbock's portraiture: it insists on a present-tense relation between author and subject, refuses the authority of the historical, "objective" stance, and subverts the chronological continuity of the subject's life. *Quest for Corvo,* Symons's brother Julian writes in an introduction, "blows the gaff on biography, as it were, by refusing for a moment to make the customary practice of detachment" (*Quest* 9–10).

Symons blows the gaff more explicitly in his 1929 lecture, delivered as part of the well-known series "Tradition and Experiment in Present-Day Literature," at which Edith Sitwell, Rebecca West, and T. S. Eliot were also speakers. The essay, which makes Symons a major spokesman for modernist biography, eloquently rejects the work of past biographers, with the exception of Strachey's, as artless panegyric. The problem, he suggests, has been the pretense of objectivity, of completeness. Recording without omission is impossible, yet past biographers have suppressed the selectivity of their task, producing formless compendia that remain selective in any case, and ugly besides (*Essays* 4). Related to this problem has been the excessive reliance on chronology as a structuring principle (a reliance similarly ridiculed by Woolf in *Orlando*). The result, according to Symons, has been a hackneyed conceptualization of the life-plot:

> Constructed on the simple formula of chronological sequence, they begin, for the most part, with their subject's birth, and describe his curly headed innocence, his sailor suit. Chapter 2 and 3, which show no diminution of the one or discarding of the other, are headed "Schooldays" and "Alma Mater," and precede "Early Manhood" in which a passing reference to "wild oats" shows that the author also has experienced much! and then chapter 5, "Marriage," sets us on the trail for home. "Life in London," "Early Work," and "Later Work" lead naturally to "Last Days": a deathbed scene, several moral reflections, a list of the books or acts of the victim, and one more biography is on the shelf, probably to stay there. (*Essays* 2)

The biographer, Symons argues, need not conform to cliché. His freedom is nearly equal to the novelist's, for while bound by fact rather than probability, he still has the freedom to choose his subject and to express his own character. Since all literary production mirrors its author, "A biographer should choose his subject as a dandy chooses his suit, remembering cut and tone as much as texture; and his subjects should fit his talent as the suit fits the dandy's body: exquisitely" (6).

The analogy is apt, for even more than Lubbock, Symons, like the dandy, sees the life as art and selects his subjects for the strangeness and beauty of their carefully cultivated selves. Stanley, he tells Eddie Marsh, sending him his brief biography of the explorer, was "as rare a flower of personality as Corvo was," the metaphor suggesting not merely natural growth, but also refined gardening techniques.[10] There is no hint in Symons of a God-given potential to be fulfilled, as in James, but only the amoral aesthetic artifact one makes of one's life, to be judged by no other criterion than its coherence and originality. Symons grants the individual self a great deal of autonomy. James and Lubbock both agree in distinguishing it from the actions ordinarily deemed to express and shape it, but Symons grants his subjects tremendous wills as well, so that they are empowered to create themselves on a titanic scale. Julian Symons and Harold Fisher have both called Symons "Carlylean" because of his taste for strong-willed, larger-than-life figures (*Symons* 31, 115). But the comparison, finally, is misleading, for the massive will possessed by his subjects is deflected from dynamic achievement to static self-construction. Even Stanley is portrayed as less a doer than a maker of masks. At the age of twenty-one, Julian writes of his brother, "he expressed . . . his intention to build his life 'as an architect plans a house'" (*Quest* 10). The dandy, of course, creates his persona with exactly the same care. The biographer-as-dandy, then, portrays the subject-as-dandy, and the biography becomes a dazzling mis-en-abîme of self-constructing selves.

Symons was passionately interested in the literature of the 1890s, and his great work, never finished, was to be a biography of Oscar Wilde, the original maker of masks and converter of life into art. But this view of life as art is generally incompatible with life as achievement; it suggests an insufficiency in the work alone, a gap between the self and its manifestations. Symons, who, his brother says in his biography, "itched with the consciousness of unrealized ability" (27), selects as his subjects Wilde, Poe, Edward Irving, Theodore Hook, Burton and Speke, Frederick Rolfe, and Emin Pasha, all men involved in name-change or disguise, exile or social incongruity, and exhibiting a peculiar disjunction between ability and achievement—at least as portrayed by Symons. "No one before or since ever lent greater talents to odder ends," Symons writes in his *Essays* of Theodore Hook, the brilliant talker and practical joker (81). And of the explorer Burton's near-fame he comments, "he was one of those men whose reputation always, mysteriously, stops short of his deserts" (110).

What has Symons's idiosyncratic choice of subjects to do with modern biographers in general and mediated biographers in particular? All share a tendency to view the self as a man-made aesthetic object. Symons's mysterious misfits also, like Strachey's women, provide suitable material for the dismantling of Victorian notions of willed achievement. For here are men who do, in fact, have monumental wills, yet who willfully misuse them or are willfully misused by fate so that even when they do rule Africa, discover lakes, or write great books, their true selves are elsewhere, disguised and indecipherable.

Their indecipherability is what makes them suited to mediated rather than novelistic biography. Their perversity is, in the end, unplumbable, and the incomplete account of an internally focalized narrator (or, in a sense, a series of internally focalized narrators, the letter-writers) allows them to retain their final mystery. Those responding to Symons's inquiries present their perspectives; Rolfe's fiction presents another; the biographer has his own; but there is no synthesis, only collation. While Strachey dismantles adventure in *Eminent Victorians* by shifting his attention from deed to motivation, Symons shifts his from deed to biographic detection. "To some men adventure can be found only in the trackless desert," Symons writes in his *Essays*, ". . . but for me there has always been sufficient danger in the unexplored pages of the dictionary, sufficient discovery in the tell-tale fact which, paired with another fact, forms a recognizable fragment of some jigsaw puzzle of the mind" (104). By dramatizing as a "jigsaw puzzle of the mind" not his subject's psyche but his own narrative work, he allows his subjects greater freedom than Strachey. And the notion of adventure, transposed from Africa to the biographer's writing desk, retains its validity. In contrast to the novelistic biographer's omniscience, Symons emphasizes his ignorance, ending his biographies in uncertainty, with the designation of gaps and remaining mysteries. *Quest for Corvo*, Ira Grushow writes, is "an artistic reconstruction of the process of biographical research, complete with dead ends, reticules, and conjectures, leaving us to conclude that so bizarre a figure as Corvo can never wholly be comprehended" (159). Symons's subjects are men who have spent their lives elaborating and disguising themselves, leaving behind a trail of false clues. Symons's goal is less to expose the falsity than to admire it. His concern is not with "truth," but with delineating the lies.

Histories of neurotics bear an odd relation to truth. As the true story of someone whose life was a process of distortion and disguise, *Quest for Corvo* has an eerily fictive quality. It tells the story, for example, of how Corvo first became known as the author of "How I was Buried Alive," a fiction masquerading as truth in a magazine whose slogan was "Truth is stranger than fiction." It quotes from Rolfe's novels, presenting them as frequently autobiographical, though the autobiographical writing of a paranoid has a somewhat equivocal connection to its extratextual referents. It quotes from Rolfe's letters, which seem to invent the information they purport merely to convey.[11]

Since Rolfe is also his chronicler's mirror image, it is not surprising that the account of Symons's own involvement in his story is less than perfectly factual: "My quest for Corvo," the biography begins, "was started by accident one summer afternoon in 1925, in the company of Christopher Millard" (15). But in his biography, Julian Symons points out that the quest's outset could not have been entirely accidental since his brother had actually already read much of Rolfe's work (116).

Symons's odd choice of subjects, then, allows him to aestheticize the self, freeing it from the straitjacket of chronological development. By emphasizing their mysteriousness, he compromises the power of historical explanation, questions the notion of historical truth, and fragments his own narrative. Because their self-creation mirrors his biographical activity, they seem to break the boundaries of the book itself.

Particularly in *Quest for Corvo*, the book's structure enhances still more the subject's disruption of historical discourse. For one thing, the structure itself refuses to remain invisible, occasionally displacing both subject and biographer as topic of discussion. When, after the first seven chapters, a change in method becomes advisable, Symons boldly announces it in an italicized note: "The evidence concerning [Rolfe's] career immediately after the Holywell episode came into my possession in fragments, over a long period of time. To present it as I obtained it would set so great a task to the reader's attention that the resulting knowledge would almost certainly seem insufficient reward" (116). The shift in chapter eight could be described in Genette's terms as a change in mood from internal, multiple focalization to nonfocalization, then back to internal focalization with chapter eighteen. By insisting, for the first eight chapters, on the fragmented, limited information available from the various viewpoints, as expressed in letters that reflect each letter-writer's personality as much as his subject (37), Symons gives the book's more synthetic central portion a tentative quality that compromises its narrative authority.

With chapter eight, then, the witnesses with their personal testimonies drop out of sight: the letters printed are not those addressed to Symons, but those written and received by Rolfe. The book, in other words, becomes more novelistic. But given the opening chapters, with Millard and the various letter-writers serving virtually as secondary (or metadiegetic, in Genette's terms) narrators, this central portion can be seen not as diegetic—narrated single-handedly without an intermediary—but as pseudo-diegetic: narrative whose "metadiegetic way station" has been omitted. Its origination in a secondary narrator, in other words, has been suppressed, its information appropriated by the first-degree narrator, in this case the biographer. In *Narrative Discourse* Genette describes the process in *A la recherche du temps perdu* where, in contrast to *Jean Santeuil*, metadiegetic narrative has been almost entirely eliminated (237–39). Obviously all biography is, in a sense, pseudodiegetic; but by prefacing his conventional middle with a metadiegetic start, and by prefacing chapter eight with an explanatory note, Symons emphasizes the narration's "pseudo" quality: the artificiality of the synthesis it reflects.

Like Story and Calderon, Rolfe is presented as unfolding rather than developing, his life less a history than a series of repetitions. Symons uses the image of Ixion's wheel throughout the text to suggest this; he writes of his meetings with Pirie-Gordon, "I was able to piece the story together, to watch another rotation of that wheel to which Rolfe was bound" (*Quest* 186). "In all human lives," Symons writes, "there is a recurring pattern, sometimes difficult to perceive, sometimes on the surface; and the pattern is drawn from within" (173). Such symbolically charged images as Ixion's wheel—along with tarantula and crab metaphors—not only sum up the pattern but, with their recurrence, recreate it, indicating that it operates independently of time and circumstance.

The origin of this pattern Symons sees in Freudian terms as an initial repression of sexual abnormality. On top of this repression, layer on layer of compensating fictions—delusions of grandeur and paranoia—have been elaborated (257). The biographer then becomes an archeologist, the role Freud aspires to in *Dora*. But if Symons uses Freudian terminology to organize his perception of Corvo, he does not attempt to *explain* him. Rolfe's "peculiar inner energy" remains unanalyzable. Only "the external events of his life, and his reactions to them, can be collated and made comprehensible" (257). The only effect of time is to multiply the fictions. As for the Carlylean free will detected by Julian Symons and Harold Fisher, it is free not at all with regard to the initial repression, but can operate with magnificent effectiveness in producing stories to disguise it. "It is essential, if Fr. Rolfe is to be understood," Symons writes, "to realize that he did not *choose* his condition: that it possessed him from early years, and that he was almost powerless to change it" (258).

"The secret lies in the sequence," Symons wrote to Edward Wadsworth, explaining his story's fascination (*Symons* 117). But R. P. Blackmur is more precise when he suggests, in a contemporary review of the book, that it fascinates because the fragments of knowledge "remain partly undisclosed and often have no satisfying context whatever" (135). Symons brilliantly suggests that what he does not know (or tell, in the case of the Venice letters too obscene to print) is even more interesting than what he does: "There were a dozen tantalizing gaps in his narrative which left my curiosity rampant," he writes of Shane Leslie (31). His own biographical efforts seem as odd and mysterious as his subject's life; he consistently downplays his control, insisting instead that "chance helped astonishingly" (155) and that his sources were themselves full of unknown elements. Since they are quoted directly, without omniscient narration to explain them, they retain that unknown quality, and the gaps between their accounts are allowed to proliferate, drawing the reader in. Placing Symons in a larger literary context is not easy. Clearly he was influenced by Strachey and by Freud—or perhaps by Strachey's use of Freud in *Elizabeth and Essex*. But as Julian Symons points out, his initial version of *Quest*, a talk delivered to the Sette of Odde Volumes in 1926, was more Stracheyan than the 1934 version. It is a concise, cleverly written chronological account of Corvo's life, more speculative in its portrayal of what Symons could not know, without any bibliographic subtext. There is also no hint of Freudian interpretation or of sympathetic identification.

Julian Symons has written that his brother disliked modern literature—Joyce, Proust, Eliot, and Auden—for its violence and disorder (Symons and Holland 261). Vyvyan Holland calls him a throwback to the 1890s (Symons and Holland 271). Certainly his interest in perversity seems more Wildean than Dostoievskian—as proposed by David Garnett, who compares *Quest* to *Notes from Underground* ("Review" 230). Symons was interested in Corvo's masks rather than his madness, for Symons, too, disguised aspects of his life—his Jewish father and assumed family name and his poverty (J. Symons, *Essays* introduction). During the eight years between talk and book, I suspect, Symons became increasingly aware of his identification with Corvo as mask-maker, and out of this identification, along with a typically post-Jamesian concern with point of view, grew the strategy of doubling, through the portrayal of his own story, his subject's search for and creation of a self. He immediately recognized his strategy as new, telling a friend, "All I can tell you about the book, my dear fellow, is that it will be unlike any biography ever written" (*Symons* 131).

The strategy had appeared in fiction though: in Conrad's *Lord Jim* and *Heart of Darkness*. Symons's narrative persona, like Marlow, must piece together his subject from witnesses and documents. Always there is someone just ahead of Symons, knowing a bit more a bit sooner, only slightly less elusive and mysterious than the man he describes. Thus Christopher Millard and Maundy Gregory, critical instigators of Symons's quest, seem already to have ventured further than he into the unknown, to have been always already beyond. Christopher Millard was himself a mysterious, multinamed figure known also as "Stuart Mason," and Maundy Gregory was a shady financier. The story we get of Corvo, then, is mitigated by its belatedness and its vicariousness, as Marlow's is of Kurtz. Its essence remains permanently unavailable to narration.

Symons, like Conrad, was fascinated by Africa and its explorers. His 1933 biography of Stanley even includes a textbook description of the continent's blankness that recalls Marlow's map with its huge unexplored area. He describes the grotesque incidents of Stanley's voyages—and, elsewhere, Burton and Speke's and Emin Pasha's—with lavish detail again reminiscent of *Heart of Darkness*. Symons also uses a particularly Conradian version of the disjunction between intention and achievement. All the explorers he describes are effectual only in Africa, only when in motion. Like Lord Jim, who can act out his self-image only as he moves farther and farther east, these men can exercise their powerful wills only as long as they remain outside Europe. Keep them immobilized in Europe and they lose their fame; their disguises are exposed; their courage is questioned; their explanations doubted.

Whether the influence of Conrad on Symons was direct or not, it seems clear to me that Symons's work reflects Conradian as well as Wildean elements. Together, this view of the self as mask and the truth as vitiated by distance and belatedness, told from a particular, limited perspective, results in a new variation on mediated biography.

Unlike the novelistic biographer, then, the mediated

biographer keeps the drama of biographical perception separate from his subject, to whom his relation is one of mirroring rather than identification. The biography that results questions traditional historical narration through technique rather than theme, and thus provides a more flexible experimental alternative than novelistic biography.

V

Feminism and Biography:
Orlando and *Flush,*
Virginia Woolf's "Jokes"

*History is too much about wars; biography too
much about great men.* (Woolf, *A Room of
One's Own* 112)

As a modernist and particularly as a feminist, Virginia
Woolf was eager to alter the conventional method and content of historical and biographical writing, but to do so, she
settled for neither novelistic nor mediated approaches.
Compromising historical narration by making the narrator
himself more prominent, superimposing his sense of time
and his perceptions on the subject's, could not appeal to an
author intent on suppressing a personalized narrative presence. Nor could the author of "The New Biography" easily follow the novelistic biographers in combining factual
material with fictional techniques. But since traditional
biography was obviously untenable, she was faced with a
dilemma: how could she appropriate the influence and
ideological weight carried by biographical writing without
either succumbing to its traditional values and methods, or
vitiating its effectiveness by losing her audience's trust?

Her answer was to combine granite and rainbow but to do so as a "joke."

What Woolf called the "great Victorian fight . . . of the daughters against the fathers" (*Three Guineas* 64) was for Woolf waged in relation to biography. It is for this reason that three of her books are subtitled "a biography": *Orlando* in 1928; *Flush* in 1933; and *Roger Fry* in 1940; and that so many of her novels (*The Voyage Out, Night and Day, Jacob's Room, The Waves*) contain direct references to the writing of lives. Many of her essays are biographical, including her lives of the obscure, and two make important contributions to biographical theory. Biography and family memoirs were her favorite reading material; she belonged to the Memoir Club, for which each member prepared autobiographical recollections. Biography mattered to Woolf; in her writing about it and in experimenting with it, she was redefining her relation to her father and, on a larger scale, the relation of women to history.

From her earliest attempts at fiction, Woolf had been concerned with the relation of women to history and historical writing. The two meanings of *history*—past events and writing about past events—were, for her, one, and she saw the exclusion of women from historical action as not only reflected but reinforced by the exclusion of women from historical commentary. Her unfinished 1906 *Journal of Mistress Joan Martyn* reflects just these concerns. The historian Rosemund Merridew insists that domestic life, too, can be of interest to the scholar and that history viewed from a woman's standpoint is different but illuminating: "A sudden light upon the legs of Dame Elizabeth Partridge," she argues, "sends its beams over the whole state of England, to the King upon his throne" (Squier and DeSalvo 241). But the medieval woman whose diary Merridew discovers, Joan Martyn, has abruptly stopped writing, leaving only a fragmentary picture of her life. The diary, invaluable and fascinating to the modern historian, was to its author—and to her descendent Mrs. Martyn—commonplace, so commonplace, Louise DeSalvo suggests, that Joan Martyn stops writing, preferring instead to hear the more exciting tales told by men of men's adventures ("Shakespeare's" 76). The result of such silencings has been a skewed record of human experience, affecting not only historians but novelists as well, who draw on history for their raw material. "In all the libraries of the world," Woolf writes in a 1920 essay, "the man is to be heard talking to himself and for the most part about himself" (*Books* 28).

From an early age, Woolf felt the need to right the balance. At fifteen, according to Ellen Hawkes, she read *Three Generations of English Women* and began her own "history of women" (43). The history of men, even when enlightened, had been dull or at the very least irrelevant to the experiences of women. Thus Rachel Vinrace dozes over Gibbon in *The Voyage Out*, and in *The Pargiters*, Kitty Malone spills ink on her father's manuscript about men at Oxford. Her father's response, "You share the inability of your sex, my dear, to grasp the importance of historical facts" (93), only increases the tension—and apparent polarity—between women and history.

Serving as images of this polarity are two figures, both biographers, husbands, and Victorians: Thomas Carlyle and Leslie Stephen. Biography for Woolf was, above all, the genre of Carlyle, who argued that history was made by "Great Men," of her father, and, overall, of an exaggerated belief in the power of human will and an oversimplified view of what the self is. Carlyle served Lytton Strachey similarly, as a vehicle through which to attack the Victorian age as a whole. He wrote of it, in an essay on Carlyle, as a time "when gas-jets struggled feebly through the circumambient fog, when the hour of dinner might be at any moment between two and six, when the doses of rhubarb were periodic and gigantic . . . when an antimacassar was on every chair, and the baths were minute tin circles, and the beds were full of bugs and disasters" (*Biographical Essays* 255). Woolf's anti-Victorianism emerged more gradually, and her 1932 essay about her father is extremely affectionate. By the late nineteen thirties, however, in *The Years, Three Guineas,* and in her autobiographical writing, she is bitterly anti-Victorian and critical of her father. Like Strachey, she equated what she most disliked about Victorianism with the form and content of the traditional biography—a massive, artless compendium of letters and chronicle, compiled by an awestruck disciple.

Neither Carlyle nor Stephen in fact write biographies of this kind. But both represent, for Woolf, an excessively externalized and intrinsically antifeminist approach to biography. Carlyle's admiration of great men, his perception of life as battlefield, and of the biographical subject as epic hero (*Critical Essays* 4:26) overvalued conflict and outward achievement and larger-than-life egos. "I hate great men," Ralph Denham says in *Night and Day.* "The worship of greatness in the nineteenth century seems to me to explain the worthlessness of that generation" (20). Carlyle is also the man who, Woolf complains in her 1924 essay "Mr. Bennett and Mrs. Brown," thinks it proper for his wife to chase beetles rather than write books. In *Flush,* he becomes an image of all that is most oppressive in Victorian life: his wife's dog Nero throws himself out a window, attempting suicide, overcome by the "strain of life in Cheyne Row"— a strain evoked, in terms strikingly similar to Strachey's, as "The confinement, the crowd of little objects, the black beetles by night, the bluebottles by day, the lingering odours of mutton, the perpetual presence on the sideboard of bananas—all this, together with the proximity of several men and women, heavily dressed and not often or indeed completely washed" (147).

The Great Man can afford to neglect personal relations; for this reason Woolf condemned Carlyle, and for the same reason her father feared to resemble him (Annan 128). Like Carlyle, Stephen plays the twin role of patriarch and biographer. He was editor, from 1882 to 1891, of the *Dictionary of National Biography,* for which he wrote 378 entries, and the author of various other biographies—of Swift, of his brother, of his friend Henry Fawcett, among others. Although not close to Carlyle, he did know him, and was in some ways a disciple; he based his own biography of Fawcett consciously on Carlyle's of John Sterling, and when he wrote about Carlyle himself for the *Dictionary of National Biography*, he did so in Carlylean terms, concentrating, he says in a letter, on "Carlyle's hard struggle for life and independence" (Maitland 386, 388). The emphasis on action, on vocation, and on conflict is characteristic of both Victorian biographers, and anathema to Woolf. In "A Sketch of the Past," in fact, Woolf complains that her father was incapable of analyzing character at all. "Give him life, a character," she writes, "and he is so crude, so elementary, so conventional, that a child with a box of coloured chalks is as able a portrait painter as he is" (*Moments* 126).

Recently such commentators as S. P. Rosenbaum, Katherine Hill, and Lyndall Gordon have emphasized common strands in the work of father and daughter. Both, for example, see literature in relation to larger social issues, as Hill and Rosenbaum point out, and Rosenbaum argues that Bloomsbury's Utilitarian liberalism comes by way of Leslie Stephen ("Educated Man's Daughter" 43–46; "Intellectual Origins" 18–19). Gordon writes of Stephen as Woolf's "first and most enduring intellectual model" (77). But that her father, to some extent, shaped her mind, is no argument against her rejection of him; it merely intensifies, as Gordon points out, her predicament: her need to reconcile her father's influence and her own views (59). Such a predicament would explain her repeated return to the issue of biography and her desire to pinpoint just where her father's methods fell short.

As a woman, Woolf felt herself an Outsider; in *Three Guineas* she insists on this outsideness as the defining characteristic of women's situation. Her father, regardless of the fact that he fostered her intellectual growth, was an insider, and he wrote as one. "Insiders write a colourless English," Woolf writes in her *Diary:* "They are turned out by the University machine. I respect them. Father was one variety. I dont love them. I dont savour them. Insiders are the glory of the 19th century. They do a great service like Roman roads. But they avoid the forests & the will o the wisps." (V : 333).

The *Dictionary of National Biography,* for Woolf, was a gigantic Roman road. When it appears in her writings, it is always juxtaposed with the excluded will o' the wisp. In *Orlando,* for example, in "Harriette Wilson" and "Lady Hester Stanhope," its condensed and superficial version of experience is made to appear ludicrously oversimple. Throughout Woolf's early fiction, in fact, the very idea of biography conjures up a misguided effort to pin down an essentially indefinable self. In *The Voyage Out,* Terence Hewet, Rachel Vinrace, St. John Hirst, and Helen Ambrose laughingly give mock biographies of themselves, fully aware of how little the facts actually reveal. "That's all very interesting," Helen says, "But of course we've left out the only questions that matter" (144). The self portrayed in *The Voyage Out* is not the predictable circle envisioned by the narrowly intellectual Hirst, but an indescribable, unknowable bubble. "You can't see my bubble," Hewet tells Hirst. "I can't see yours; all we see of each other is a speck, like the wick in the middle of that flame. The flame goes about with us everywhere; it's not ourselves, exactly, but what we feel" (109). If the self is not objectifiable, but a kind of mobile consciousness closer to light than matter, traditional biography becomes pitifully inadequate.

The crime of materialism with which Woolf charges Bennett, Galsworthy, and Wells in "Modern Fiction" resembles the biographer's assumption that the accumulation of facts is sufficient to convey a life. But a life truly perceived will be absent from such factual accretions, for a life truly perceived, Woolf argues in *Night and Day,* her second novel, is nothing other than a life imagined. "You're a romantic," Katharine Hilbery tells Ralph Denham, "making up stories about me," and he replies, "That may be what we have to face. There may be nothing else. Nothing else but what we imagine" (382). The wise if flighty Mrs. Hilbery has long ago come to the same conclusion, and as a result, her biography-in-progress of her father has come to a standstill. Or rather, it has become an endless process of elaboration, "a wild dance of will-o' the wisps, without form or continuity, without coherence even, or any attempt to make a narrative" (43). The things she happens to know about her father, a famous poet, have no intrinsic shape, nor do the copious manuscripts and letters on which she is to base her work. There are problems with propriety (the poet was a passionate man) and with veracity (for "the facts themselves were so much of a legend" [102]). Even in calling up her own memories of her father, Mrs. Hilbery "no longer knew what the truth was" (103).

If, as *Night and Day* suggests, life is an essentially imaginative act and the self an intangible bubble, traditional life-writing has failed to convey it. "Mr. Bennett and Mrs. Brown," Woolf's call for new methods of characterization, reveals that intrinsic to this failure is the distortion or neglect of women's experiences. In December 1910, Woolf notoriously states, human personality changed.[1] Not so well-known, though, is the feminism underlying her perception of the change.[2] Her three pieces of evidence all reveal the changing position of women: the cook, Clytemnestra, and Jane Carlyle are now understood on their own terms, she says, not merely in relation to others. The changing position of women is what inspires Woolf's call for new conventions and her rejection of outmoded methods of characterization—the characterization by "house property," she calls it, of the Edwardians, who provide an accumulation of extrinsic details rather than insight into personality.

Mrs. Brown, depicted in her railway carriage by Galsworthy, Bennett, and Wells, eludes them all. This imposition of an imagined character on an actual figure in a railroad carriage occurs several times in Woolf's work, and most often it is a man's fiction imposed on a woman. When characterization is inadequate, it is women whose experience is excluded. The new role of women, therefore, must be accompanied by new characterizational conventions— that permit the transmission of personality, of perception, not just action and accoutrements. Arguing along similar lines, Lyndall Gordon writes of Woolf's desire to "light up a woman's uncharted nature" (33) and her espousal of a biography concerned with "hidden moments and obscure formative experiences in a life, rather than its more public actions" (94).

Such a view directly contradicts the Aristotelian assumption of traditional biography that character does, in fact, express itself in externally evident ways. Sidney Lee, Stephen's successor as editor of the *Dictionary of National Biography*, sums up the view in his *Principles of Biography:* "Character which does not translate itself into exploit is for the biographer a mere phantasm" (9). Woolf's mock biographies launch a direct attack on this judgment, exposing the absurdity of exploits, the intense reality of phantasm.

For Woolf does not simply reject biography. "Men in clubs and cabinets," according to the narrator of *Jacob's Room*, label character drawing "a frivolous fireside art, a matter of pins and needles" (155). But it is precisely their dismissal of sensitive character drawing, the "women's work" of "pins and needles," that enables men to act cruelly, in particular, to wage World War I, in which Jacob Flanders dies: "Like blocks of tin-soldiers the army covers the corn-field, moves up the hillside, stops, reels slightly this way and that, and falls flat, save that, through field-glasses, it can be seen that one or two pieces still agitate up and down like fragments of broken matchstick" (156).

For Woolf, unimaginative portraiture and those tin-soldiers are akin. They are able to kill and die because others are as unreal to them as they are to themselves. If character drawing could succeed, Woolf writes in her *Di-*

ary, if we had access to others through their perceptions rather than through a reified, oversimplified self, we would have so vivid a sense of each other's consciousnesses that war would be unthinkable (1 : 186). On the table in Jacob Flanders' room at Cambridge is an essay entitled "Does History Consist of the Biographies of Great Men?" We never find out how Jacob answers the question, but *Jacob's Room* is the story of how the kind of history that does consist of just that is also the kind that kills the young men who are heir to it. Sidney Lee, speaking in 1918, makes the connection himself. He urges a surge of biographical activity as a fit response to World War I: "The great events which are striking all our minds give the commemorative instinct of all nations . . . a vital energy, and a range for exercise, exceeding anything which has been previously known" (81). Praise of biography, overvaluation of action, and idealization of war are linked, by Lee and by *Jacob's Room.*

In her 1938 *Three Guineas,* Woolf makes the connection between patriarchy, war, and biography explicit. Here she argues that biographies in the past have dealt primarily with men and have portrayed their lives in terms of battle or struggle. Where such a conception of life is the only one imagined and published, she asserts, history will deal with what she calls in an earlier essay "Wars and Ministries and legislation," and women will be excluded; "We are left out, and history, in our opinion, lacks an eye" (*Books* 23). But a history with nothing to say about women is askew; it not only reflects their absence from history but reinforces the values that excluded them. Simply to reject biography is to facilitate that exclusion.

The traditional view of Woolf is that she did reject biography, that she felt uncomfortable working with factual material and that she failed when she tried to do so. Her own father felt a "grasp of facts" to be inherently masculine (Annan 307), a view echoed by Kitty Malone's father in *The Pargiters* (93). Yet Kitty is fascinated by history when she has time away from entertaining visiting Americans and has a chance to study with a woman she respects. To some extent, Woolf accepted the polarity posited by Kitty's father and attacked throughout her writing the narrow, fact-obsessed, aggressively intellectual male—St. John Hirst, for example, who puts Rachel to sleep with his Gibbon. She values instead the intuitive, boundary-less fluidity she associates with femaleness. But the cost of accepting this dichotomy is high, and finally she rejects it. Seeking a middle ground between St. John Hirst and Mrs. Ramsay, Woolf returns again and again to the practice and discussion of biography and, more broadly, history. After finishing *Orlando,* she contemplated writing a history of women at Newnham—a symbolic answer, perhaps, to Professor Malone's history of men at Oxford.

Throughout Woolf's career, then, nonfictional writing remained a challenging possibility. She could not simply reject the realm of facts. That would be accepting her own exile from history. She could not simply echo male nonfictional writing; that, again, would continue the exclusion of women from the historical record. She needed what Myra Jehlen calls an Archimedean lever—a standpoint outside the language which, if used, would endorse the polarities she sought to repudiate, but a standpoint whose outside-ness would not simply facilitate the exclusion she struggled against (189–90).

The question for Woolf was how to revise biography so that it could include women as subjects and reflect women's differing perceptions without its being either co-opted by masculine terminology or ignored as eccentric and "feminine." Woolf's "joke" biographies are her answer. In them, she can appropriate the factual realm of her father through the standard biographical features of preface, index, footnotes, photographs, and pedantic narrator. But by writing about a woman and a dog and by openly ridiculing her own narrator, she can also defy the sobriety and objectivity overvalued by traditional biographers.

M. M. Bakhtin has defined parody as a "dialogized hybrid," a deliberate mixing of genres and languages that corrects a genre's tendency toward authoritarian single-voicedness (76). Often parody uses a codified genre—epic, for example—for an inappropriate subject; The War between the Mice and the Frogs is Bakhtin's example. In a sense, then, any biography of a woman is parodic, just as women and dogs in Cambridge chapels seem, inevitably, a mockery: "No one could think of bringing a dog into church," thinks Jacob, a student at Cambridge, in *Jacob's Room:* "For though a dog is all very well on a gravel path, and shows no disrespect to flowers, the way he wanders down an aisle, looking, lifting a paw, and approaching a pillar with a purpose that makes the blood run cold with horror . . . a dog destroys the services completely. So do these women" (33). With *Orlando* and *Flush,* Woolf again pairs women and dogs as mockers of a solemn institution, the "church" of biography.

Any depiction of female achievement must in any case be a joke because of its implausibility. In *Night and Day,* Mrs. Hilbery has what she calls her "little joke" about Shakespeare; her theory that actually Ann Hathaway wrote the sonnets. Woolf has her own Shakespeare joke in *A Room of One's Own:* her discussion of the playwright's imaginary sister. This sister won't turn up in "Sir Sidney Lee's life of the poet," but that is precisely the point (*Room* 117). The jokes are the only way available to Woolf to assert that women do, in fact, have a past and a tradition on which they can draw for wisdom and inspiration.[3]

Woolf's mock biographies also grow out of her relation to Lytton Strachey. "I wanted to play a joke on Lytton," Woolf writes of *Flush* in a 1933 letter, "it was to parody him" (*Letters* 5:162). Strachey had initiated a biographical revolt with his *Eminent Victorians,* but he had done so initially in the name of eighteenth-century values about which Woolf had her doubts, as she indicates through her portrayal of St. John Hirst in *The Voyage Out.* She blamed Nicolson's 1923 biography of Tennyson, which she hated, on his influence (*Letters* 3:62), and in her 1927 "The New Biography," written just a year before the publication of *Orlando*, she expressed her doubts about his methods.

The Victorian biographer, she writes, exaggerated his subject's virtues and produced endless, formless compilations of data—complaints echoing Strachey's in his preface to *Eminent Victorians*. With the twentieth century, though, there has come a change, according to Woolf. Biographies are shorter and are narrated by an equal rather than by a sycophant. The new biographer "chooses; he synthesizes; in short, he has ceased to be the chronicler; he has become an artist" (*Granite* 152). Woolf does not fully endorse the change. "A little fiction mixed with fact can be made to transmit personality very effectively," she admits, but as a consequence, the larger-than-life-sized Victorian subject becomes a shrunken figure trapped by his chronicler's rather satiric view of him (154). The reader's credulity is also sacrificed, as fact and fiction pull apart in his mind.

To a large extent, Woolf is in agreement with Strachey about what a biography should do, and *Orlando* and *Flush* can be easily read as novelistic biography taken to its logical extreme. Meisel has called *Orlando* a "consummate Paterian portrait," linking it to other new biographers' Paterian roots (*Absent Father* 44–45). There are parallels in the way Pater, the novelistic biographers, and Woolf in *Orlando* depict the self. But one crucial difference lies in Woolf's unwillingness to shrink her subject, to appear more knowledgeable about Orlando and Flush than either is about himself. She rejects the overpowering narrative authority with which the novelistic biographers tell their stories and probe their subjects' minds. She allows her subjects the integrity permitted by mediated biography, with its incomplete, particularized vision, without thrusting herself forward as a narrative persona. This she does by satirizing the entire enterprise: creating an obtrusive narrator in *Orlando* but making him a fool, allowing the narrator of *Flush* access to his subject's inner life, but making that subject a dog. Supporting Strachey's revolt against traditional biography, she is eager to take it a step further, a step closer to accommodating female experience and female vision. She thus combines aspects of novelistic and mediated biography, taking from the former its interest in describing an inner life invisible to the purely external observer, and from the latter its respect for the integrity of its subject.

This connection between feminism and parodic biography began as early for Woolf as her mock biographical sketch of Violet Dickinson, the close friend of her early twenties. In *Orlando,* of course, her subject was Vita Sackville-West, with whom she had been intimately involved for several years when she wrote to her announcing she had suddenly realized how she could "revolutionise biography in a night" (*Letters* 3:429). Used in the past to commemorate an admired dead person from a great distance, biography for Woolf becomes an act of communication between two living, loving women. Such a transformation of biography into love letter is at least as subversive, in its way, as placing a dog in a Cambridge chapel.

Orlando is dedicated to Sackville-West (herself a biographer and married to the biographer Harold Nicolson) and is based on her family history. Much of it is derived from Sackville-West's own account of her family and their estate, *Knole and the Sackvilles* (see Baldanza). There is, then, a certain amount of factual material in *Orlando*, particularly the descriptions of Knole and its furnishings. There are also roman-à-clef-like correspondences: Sasha the Russian princess is also Violet Trefusis, Sackville-West's lover; Orlando's poem "The Oak Tree" is also Sackville-West's prize-winning poem "The Land." These extra-textual ref-

erences, along with photographs, preface, index, and subtitle, are important to Woolf because they establish what
Philippe Lejeune calls a "referential pact" with the reader;
they announce that what follows is nonfiction (155). Book-
sellers responded by placing it on the biography shelf in
their stores, even though they warned this would reduce
sales. Woolf was chagrined at the thought of selling fewer
books, but the pretense of referentiality had clearly been
part of her plan (*Diary* 3 : 198).

Orlando was written in the months immediately following the publication of *To the Lighthouse*, the book which
laid to rest her parents' ghosts in her mind. "And now he
comes back sometimes," Woolf writes of her father in her
Diary at this time, "but differently. . . . He comes back now
more as a contemporary" (3 : 208). In *Orlando* Woolf seems
to be meeting her father halfway: accepting his allegiance
to the facts halfway, borrowing his narrative persona halfway, imitating his emphasis on gender roles halfway. Most
importantly, though, in *Orlando* Woolf begins to reclaim
for her sex the realm of fact, meeting her father at last on
his own turf, "more as a contemporary," i.e., no longer as a
father to be resisted, but as an equal to be absorbed. "*Orlando*," she later wrote in her diary, "taught me how to
write a direct sentence; taught me continuity & narrative,
& how to keep the realities at bay" (*Diary* 3 : 203). To her
repertoire of "feminine" qualities like suggestiveness, lyricism, fragmentation, and fantasy, in other words, she had
now added "masculine" directness, continuity, and control
of factual material. "I want to write a history," she adds in
the same diary entry, "say of Newnham or the woman's
movement, in the same vein."

This referentiality, though, for traditional biographers a
matter of simply collating documents and checking sources,
is for Woolf a far more complex affair. Traditional biography, single-voiced, portraying a completed, valorized past,
a "world of fathers and founders of families," in Bakhtin's

terms (13), is subverted in *Orlando* by a multiplicity of narrators, the eruption of present into past, a challenge to hierarchy, and a biographical referent so problematic that her identity must be established by law suits.

Orlando's identity is problematic because at the age of thirty she changes sexes, then disappears for a time when she takes up residence with gypsies. Sackville-West's identity was problematic because she was bisexual and had at times dressed as a man and thus blurred gender boundaries, and because her ancestral home, Knole, had been the subject of litigation, the question being whether her grandfather had married her grandmother. At the time *Orlando* was written, Sackville-West was about to lose Knole; because she was a woman, she was ineligible to inherit.

Inheritance—the passing on, from father to son, of authority and wealth—is an issue central to biography, which tends to be written from a filial viewpoint. The narrator-son, in commemorating the father-subject, also integrates past into present so that the biography becomes an enactment of inheritance from one generation to the next. For women, both biography and inheritance are problematic. As Woolf complains in reviewing a biography of Mary Mitford, there is a shortage of viable female subjects—or at least of subjects suitable for a "lady" to write about (*Common Reader* 192). In any case the role of inheritance is to provide continuity from the valorized past described by Bakhtin to the present, and that past's value rests on its exclusion of women.

The epic values that exclude women also kill men. *Orlando* alludes to two epics in which sons die on account of a father or father figure: *The Song of Roland* and Matthew Arnold's "Sohrab and Rustum." When *Orlando* opens, its subject is playfully slashing at a shriveled Moor's head which swings from a rafter. Roland's epic exploit, his death as he kills Moors for his king, becomes Orlando's play. "No life of a man, faithfully recorded, but is a heroic poem of its sort, rhymed or unrhymed," according to Carlyle (*Critical* 4 : 26). *Orlando* questions the logic of associating heroism with life and legitimacy.

Oddly, it is as a woman that Orlando has her actual adventure, when she lives with gypsies, one of whom is named Rustum. Arnold's Rustum is killed by his father in single combat, father and son virtually forced to battle each other by their pride and prowess. Rustum's father, of course, does not recognize his son; told that his child was a girl, he has no reason to suspect such a son exists. The situation suggests that women are by definition marginal in the world of fathers and sons; had Rustum actually been the "puny girl" his mother said he was, he could never have faced his father in battle. Had Vita Sackville-West not been the girl she was, she could have inherited her ancestral home, participated in the world of fathers and sons, and been the subject of ordinary, not mock biography.

Orlando has yet another literary referent related to issues of inheritance, Shakespeare's *As You Like It*, a depiction of disrupted inheritance put right by cross-dressing and marginalization in the Forest of Arden (Moore 341n; Delattre 189). Orlando, placing love-letters on trees, suggests Woolf's Orlando, with her poem "The Oak Tree"; his complaint that he has been deprived of his rightful inheritance suggests Sackville-West herself. Rosalind's disguise as Ganymede acting the part of Rosalind resembles Orlando's transformation into womanhood, which she occasionally undoes by dressing herself as a man. One night, in fact, she is picked up by a prostitute (as Ganymede attracts Phebe). When she reveals that she is a woman, Woolf writes, "Nell burst into such a roar of laughter as might have been heard across the way" (217). They brew some punch, invite Nell's female friends, and tell each other their life stories. These casual biographies, shared among intimates in a room with a carefully closed door, provide a powerful alternative to male-oriented biography. And though none has a respectable lineage, "None was too wretched or too poor but to have some ring or handkerchief in her pocket which stood her in lieu of pedigree" (219).

Biography as communication among intimates; inheritance as chosen or created rather than dictated: these are the alternatives available to women who, like Celia and Rosalind, ignore the hierarchy established by others and form their own affiliations. "Many were the fine tales they told," Woolf writes, "and many the amusing observations they made, for it cannot be denied that when women get together—but hist—they are always careful to see that the doors are shut and that not a word of it gets into print" (219).

As You Like It, of course, winds up validating, not repudiating, orderly biological inheritance; the trouble there was usurpation, not the laws themselves. For women in Woolf the trouble runs deeper, but an Arden of sorts offers them alternatives: the underworld of solidarity with prostitutes, and to some extent the world of art, as well.

At the center of Orlando's home is a tapestry portraying the flight of Daphne from hunters. Her only escape, we know, is to turn into laurel, symbol of art. As art can provide Sackville-West with Knole, it can also provide an alternative, freely chosen inheritance.[4] As she lives from sixteenth to twentieth century, Orlando carries with her a single manuscript, her poem "The Oak Tree." Pressured and changed by the times through which she lives, Orlando finds what identity she has through her literary efforts—as an artist, a figure Woolf compares to a traveler trying to get a box of cigars through customs. This illicit sneaking through of possessions (phallic possessions at that) is Woolf's alternative to the legal inheritance of fathers and sons.

Humor, illegality, secrecy, anonymity, casual conversation: these are the sources of feminist power in opposition to male, ego-oriented, authoritative history. Critics have pointed out the important role played by old garrulous women as alternatives to male univocalism in Woolf's work

(Neuman 74; Lyndall Gordon 260) and Woolf's stubborn opposition to the "masculine voice of the omniscient narrator" (Blain 119). In *Orlando* she traces the masculine voice to its source in epic, epic biography, and the exclusion of women.

Woolf challenges the voice not merely by complicating her subject but by multiplying her narrator as well. In an essay on DeQuincey, Woolf writes that the biographer or autobiographer "must devise some means by which the two levels of existence can be recorded—the rapid passage of events and actions; the slow opening up of single and solemn moments of concentrated emotion" (*Second Common Reader* 125). This kind of dichotomy turns up whenever Woolf writes about life-writing. Traditionally only the passage of events and actions had been recorded—the "granite" of facts—but the "rainbow" of personality should also be communicated, if only it is possible. In *Orlando* Woolf provides two narrators to fulfill the task: a document-obsessed *Dictionary of National Biography*–style narrator and a Proustian one.[5] Since the document-narrator is undercut by an ironic tone, though, this duality is itself an oversimplification. One moment the narrator is providing a drop by drop description of rain, in an obviously Proustian passage; the next he is pompously complaining about gaps in his sources: "It is, indeed, highly unfortunate, and much to be regretted," the narrator comments, "that at this stage of Orlando's career, when he plays a most important part in the public life of his country, we have least information to go upon" (110). The documents, it turns out, have been destroyed by fire and revolution, and as a result, "it has been necessary to speculate, to surmise, and even to use the imagination."

The elusive Orlando is inconvenient for this plodding, DNB-narrator, for she fits into no preconceived life-plot. As man, she performs no visible exploits; as woman, she spends most of her time writing and thinking, rather than loving, as she ought: "As long as she thinks of a man," the narrator comments, "no one objects to a woman thinking" (242). Nancy Miller points out that women's plots that reject this dichotomy between male ambition and female eroticism have been accused of "implausibility"—an implausibility Woolf flaunts and ridicules (40). "If then," her narrator comments, "the subject of one's biography will neither love nor kill, but will only think and imagine, we may conclude that he or she is no better than a corpse and so leave her" (242).

In the ordinary biography, of course, death is the climax, the moment when the life takes on its fullest meaning, now that it can be seen in retrospect, as a completed past. A. O. J. Cockshut has described the importance of deathbed scenes in nineteenth-century biography: the moment when both life and book achieved full coherence. Without death, in fact, there is no biography: "The intervention of death alone," writes Sidney Lee, "brings the career within the lawful range of biography" ("Perspective" 77). In *Orlando*, though, death is robbed of its finality, its power to confer meaning. Twice Orlando sleeps for a solid week, then awakens refreshed. And far from ending with a death, *Orlando* ends with the aggressive eruption into the biography of the present: the storytelling pace slows, the chimes of clocks pound the time into Orlando's head, and the Proustian narrator takes over, portraying consciousness as a hodgepodge of unfinished thoughts and perceptions. The department store and the automobile, two very modern inventions, convey this feeling of fragmentation and incongruous juxtaposition. Traveling rapidly out of London, Orlando can make out only parts of signs, their incompleteness mirroring the incompleteness of her own life story.

If *Orlando's* ending is aggressively un-ending-like, its overall shape similarly resists conventional biographical patterns. In *Three Guineas*, Woolf urges that as women enter public life they transform it, rather than accept male status-consciousness and competition. She urges that they refuse ribbons and awards, as she herself did, when they were offered her. Orlando does accept the Burdett Coutts Memorial Prize—as Sackville-West accepted the Hawthornden prize for "The Land"—but humorously and in parentheses, causing her biographer (the document-one) to complain: "We must snatch space to remark how discomposing it is for her biographer that this culmination to which the whole book moved, this peroration with which the book was to end, should be dashed from us on a laugh casually like this; but the truth is that when we write of a woman, everything is out of place—culminations and perorations; the accent never falls where it does with a man" (280). *Discomposing* is the perfect word for it; for in making her biographer uncomfortable, Orlando is also unwriting traditional biography, refusing to let her life take on the familiar, climactic shape.

Woolf's rejection of biographical conventions in *Orlando* has been noted by such commentators as Edel (*Literary Biography* 94), Naremore, who calls *Orlando* an attack on the "deadening empiricism of most biographical literature" (193), and Fleishman, who terms it a "debunking novel" (*Historical Novel* 233). The traditional biographer's reliance on documents, on chronology, on facts and even on a coherent concept of a "self" is ridiculed.

The self, for Woolf, is defined by the act and objects of perception: what Orlando reads, wears, and sees around her. It is because its boundaries are so permeable that the self is describable at all; that part of us formed by our sense impressions must be accessible to others who have perceived the same objects. In "The Narrow Bridge of Art," published the same year she began work on *Orlando*, Woolf called for a new novel that would describe the less personal aspects of an individual's response to his environment: "the power of music, the stimulus of sight, the effect on us of the shape of trees or the play of colour, the emotions bred in us by crowds. The obscure terrors and hatreds which come so irrationally in certain places or from certain people, the delight of movement, the intoxication of wine. Every moment is the centre and meeting-place of an extraordinary number of perceptions which have not yet been expressed" (*Granite* 23). The mind, then, has a constant, indefinable relation with external objects, whose exact impact has yet to be pinpointed and which may even, to a large extent, *constitute* the mind. Claire Kahane contrasts this idea that "perceptual objects themselves help to define the self" with the more traditional philosophical distinction between subject and object associated, through Tansley and Bradshaw, with masculine insensitivity (72–73). This emphasis on the mind as a receiver of sense-impressions anticipates Woolf's later interest, in "A Sketch of the Past," in the larger, social forces that define people: the "invisible presences" of friends, family, surroundings, epoch (*Moments* 80). *Orlando's* depictions of fashion—in clothes, furniture, or art—dramatize this interplay of perceiver and perception, of individual and influence, of past and present. Evoking Edwardian England, she writes: "The dryness of the atmosphere brought out the colour in everything and seemed to stiffen the muscles of the cheeks. It was harder to cry now. Water was hot in two seconds. Ivy had perished or been scraped off houses. Vegetables were less fertile; families were much smaller" (*Orlando* 267). The absurd juxtapositions and parallels at once hint at and mock causality. Woolf ridicules the tracing of continuities, the traditional task of historical narrative.[6] Instead she describes objects as if they were accretions of their contexts and uses. The magical mingling of human and nonhuman behavior offers the feminist biographer a subtler, less ego-oriented, less simplistic method of portraying the self than either neglect of inner experience or an omniscient and intrusive depiction of it.

If *Orlando* is read as a kind of "macrohistory," dealing with the "impersonal content" of individual subjects, the "common denominator of perceptions and attitudes produced by a specific culture," in Saul Friedländer's words, its contribution to biographical theory becomes more clear and its peculiarities make more sense (113). Woolf's reveling in Sackville-West's aristocracy, for example, need not be seen as snobbery, for the aristocrat, as Morris Philipson points out, is more aware of his relationship to history and his debt to forebears (247). Tracing in Sackville-West's face the features of her ancestors, examining in her home their possessions, Woolf found vivid evidence that the self, as a kind of repository, could be depicted simultaneously from without and within.

This view of history and the self makes *Orlando*, in Fleishman's words, a "genuine fusion of fiction and biography" (*Historical Novel* 137). As such, it bears a close relationship to the novelistic biography of Strachey. Certainly the Paterian concept of the "imaginary portrait," melding historical moment and psyche, underlies both. But *Orlando* differs in that it ridicules the historical continuity it seems to seek, undercuts its own narrative authority, and, where novelistic biography "shrinks" its subject, grossly exaggerates its own, opening out the notion of personality to include an entire world. Like Mrs. Hilbery's joke about Ann Hathaway, *Orlando* is a joke with a point. For in making a joke of biography Woolf is defusing its power to exclude women from history, to dictate to men a life-plot of competition and aggression, to denigrate thought as somehow different from life.

Flush, like *Orlando*, Woolf belittled as a joke. Backed up by research and endnotes, it is more recognizable as biography, but it has at least as unlikely a subject: Elizabeth Barrett Browning's dog. Here again, Woolf's choice of a subject produces, inevitably, parodic biography. The joke this time is angrier, though, for as Woolf grew older she became more willing to abandon what she called her "teatable" training (see Heilbrun, "Woolf").

Carlyle and Barrett's father appear in *Flush* as images of an oppressive patriarchy. United against them are women—Barrett and her maid Lily Wilson, an alliance crossing class barriers; and Flush—who seems tamed and co-opted but whose physical presence casts an absurd light on all that surrounds him. At one point the Brownings, with Flush, are returning to Italy from a visit to England. On the tossing deck, Flush sees a "stern, tall man": "'Mr. Carlyle!' he heard Mrs. Browning exclaim; whereupon— the crossing, it must be remembered, was a bad one— Flush was violently sick" (150–51). This vomiting dog confronts Carlyle's concept of epic biography with epic-resistant reality, with what Bakhtin calls the laughter that opposes hierarchy.

Flush depicts defiance and laughter; Nero, Jane Carlyle's suicidal dog, depicts the victimization which is the other possible response of women to oppression. Nero's attempted suicide echoes others in Woolf's work: Eusebius Chubb in *Orlando* is driven to a gas oven by similar stimuli. Septimus Smith in *Mrs. Dalloway* (and Woolf during a 1904 breakdown) uses a window to flee a forcibly imposed sense of "proportion." Holmes and Bradshaw represent a vacuous social conformity particularly oppressive to women; Bradshaw's wife has long since "gone under," in Woolf's words. Nero's leap from the top-story window also echoes Barrett's own flight from her father as depicted in *Flush*— a flight from a rigid social hierarchy that suffocates women to the freedom of Italy—and Woolf's own flight from what she regarded as Victorian values in general. "Woman was his slave," she writes of her father in "A Sketch of the Past," "being the most typical of Victorians" (*Moments* 125).

Flush follows the spaniel's life from the time he was presented to Barrett to his death in Italy. Its mock-serious narrator discusses the dog's ancestors, then chronicles his activities (watching Barrett write; witnessing the growth of her relationship with Browning; walking in the park; rambling around Venice), his emotions (mostly primitive— jealousy, lust, fear), and his perceptions (mostly smells).

It does all that a biography should do, according to Woolf; but its subject's limitations in height, intelligence, and freedom keep it from doing much. Flush's essence eludes biographical depiction in part because understanding across species is limited; but the difficulty in understanding across species lines is only slightly greater than understanding across ego boundaries, and Flush's limited range of experience and understanding is, in any case, scarcely more limited than that of the "educated man's daughter," of whom Woolf writes in *Three Guineas*, whose view is restricted to the drawing room window. In giving up the freedom to roam which he had with his first owner, in learning about rank and breeding among dogs, Flush mimics the entrapment of women who, cut off from freedom, become complicitous in their own oppression; complacent, narcissistic, class-conscious, Flush no longer rebels against his chain, but preens on it. Like *Three Guineas*, *Flush* makes a connection between patriarchy and social oppression; the impulse that keeps all real experience of life away from women insists, in particular, that the actual juxtaposition of wealth and misery be kept hidden. When a woman breaks out, as does Barrett when she rescues the kidnapped Flush, this juxtaposition is the first thing she notices; hidden behind stern Wimpole Street is the poverty of Whitechapel. "Mixed up with that respectability was this filth," the narrator comments (88).

But *Flush* also depicts a triumph of daughter over father. By eating the dinner Barrett could not eat herself, Flush spares her her father's wrath (an incident with resonances of Woolf's own eating disorders) and helps her to deceive him. Similarly, Wilson helps her retrieve Flush from his kidnappers, marry, and leave England, all in defiance of Mr. Barrett. By discovering what her culture defines as alien to her and uniting with it—sexual passion, dog, maid, Italy: all alien to the "educated man's daughter"—Barrett becomes, like Orlando, a blurrer of hierarchical distinctions. For Barrett's first reaction on confronting the squalor of Whitechapel is to identify not with her social class but with her gender: "Here lived women like herself," she thinks (104). Her alliance with Lily Wilson suggests the same solidarity and shows its power. When the implacably logical men around her argue that to ransom Flush from his kidnappers would mean catering to immorality, Barrett and her maid insist on the primacy of affection over morality and ride in a carriage to Whitechapel to negotiate his release. The attempt fails, but does persuade Mr. Barrett to yield; and the experience provides material, later, for *Aurora Leigh*. The alliance parallels that discerned by Susan Squier in Woolf's "Great Men's Houses"; there Jane Carlyle and her maid battle dirt and disorder, "united in one battle," according to Squier (496), while the Great Man writes.

Flush's imprisonment by his kidnappers reveals imprisonment for what it is, without the plush setting, expensive food, and lavish affection: pure misery. For Flush's imprisonment clearly parallels Barrett's own: "It was almost as difficult for her to go to Flush," Woolf writes of Barrett, "as for Flush to come to her" (98). Afterwards, Flush is more closely identified with Barrett than ever, and when they flee together to Italy, their imprisoners are paired: "There were no dog-stealers here and, she may have sighed, there were no fathers" (126).[7]

Escape from the father provides a much broader range of experiences than Wimpole Street had offered. Flush mates indiscriminately; Barrett Browning has a child. Flush no longer cares about his breeding and appearance and socializes across class lines; the Brownings entertain many visitors and experiment with table turning. Barrett's previous knowledge of life had been summed up by five busts in her bedroom: formulaic and whitewashed icons of male culture that Flush perceives as gods. But "Mrs. Browning possessed a fund of curiosity as to human life," Woolf writes in an endnote, "which was by no means satisfied by the busts of Homer and Chaucer on the washing-stand in the bedroom" (176). These busts, like traditional biography, represent a terribly limited version of culture, one that is defined by what it excludes. "One hour spent in 5 Cheyne Row will tell us more about [the Carlyles] and their lives than we can learn from all the biographies," Woolf writes in "Great Men's Houses": "Go down into the kitchen. There, in two seconds, one is made acquainted with a fact that escaped the attention of Froude, and yet was of incalculable importance—they had no water laid on" (23).

Woolf's remodeling of biography is a refusal to be defined by what excludes her. As the extratextual circumstances of *Orlando* subverted its framework, *Flush*'s endnotes—traditional proving ground of male erudition—challenge the world the biography depicts. What we need most of all, Woolf suggests, in one of nine lengthy notes, are biographies of "the inscrutable, the all-but-silent, the all-but-invisible servant maids of history" (182). In *Three Guineas*, too, another work where footnotes become a feminist weapon, Woolf calls for biographies of maids. Relegated by gender and class to the endnotes of history, maids represent for Woolf the repressed domestic underside of Victorian society. Crosby in *The Years* is one example, inhabiting a lightless basement room, her only intimate a dog, worshipping the children she serves. As the subject of a biography she would not necessarily provide new insight into her world. But the simple insertion of her life into the historical record would expose the price exacted by that world for its survival. Wilson herself, according to Woolf in an endnote, "spoke almost as seldom as Flush" (177). She requires a biographer for the very reason she provides so elusive a subject. Her silence and invisibility are also a part of human experience and deserve the validation only nonfiction can provide. In yet another endnote, Woolf depicts an aged Lily dreaming in terms that recall Lytton Strachey's famous summing up of Queen Victoria's life through her deathbed memories:[8]

A very strange day it had been, she may have thought, as she sat in the red Venetian sunset, an old woman, dreaming. Her friends, married to farm hands, still stumbled up the English lanes to fetch a pint of beer. And she had eloped with Miss Barrett to Italy; she had seen all kinds of queer things— revolutions, guardsmen, spirits. . . . Then Mrs. Browning had died—there can have been no lack of thoughts in Wilson's old head as she sat at the window of the Palazzo Rezzonico in the evening. But nothing can be more vain than to pretend we can guess what they were. . . . (181–82)

The passage is Stracheyan until that last sentence, which repudiates all speculation. Prolific queens are easily depicted. Silent maids, like dogs, can be depicted only through parody that mocks its own pretense of understanding. The narrator's sudden refusal to describe Lily Wilson's thoughts resembles a similar self-interruption in *Orlando,* when the prostitutes' recounting of their pasts becomes abruptly inaudible: "but hist—they are always careful to see that the doors are shut and that not a word of it gets into print" (219). The lives of women are by definition inaccessible to biographical narration, maids and prostitutes representing only an extremer form of their marginality, their silence or secrecy.

But if the task of biography, for Woolf, is to describe what has been left out of biography in the past, and, at the same time, silence and secrecy are viewed as intrinsic attributes of women's experience, biography is faced with a nearly impossible paradox. In *Three Guineas,* Woolf admires Josephine Butler, who refused to allow a biography to be written of herself (76), but comments in an endnote, "It is much to be regretted that no lives of maids, from which a more fully documented account could be constructed, are to be found in the *Dictionary of National Biography*" (166). In the absence of such accounts, nothing annoys her more, in her many biographical reviews, than empty speculation based on irrelevancies or clichés— empty speculation of the sort she briefly allows herself in

159

dwelling on Wilson's memories. If women silence themselves, and biographers are refused the right to invent them, how are they to be made real for the world? The answer, Woolf says in *Three Guineas,* is to look between the lines of the biographies that do exist (77). This is what *Orlando* and *Flush* seek to do: to suggest, through their distorted echo of traditional biography, what is not in Froude, in the *Dictionary of National Biography,* or in "Sir Sidney Lee's life of the poet."

At one point in *Flush,* the dog, tormented by fleas, is shorn of his beautiful coat, leaving him "emasculated, diminished, ashamed," the mirror telling him, "You are nothing." But then "the potent spirits of truth and laughter" turn his mood around: "To be nothing—is that not, after all, the most satisfactory state in the whole world? . . . To caricature the pomposity of those who claim that they are something—was that not in its way a career?" (143). Biographical invisibility, the fate imposed on women by a narrow understanding of what, in a life, is worth recording, offered women a valuable vantage point from which to remake biography. For Woolf it was also a way not of winning the Victorian battle of daughters against fathers—for that would endorse the masculine taste for war metaphors—but of laughing it off: a far more meaningful triumph.

VI

Unweaving the Self: Psycho- and Sociobiography

Novelistic biography depicts the self from within. Mediated biography depicts a biographer perceiving a self. Both remove the biographical narrator from his traditionally invisible and inviolable position of authority and give him prominence as interpreter or at least as gatherer of impressions. But both retain, for all their innovations, a notion of the self as a characterizable entity with approximate boundaries. Pater had pointed out the continuity of the self with its surroundings, and certainly the novelistic biographers were intensely aware of the tenuousness of any momentary unity and coherence attainable by the self, but it was that unity, bounded by the "thick wall of personality" that they made their subject: "each mind keeping as a solitary prisoner its own dream of a world" (235). Similarly the mediated biographers, portraying the self as a pattern drawn from within—the life as aesthetically coherent—tended to emphasize its isolable and isolating characteristics at the expense of those formed in a free interplay between self and world.

The question then becomes: how portray the self from within without isolating it? How blend an adequate treatment of the inner life with a recognition of the demands of objectivity—demands experienced by the biographical sub-

161

ject (who did, after all, function within a society) as well as by the biographer?

These questions were certainly not ignored by novelistic and mediated biographers, who could use fate and personal relationships to link their subjects to a larger context. But they become central in the last work of Strachey and Woolf. They choose quite different ways of solving the problem, but both seek to open up the self, to dramatize its multiple elements as they interact, fragmentarily, with elements of other selves and with the environment. A single consciousness is less apt to be the subject and a single narrative perspective is less apt to be employed. Strachey relies in part on Freudian terminology to buttress his interpretation of Elizabeth and Essex, while Woolf almost entirely suppresses her narrative presence in *Roger Fry*.

There are, then, at least two possible responses to the problem of unweaving the self: to dramatize psychic mechanisms in Freudian or other psychological terms and to seek a social basis for intellectual growth and development. To a large extent these approaches overlap; in *Elizabeth and Essex*, for example, Strachey uses both. As Freud indicates in *Totem and Taboo* and *Moses and Monotheism* (and as Jung's notion of a "collective unconscious" suggests), individual and mass psychologies have a great deal in common.

The works discussed in this chapter all seem to me to be as innovative as they could be within the bounds of their theoretical assumptions. Strachey's *Elizabeth and Essex*, published in 1928, was his last full-length biography, his most disliked, and, in its use of Freud and speculation, his most experimental. Woolf's *Roger Fry*, on the other hand, is generally read as an extremely conventional biography. It is her only wholly serious biography and represents, I will argue, not a regression from innovative theorizing but an experiment in its application without departing from a literal conception of fact. It is similar in this way to Forster's 1934 *Goldsworthy Lowes Dickinson;* both biographers submit themselves to rather stringent notions of what biography ought to do, without by any means surrendering to these constraints.[1] Both I classify here as sociobiographies, by which I mean biographies concerned with placing the intellectual development of their subjects within a social context—as a dramatized interaction of social forces, not as analytical intellectual or social history. Both works embrace fragmentation as a method, relying heavily on quoted material from the subject's writings, thus emphasizing the independent interaction of various elements of the subject's life and environment.

In 1920, Strachey's brother and sister-in-law, James and Alix Strachey, went to Vienna to study with Sigmund Freud. They became psychoanalysts and on their return discussed the new psychology with Lytton. At first skeptical, Strachey was ready by 1926 to accept and experiment with Freudian analysis (Holroyd 2:586). Two years later he published *Elizabeth and Essex,* which he dedicated to James and Alix. The book unquestionably reveals the influence of Freud, who wrote Strachey after its publication, "You are aware of what other historians so easily overlook, that it is impossible to understand the past with certainty, because we cannot divine men's motives and the essence of their minds and so cannot interpret their actions" (Holroyd 2:616). The compliment appears somewhat backhanded, since Freud praises Strachey for recognizing the impossibility of what would seem to be his task as an historian, but in fact this is precisely what *Elizabeth and Essex* is about: human history as a blend of psychological and social considerations in which motive and action, interpretation and fact, are indistinguishable. In using Freud, Strachey did not seek an explanation for particular events but an internally consistent system that at least gave events a structure, linking them to a sociohistorical context and transcending the isolation of individual subjectivities.

In all his biographies Strachey is concerned with the inexplicable and uncontrollable forces governing human action. In *Eminent Victorians* he fragmented his subjects' conception of the world by revealing incongruous details or actions that gave the lie to the generalizations by which they seemed to live. In *Queen Victoria* he aligned himself with his subject's sentimentality, while suggesting all that it failed to take into account. In *Elizabeth and Essex* he turns an entire age into a psychic drama, delineating for the first time the irrational forces that he had hitherto only hinted at. Hayden White's account in *Metahistory* of the limitations of eighteenth-century historiography explains Strachey's use of Freud: "The *philosophes* needed a theory of human consciousness in which reason was not set over against imagination as the basis of truth against the basis of error, but in which the *continuity* between reason and fantasy was recognized." The problem "was to uncover the implicit rationality in even the most irrational of human imaginings" (51–52). These connections between irrational and rational cannot be found, but must be fabricated. "The difference between the Enlighteners and Nietzsche," White writes, "was that the latter was aware of the 'fictive' nature of his own Ironic perceptions" (69).

Strachey had always recognized that the historian's task was in part fictive, particularly in *Queen Victoria,* where the narrator is aligned with the subject's own self-weaving. But in *Elizabeth and Essex* he most clearly rejects any dichotomy between fact and fiction. Here he extends the notion of self-weaving well beyond the boundaries of the self, so that the entire world is seen as a network of various fictive constructs. Freudian theory, by positing a connection between reason and fantasy, a system by which the eruptions of unconscious into conscious belief could be formulated, implies that fiction-making is an intrinsic part of human activity. This, I think, is why Freud congratulated Strachey not on his accuracy, but on his uncertainty and his willingness to speculate. Freud himself once called his *Moses and Monotheism* an "historical novel" (Manuel 198), and at the end of his biography of Leonardo da Vinci he writes that he may be accused of having "merely written a psychoanalytic novel," and adds, "I am far from over-estimating the certainty of these results." (*Psychological Works* 11 : 134). Strachey's portrait of Florence Nightingale laid the groundwork for such a mingling of fact and fiction. Her daydreaming, her rejection of marriage, her invalidism allow her to reinvent herself. Elizabeth's neurosis is linked to a similar act of self-construction. But Elizabeth is not isolated by her neurosis, for it is somehow shared by her environment, with the result that her symptomatic indecisiveness functions effectively as strategy, and her distrustful vision of the world as elaborately scheming functions effectively as reality. Ordinary people, according to Freud, tend to exaggerate the distinction between fantasy and reality: "Reality seems to us something worlds apart from invention, and we set a very different value on it." But fantasies, too, "possess a reality of a sort": "The phantasies possess *psychical* as contrasted with *material* reality, and we gradually learn to understand that *in the world of the neurosis it is psychical reality which is the decisive kind*" (*Psychological Works* 16 : 368).[2]

In a sense, then, Strachey treats all of Elizabethan England as a neurotic patient. But in a larger sense he simply treats this particular era as a dynamic network of significations, an intersection of variant texts, in which the linguistic construction of events outweighs the events themselves. *Elizabeth and Essex* is a far more ambitious work in this sense than *Queen Victoria*. In the earlier work the narrator portrays a single version of experience while history itself—as a causal system—eludes both narrator and subject. In *Elizabeth and Essex,* on the other hand, Strachey portrays the meshing of conflicting viewpoints as the sole ingredient of historical action. History here is not a mysterious force running its course behind the backs of human agents, but the product of human interpretation, inseparable from human fiction-making. Fact and falsehood, strategy and symptom, historical event and text: each pair is synonymous in Strachey's con-textualization of Elizabethan England.

As a woman, Elizabeth profits from this blurring of distinctions, for it allows her to reimagine herself as she refuses to submit to a socially defined role. Clifford Bower-Shore notes this refusal in an oddly accurate, if stunningly offensive comment: "Altogether *Elizabeth and Essex* was a sad failure. Elizabeth, sex-hungry like many ugly women, lazy and often despicable, should have become the well-pierced board for Strachey's darts of irony. But in this book she evades, as her repressed body evaded in reality, total subjection to man's desire" (69). If Elizabeth escapes Strachey's irony, it is because she escaped subjection to man's desire. This escape is inseparable from her repression. Even more than Nightingale, like Woolf's Orlando, Elizabeth acts out Nancy Miller's alternative to Freud's ambitious/erotic dichotomy, choosing a dream in which "egoistic desires would assert themselves paratactically alongside erotic ones": "The repressed content [Miller writes] would not be erotic impulses, but an impulse to power: a fantasy of power that would revise the social grammar in which women are never defined as subjects; a fantasy of power that disdains a sexual exchange in which women can participate only as objects of circulation" (41). Elizabeth insists on her sexuality while retaining her power.

Elizabeth pays a price, though, for her "both-and." Strachey suggests that her conscious intent to act, to rule, to love, is disturbed by a pathological inability to commit herself conclusively, an inability that resulted from a childhood trauma. "Her sexual organization," he writes, "was seriously warped" (*Elizabeth* 20). Her mother had been beheaded by her father, and at fourteen, she was caressed by her step-mother's husband; the result, according to Strachey, was "a deeply seated repugnance to the crucial act of intercourse" (25). There was also a deeply seated repugnance to any crucial act; as portrayed by Strachey, Elizabeth's indecisiveness is a symptom of her repressed sexuality.

At times, particularly in her execution of Essex, Elizabeth seems the victim of her repression. On that occasion Essex's reference to her "crooked carcase" brutally objectifies her, shatters her vanity ("the citadel of her repressed romanticism" [262]), and brings to the surface the repressed awareness of her sexual vulnerability. This in turn triggers uncontrollable rage, and for the first time in her life, Strachey suggests, she doesn't delay, but takes her revenge: "Manhood . . . was overthrown at last" (263). The execution is portrayed as essentially self-destructive; she feels herself "a puppet in the grasp of some malignant power, some hideous influence inherent in the very structure of reality" (282), an influence recognizable to the reader as her unconscious. Strachey conflates her remaining years and we next see her speechless, paralyzed, childlike, her finger in her mouth. She seems to have been betrayed by her unconscious, her apparently triumphant fusion of power and sexuality reduced to infantile autoeroticism.

Yet the execution of Essex is quite a reasonable response to his betrayal. And indecisiveness is not merely a neurotic symptom but also the clue to her success. For Elizabeth succeeds "by virtue of all the qualities every hero should be without—dissimulation, pliability, indecision, procrastination, parsimony" (11). She uses her marital availability as a diplomatic weapon, while her sexuality becomes a kind of war-game. The decisive act will never happen, but as possibility, it is both strategically effective and erotically rewarding:

> Though, at the center of her being, desire had turned to repulsion, it had not vanished altogether; on the contrary, the compensating forces of nature had redoubled its vigour elsewhere. Though the precious citadel itself was never to

be violated, there were surrounding territories, there were outworks and bastions over which exciting battles might be fought, and which might even, at moments, be allowed to fall into the bold hands of an assailant. (25)[3]

Even her vanity can be seen as self-assertion rather than self-deception. She insists on defining herself as both powerful and beautiful; Essex's crime is that he interprets her on his terms rather than hers. As queen she has the power to insist that she be perceived as seductive.

Aiding her in this insistence is the continuity among her consciousness, her unconsciousness, and her environment. For the psyches of Essex and Elizabeth are the stages on which the Middle Ages acts out its defeat by the Reformation. "In the history of Essex," Strachey writes, ". . . the spectral agony of an abolished world is discernible through the tragic lineaments of a personal disaster" (2). And in the history of Elizabeth, the lively, the unpredictable, the inconsistent make their way through her psyche and through her society.

Elizabeth's indecisiveness and hesitation mirror the age's love of variegation, its obsession with mutability. Her repressed sexuality surfaces in elaborate flirtations; her age similarly reroutes its dark core of irrationality into stylized patterns. The Renaissance, Strachey writes, was a "double-faced age" (50): above, a "surface of caracoling courtiers"; below, "cruelty, corruption, and gnashing of teeth" (65). Popular entertainment includes bear-baiting, the legal system sanctions torture and castration, and social mores call for elaborate yet revealing dress. Game, ritual, and stylized sensuality are the Renaissance's equivalent of Elizabeth's pleasantly embattled erotic outposts, all displaced expressions of the irrationality within.

The rich ornamentation of dress and manner is an expression of tremendous energy turned from its course into endless elaborations. Nowhere is this more clear than in the Queen's—and her realm's—love of language: "The splendid sentences," Strachey writes, "following one another in a steady volubility, proclaimed the curious workings of her intellect with enthralling force; while the woman's inward passion vibrated magically through the loud high uncompromising utterance and the perfect rhythms of her speech" (18–19). Words are Elizabeth's "crowning virtuosity," and her fiercest weapon; they replace—even become—action, just as her indecisiveness replaces—even becomes—policy.

The importance Strachey gives the linguistic interpretation of experience is one explanation for his lengthy treatment of Dr. Lopez, the Portuguese Jewish doctor who is brutally and wrongly executed for treason. For torture is, in *Elizabeth and Essex,* primarily a proliferator of texts: "The proofs of guilt must not be sifted by the slow process of logic and fair play; they must be multiplied—by spies, by *agents provocateurs,* by torture" (80). The frequent betrayals result from the juxtaposition of variant texts. The final adjudicators are secretaries and lawyers, professional producers and validators of texts.

The word is, in fact, behind all the major action of *Elizabeth and Essex.* Letters, poems, Shakespeare's *Richard II,* which is supposed to fuel Essex's rebellion, the history book used as evidence against him, the depositions of tortured prisoners, Bacon's account at the trial of Essex are the true determining factors, not the deeds of "men of action." And the words culminate in the *sentence,* the final imposition of interpretation on reality (Lopez, for example, is found guilty and is, unquestionably, executed).

The word, like the symptom, is intrinsically ambiguous, suggesting and simultaneously denying the presence of the thing it signifies (Freud, *Psychological Works* 16:360). Essex the man of action and Bacon the scientist are similarly unequipped to face ambiguity, and both, in Strachey's view, pay for their simplicity. The unpoetic Bacon, who "sought to shape with his subtle razor-blade, the crude vague blocks of passion and fact" (46), fails to understand his own and others' minds. For the human mind is dominated not by reason but by desire, by motivations irreducible to logical explanation, by contradictory impulses. Bacon cannot possibly fathom Essex's motives, because according to Strachey, "The motives of the most ordinary mortal are never easy to disentangle, and Essex was far from ordinary. His mind was made up of extremes, and his temper was devoid of balance. He rushed from opposite to opposite; he allowed the strangest contradictories to take root together, and grow up side by side, in his heart" (253).

Central to *Elizabeth and Essex,* as to other histories of Elizabeth's reign, is the absence of an heir, and the resultant threat to political stability. But where other chronicles depict plots and counterplots, Strachey depicts symptoms. The absence of an heir becomes the deepest meaning of the Queen's repression, and the endless textual elaborations necessary, according to Strachey, to preserve the Queen from treason, are the results—symptoms, even—of that absence. In portraying Elizabethan England, he has portrayed a world where textual interpretation supersedes sexual reproduction. It is fitting, then, that the book ends with a glimpse of Cecil, the Queen's secretary, writing to the new king after Elizabeth's death:

> As the hand moved, the mind moved too, ruminating sadly over the vicissitudes of mortal beings, reflecting upon the revolutions of kingdoms, and dreaming, with quiet clarity, of what the hours, even then, were bringing—the union of two nations—the triumph of the new rulers—success, power, and riches—a name in after-ages—a noble lineage—a great House. (286)

The future is conceived as a linguistic construct in the mind of the secretary, yet it is precisely this future that will, in fact, be realized. True continuity is offered not by monarchs, who act, but by writers, who make the connections between events and actually summon kings out of Scotland, ensuring a smooth transition.

Strachey contextualizes his subject by dramatizing her psyche and positing a continuity between psychic and social mechanisms. Forster and Woolf, while interested in those factors that de-individualize the subject, turn their attention to intellectual rather than instinctual issues. In doing so they face similar problems and find somewhat similar solutions.

Their subjects, for one thing, were similar. Goldsworthy Lowes Dickinson and Roger Fry were Cambridge contemporaries, friends of each other and of their biographers. Both left autobiographical fragments and many letters. Both had unconventional sex lives, an aspect both biographers chose to underplay. Both gained distinction primarily as teachers or inspirers; their own adventures and achievements were not large scale, and their lives were in many ways ordinary. Both men were heavily influenced by others, and for both friendship and discussion were vitally important. Both were singularly unegotistic. To understand them, one must understand what interested them as much as what went on within them.

Forster and Woolf to some extent brought shared values to their similar subjects. They shared a dislike of "great men," of war, of self-importance and egotism, a preference for thoughtfulness over hyperactivity. Dickinson and Fry were thus particularly suitable subjects, but their very suitability also made them difficult. Dickinson the "bird of passage" and Fry the "hawk-moth" were in constant motion. How could such fuzzily defined and receptive selves be fixed in language that would not distort them? How could their lives, devoid of drama and suspense, be made interesting and meaningful—but not so interesting as to exaggerate their accomplishments? As Forster and Woolf work at these problems, they move in the direction of sociobiography. Each portrays a self in constant interaction with his environment and past, employing what Forster calls a "halting narrative": one that does not emphasize crucial turning points, but that pauses to describe significant intellectual discoveries. Narrative continuity and authority are deliberately questioned; the subjects are frequently and extensively quoted, and recurrent images originate in the subjects' own texts. Each subject's unity as a self emerges not through authorial delineation (although, particularly in Forster's case, there is some of that), but through the recurrence and repetition of ideas, images, concerns. The underlying metaphor for the self in both biographies is musical—a metaphor characteristic of sociobiography.

Goldsworthy Lowes Dickinson and *Roger Fry* are sociobiographical, then, in that each depicts a mind intersecting with other minds, defined by perception rather than action, in free interchange with an environment. In some respects, such a description fits mediated biography as well: like mediated biographers, sociobiographers reject narrative omniscience and the speculative portrayal of their subjects' inner lives. They grant their subjects a certain amount of unknowability or at least unconveyability and show an interest in the biographical process itself. But the differing role of the narrator makes a crucial difference. In sociobiography, even when, as in the case of Dickinson and Fry, the authors knew their subjects, the narrator's role is minimalized. His contact with the subject is simply another aspect of the play of influence and affinities operating within the text. This is very different from the synthesizing role played by James's and Lubbock's and Symons's narrators, each of whose particular angle of vision dominates the portrait.

Recognizing their common aim, Forster praised *Roger Fry* for its musical quality (*Two Cheers* 244). While Woolf was unimpressed by *Dickinson*, it provides a precedent for her approach (it was published six years before *Roger Fry*) and an additional example of how, for the modern novel-ist, nonfiction poses the same technical problems as fiction, and thus invites similarly innovative responses.

For Dickinson, Forster writes, "as for the Victorians, life was a pilgrimage not an adventure" (99). A pilgrimage gains its meaning from its completion; the whole point is to arrive at a destination. A life story told as pilgrimage would relate all it included to its end. There would be cru-cial, revelatory moments followed by a sense of vocation, achievement, and the all-important deathbed. But Dickin-son, despite his nineteenth-century concerns, "was some-how freer and less glum": "As soon as it came to the ques-tion of his own death, his own fate, he turned easy and modern, and one of the reasons that attracted the young to him was that he never gave them the sense of nursing a private destiny. He was not only selfless here, he believed in the imagination—believed in the sense that he was interpenetrated by it, and so was not personally mortified either by the victories or by the defeats of reason" (100).

Dickinson's lack of a private destiny and his broad imag-inative sympathy counteract the pilgrim in him, and For-ster structures his biography as a combination of pilgrim-age and adventure. Dickinson's life is, to some extent, a steady movement toward his rightful cultural inheritance; through Greek poetry, for example, he glimpses the "land which was his home" (18). But it is also a series of false starts, each with a reward of its own. Forster's own interest in the texture of life rather than its turning points turns attention away from the steady movement. Dickinson's suc-cess as a teacher emerges unobtrusively from the book's central chapter after a series of vividly described failures.

Dickinson's life is structured with the same oddity of em-phasis as Forster's novels—an oddity Christopher Isher-wood labeled "tea-tabling," characterized by a "new kind of accentuation": big scenes are underplayed "until they sound like mothers'-meeting gossip" (174). Thus Dickin-son's emergence as a teacher is presented undramatically, overshadowed by his earlier experiments as farmer, lecturer, and doctor. False starts are presented as vividly as true ones, and for Dickinson are as meaningful: "It is characteristic of Dickinson that, even when appearing to fail, he should gain something of permanent value" (47). The intellectual discoveries that form the substance of Dickinson's self-discovery are repeatedly compared to a door opening: Dickinson's image, originally, but Forsterian also in its low-keyed mundanity. The word *crisis* Forster uses only ironically, to describe Dickinson's unwitting offense against an absurdly puritanical provincial audience.

Forster is famous for denigrating plot in his 1927 *Aspects of the Novel*. That same year he wrote in his Commonplace Book, "Abjure freshness, underemphasize surprise. Each incident should fall on to a thick bed of previous impressions, like the tree on to mould that has been formed by its own dead leaves" (P. J. M. Scott 194). In a sense he un-plots the life-plot, providing the few events in Dickinson's life with a thick bed of conversation, intellectual context, and even nonsense, which he says is "too seldom recorded" in biographies (*Dickinson* 113). Such major events as Dickinson's trips to America, India, and China are presented as chronological digressions, and are seen through letters and conversations as a series of personal relationships rather than voyages of exploration. According to Forster, "the movements of a tourist's body are not worth recording unless they generate movements inside his mind" (121). Preferring reaction to event, he goes on to quote Dickinson's poem about a Peking temple. Chapter headings, also, tend to be stubbornly mental: among particularly important chapters are the undated "Shelley, Plato, Goethe" and "America, India, China," and the story of Dickinson's return to Cambridge entitled not, melodramatically, "Dickinson finds his true self," but, obscurely, "The Socratic Method."

As he leads towards Dickinson's death, Forster maintains his reluctance to accentuate. In summing up his accomplishments he writes, "The list of his little honours might be extended, but I am unwilling to make it sound important, for he was not interested in posts or in having letters after his name" (167). Similarly, Forster will quote no eulogies, preferring instead to quote Dickinson's "former bedmaker at Cambridge," who said simply, "He was the best man who ever lived" (197). Death itself slips in unobstrusively, as the result of an operation from which Dickinson seemed to be recovering. But then for Forster death, above all, requires tea-tabling, for it is the ultimate plot-creator, appending a naturally emphatic resolution to whatever precedes it. Dickinson's death, therefore, is portrayed through a series of negations: "There was no self-consciousness or cynicism in his departure, no sentimentality, and no 'message'; it called for no special tone of voice because he had never used one" (198). The "no special tone of voice" matches the lack of a "private destiny." The life without climax, for Forster, is one better able to respond sensitively, unegotistically, to its surroundings.

Dickinson's openness to intellectual experience differs greatly from the self-limiting, starkly outlined selves depicted by novelistic biographers. As a learner, he is often passive, accepting a role sometimes of comic helplessness or inadequacy. As an absorber and transmitter of inherited culture, he places little value on originality for its own sake. His self seems more a meeting place of influences and reactions than a clearly defined entity.

Most of all, Dickinson is not static. He is most himself when he talks, not when he writes: "When he spoke to his friends or spoke of them all altered at once; he vibrated to wave after wave. . . . That was his strength, that was his glory, and if that could be communicated in a biography, he would appear for what he was; one of the rarest creatures of our generation" (171). The "vibration" comes from the interaction of minds, from dialectic. It is the opposite of the monovalent, authoritative rhetoric of the written page. Dickinson refuses to impose or emote; he becomes more "tentative" as he grows wiser. In the crucial "Socratic Method" chapter Forster writes, "It is as a teacher who was constantly being taught that he must be regarded during these twenty-one years" (76). In this, of course, he is Socratic, a comparison Forster makes again in what is virtually the book's last sentence. In his goodness, his insistence on dialogue, and his role as catalyst, Dickinson resembles Socrates. To capture such a figure his biographer must also, to some extent, resemble Socrates.

Forster does, in fact, abjure narrative authority. In all his nonfiction, as S. P. Rosenbaum points out, his tone tends to be conversational, inviting dialogue rather than asserting authority ("*Aspects*" 74). In *Dickinson* Forster maintains this tone by occasional appeals to his reader ("May one . . . ?" he occasionally asks), by concluding with a dialogue between himself and Mephistopheles, "who should inhabit a cranny in every biography," and by self-interruption.

This self-interruption is in part the "halting narrative" Forster himself describes in his preface: the interruption of chronological by conceptual account, as in the undated chapter on Shelley, Plato, and Goethe. The "life in time" is thus supplemented by "the life by values," terms Forster uses in *Aspects of the Novel* (19). He sometimes interrupts himself with lists and ellipses, as when he describes the fragmented experiences of Dickinson at sixteen: "Memories of the 'Messiah' and better still the 'Elijah' . . . excerpts from a queer new thing, 'The Ring', and the composer embracing the conductor afterwards. . . . May liked 'The Ring', he could make nothing of it . . . the Bancrofts in 'Caste' . . ." (20; Forster's ellipses). In addition, frequent excerpts from Dickinson's *Recollections* (then unpublished) and letters create a counterpoint to his own voice, emphasized by his borrowing of Dickinson's own imagery and language, as in the case of the "opening door." His method, finally, is the same he attributes to Dickinson, that of the "dialogue-writer," not novelist. For while the novelist, according to Forster, describes his characters' surfaces to suggest their inner lives, Dickinson—and Forster, in writing of him—"begins from within" (59).

In the epilogue to *Dickinson,* Forster's Mephistopheles wonders why a biography of so minor a life was necessary. "It is difficult to think of a life where so little happened outwardly" (199), Forster concedes, but a man is more than the sum of his parts. Goldie, he argues, was unique: "he left us more alert for what has not yet been experienced and more hopeful about other men because he had lived." A biography of Dickinson, Forster writes, "if it succeeded, would resemble him; it would achieve the unattainable, express the inexpressible, turn the passing into the everlasting." He has not succeeded, Forster concludes, "And perhaps it only could be done through music. But that is what has lured me on" (201).

Forster here is not literally confessing failure. According to Stallybrass, his letters about the biography were cheerful (xii), and he was contented with the finished product (xi). His aim is to convey the unity of Dickinson's character without reifying it. Like the wild goose of *Orlando,* Dickinson's "indescribably rare being" remains just beyond his chronicler's grasp. Dickinson's role had been catalytic rather than creative, so it is fitting that his biography end with the words "lured me on," with their hint of unfinished motion and Goethean striving. Dickinson's unity, paradoxically multivalent, can only be evoked.

Music, Forster suggests, would evoke it most effectively, in part because Dickinson was himself in love with music. Music also plays a major role in Forster's work, for reasons most clearly explained in his essay "The Raison d'Etre of Criticism in the Arts." There he explains that only music can be heard both sequentially and architecturally; "It exists in time, and also exists outside time, instantaneously" (*Two Cheers* 120). The listener hears each note individually, but also as part of a larger, overarching structure. Biography, like the novel, aspires to a similar duality, combining chronology with timelessness. In *Aspects of the Novel,* Forster discusses two ways of giving prose an element of time-lessness: through the patterning of plot elements and through the rhythmic recurrence of objects or themes. Rhythm turns out to be the preferable method; as S. P. Rosenbaum points out, Forster favors musical over visual analogy ("*Aspects*" 72).

Pattern, Forster suggests, works by exclusion, creating aesthetically pleasing form at the expense of life. Rhythm, on the other hand, creating coherence by mere recurrence, leaves plenty of room for the accidental and irrelevant. Only music offers both coherence and expansion, "not rounding off but opening out," the notes finding, at piece's end, "in the rhythm of the whole their individual freedom" (Forster, *Aspects* 116).

Forster's biography, then, aspires to the condition of music, seeking to convey a personality both open-ended and coherent. He is not the only person to see in music an apt metaphor for human identity. Norman Holland borrows from Heinz Lichtenstein the notion that music is a crucial metaphor for talking about the "dialectic of sameness and difference" of which identity consists. "Each action," Holland writes, "is a variation on a theme which we learn by seeing the theme in its ever new variations" (452). And Virginia Woolf makes a similar connection in a 1940 letter to Mrs. R. C. Trevelyan, whose comparison of *Roger Fry* to music she endorses. The horde of details, Woolf writes, she abstracted into themes, which are stated in chapter 1, then developed with variations throughout (*Letters* 6 : 426). Woolf follows through on the metaphor more consistently than Forster and writes, I think, a more involving biography, but it may have been Forster's lead she followed.

The pilgrimage element in *Goldsworthy Lowes Dickinson* is what keeps it, finally, from being as innovative as Woolf's *Roger Fry*. While placed in relation to a past and to his friends, Dickinson's self is not as decentered as Fry's, his life-plot not as shapeless. At the heart of the contrast, I suspect, is less a distinction between the two subjects than between their biographers. Until he reaches Cambridge, Dickinson is in exile from his true home: the land of culture and beauty represented by Shelley, Plato, and Goethe. At Cambridge, he finally claims for his own "our heritage," finding in the books and people there a "magic fusion" that satisfies him completely (30). Related to this concept of "home" is that of the "centre," an essential self sometimes "covered with rubbish and worry" (16), but always there, waiting for the opportunity of Cambridge to emerge. As a feminist, Woolf could not find in Socrates a parallel or in Cambridge a home. She also speaks often of her subject's "centre," most often as an absent center. This absence lends Fry his openness and her biography its radically open-ended quality.

While she was writing *Roger Fry*, Woolf occasionally took refuge in "A Sketch of the Past," an autobiographical fragment that serves also as theoretical commentary to the biography. In "Sketch," Woolf writes of her mother:

> She was one of the invisible presences who after all play so important a part in every life. This influence, by which I mean the consciousness of other groups impinging upon ourselves; public opinion; what other people say and think; all those magnets which attract us this way to be like that, or repel us the other and make us different from that; has never been analysed in any of those Lives which I so much enjoy reading, or very superficially. (*Moments* 80)

These invisible presences are central to Woolf's conception of the individual self, and in writing about Fry she felt the lack of some theoretical framework with which to understand and describe these forces. She is groping toward a sociology of knowledge as a basis on which to depict the social—i.e., shared or inherited or influenced—aspects of intellectual life. She recognizes that her own formation by society limits her understanding of it. As a "fish in a stream," she cannot abstract herself from her context and see the stream itself, nor can she think independently of her ancestors and environment.

Woolf, of course, had long recognized the impersonal and transpersonal elements in each individual. In *Jacob's Room*, for example, Jacob is to a large extent not Jacob but "Richard Bonamy—the room; the market carts; the hour; the very moment of history" (73). Recent critics have suggested that in fact her interest in social context is traceable in part to her father's interest in social history (Hill 355). Noel Annan argues that Stephen's awareness of how social circumstances condition thought makes him a "little Marx" (229). But Woolf in the late nineteen thirties was surrounded by theories linking not just ideas but the very fabric of the self to social, psychological, and cultural contexts. Woolf's invisible presences may be related to Stephen's sense of history as shaped by "forces dimly perceived" (Annan 206), or even to Pater's "Child in the House," for whom "inward and outward being [are] woven through and through each other into one inextricable texture" (173), but they have more in common with the work of the psychologists and anthropologists she was reading towards the end of her life, who offered a more rigorously analytical view of the self.

During the time that Woolf worked on *Roger Fry*, she finished *The Years* and began *Between the Acts*. She also wrote "A Sketch of the Past" and various essays. She read many biographies "to see how biographies are written" (*Letters* 6:261), and she was "gulping up Freud" (*Diary* 5:249). She and Leonard visited Freud at Hampstead, and she read *Moses and Monotheism* (*Letters* 6:346) and "Freud on Groups" (*Diary* 5:252). Immediately after finishing the biography, she read, "with pressure of suggestions," Ruth Benedict's *Patterns of Culture* (*Diary* 5:306). Clearly she was fascinated by the possibility that, as Freud seems to her to suggest, we are all "whirlpools" (*Diary* 5:250), driven by shared forces, formed out of shared material.

In *Patterns of Culture,* Benedict argues against the nine-teenth-century habit of pitting the individual against so-ciety, when no such dualism can exist: "His culture," she writes, "provides the raw material of which the individual makes his life" (251). Freud in *Moses and Monotheism* ap-plies terms derived from work with individuals to mass psychology, suggesting that individual experience includes "fragments of phylogenetic origin." Each of us, he argues, possesses an "archaic heritage," which includes disposi-tions and "memory-traces of the experiences of former generations" (157, 159). Benedict would argue the claims of culture against inheritance, but both writers insist on re-moving the individual from isolation. Something similar is on Woolf's mind, I think, when she writes, near the start of "A Sketch":

> Who was I then? Adeline Virginia Stephen, the second daugh-ter of Leslie and Julia Prinsep Stephen, born on 25th January 1892, descended from a great many people . . . born into a large connection . . . born into a very communicative, literate, letter writing, visiting, articulate, late nineteenth century world; so that I could if I liked to take the trouble, write a great deal here not only about my mother and father but about uncles and aunts, cousins and friends. (*Moments* 65)

In a 1911 essay on Victorianism, Forster wrote rather vaguely of "That idea of comradeship . . . that idea of so-ciety as a whole and a fluid whole . . ." which would have seemed to the Victorians "fantastic and faintly improper" (*Albergo Empedocle* 112). He is referring, I think, not only to a loosening of conventions, but to a more generalized sense that social interchange is essential to growth and any pretense of isolated grandeur is mere pretense. Woolf's concern with invisible presences is farther along on the same continuum, a more radical attempt to deconstruct yet depict the self by ignoring the "I" as a misleadingly uni-tary concept and focusing instead on the mother, father, uncle, and friends. In writing about Fry she is careful to suppress her own narrative "I" (and earned Forster's praise for her self-suppression [*Two Cheers* 249]) and to some extent Fry's "I" as well. Like Forster on Dickinson, she hints at a Fry she has not quite captured. It is not Fry's magical unity that baffles her, however, but his complexity.

Roger Fry is the only book by Virginia Woolf that most critics would agree is, in fact, a biography. She herself commented in her diary, "I'm rather proud of having done a solid work" (*Diary* 5:306). Whereas in *Flush*, she felt herself free to conflate the dog's three separate kidnappings into one, she wrote *Roger Fry* with a fairly conventional sense of the "truth" and her obligation to it. She depended heavily for her material on letters, on Fry's own writings, on her own acquaintance with him, and on the accounts of others. She described Fry's family heritage, his childhood, education, achievement and death, all topics of traditional biography. She was even so traditional as to be reticent about his love affairs, perhaps because she would have had to include her own sister among his "twenty mistresses," but also because Fry's relatives were looking over her shoulder (*Letters* 6:104).

The circumstances and shape of the biography, then, do not suggest innovation. Those who have written on Woolf's biographical theory generally characterize it as regressive, a falling away from her own theoretical advances.[4] Michael Rosenthal calls it more an appreciation than a biography (214). And in *Literary Biography*, Leon Edel, after an admiring discussion of *Orlando*, calls *Roger Fry* "wooden" (98), though a few years later at the National Gallery, he evinced more enthusiasm for it.[5] Leonard Woolf himself thought the book a failure and a terrible burden his wife should never have taken on: "The orderly presentation of reality, which remorselessly imposes its iron pattern upon the writer who rashly tries to discern and describe in it the infinite kaleidoscope of facts, was not natural to Virginia's mind or method" (*Journey* 40). Jean Guiget agrees, complaining that the book lacks "material solidity" (351).

Published as she worked on *Roger Fry,* Woolf's 1939 essay "The Art of Biography" is generally understood to reflect her unhappiness with the genre, her resigned sense that it is craft, not art (Lewis, "Combining" 321). As early as "The New Biography" eleven years before, Woolf had been skeptical about the possibility of combining fact and fiction; here she announces that biography's first allegiance must be to fact. Strachey's *Queen Victoria* succeeds, she says, because it is based so carefully on evidence. His *Elizabeth and Essex* fails because it mingles invention with actuality. Complaining that Elizabeth "moves in an ambiguous world, between fact and fiction" (*Death* 192), Woolf certainly seems to be ceding the ground she had won in *Orlando.*

Alice Fox has suggested other grounds for Woolf's dislike of *Elizabeth and Essex.* Calling it "antifeminist," she argues that Strachey described and analyzed, through Elizabeth, Woolf's own sexual history (41–42). But there were less personal reasons for Woolf to distrust its ambiguity. Writing for her was always, above all, a means of communication. Anything that strained the relation between writer and audience might disrupt this communication. This was the charge she brought against Strachey, Eliot, and Lawrence in "Mr. Bennett and Mrs. Brown." When she herself mingled fact and fiction, she did so as parody and thus violated no bond with her reader. Strachey, in the interest of drama, had sacrificed credibility.

Fact is not fiction, she argues: "you must choose, and you must abide by your choice" (194). But the essay is not a rejection of innovative biography, nor does it diminish the importance of biography as a genre. Verifiable facts are to be the raw material of biography, but "these facts are not like the facts of science—once they are discovered, always the same" (194). The selection, the evaluation, and the organization of facts change over time; the biographer's choices in these matters determine how we view the world. Biography's power, then, is immense, and it rests in the relation between reader and writer.

Biography, she writes, can provide the "fact that suggests and engenders" (197); it can alter what we regard as truth, whom we regard as important. The biographer "must go ahead of the rest of us, like the miner's canary, testing the atmosphere, detecting falsity, unreality, and the presence of obsolete conventions" (195). Limited by his obligation to widows, friends, and facts, the biographer has, nonetheless, tremendous power. There may be a difference between creation and verifiable evidence, but even verifiable evidence is subject to varied interpretations. The grounds of the granite-rainbow distinction have shifted, but not the essential point.

Roger Fry, then, is not the product of a disappointed writer resigned to fulfilling a personal obligation by producing an unambitious, conventional biography. Her own summing up of her accomplishment was as triumphant as it was apt; *Roger Fry,* she wrote Ethel Smyth, is an "experiment in self-suppression; a gamble on Roger's power to transmit himself and so rich and to me so alive and various and masterly was he that I was certain he would shine by his own light, better than through any painted shade of mine" (*Letters* 6:417). And, she concludes, "I succeeded!"

The success did not come easily, however. In "The Art of Biography" she suggests that the old chapter headings of "Life at college, marriage, career" were no longer useful (194). But what was the alternative? Among her unpublished papers is a short note: "The method should be to find out what his qualities were and proceed to illustrate that by events. To be very free with the sequence of facts" (quoted by Lewis, "Combining" 319). In fact, though, *Roger Fry* is for the most part structured chronologically, and its chapter titles—"Cambridge," for example, or "Chelsea: Marriage" and "Work" resemble those she questioned.

Gradually Woolf groped toward an appropriate structure and method for her biography. From *Flush* Woolf derives a kind of antibiographical plot, allowing her to depict Fry's life as in part a flight from his father, who, like

Mr. Barrett, is aligned with an oppressive social order, and from a Victorian (and particularly Carlylean) idea of vocation as essential to life. From *Orlando*, reinforced by later reading, comes an inordinate interest in the play of influences on Fry's sensibility—his Quaker ancestry, his friends—the invisible presences she describes in "A Sketch of the Past."

Essential to her method are two elements: the musical analogy and what she calls her "compiling method": "I think I see how it shapes," she writes in her diary of the biography-in-progress, "& my compiling method was a good one" (*Diary* 5:215). The compiling results from her deliberate suppression of her own narrative voice and characteristically lyric tone. She does little summarizing or synthesizing, nor does she dwell on her own responses to Fry. Considering how well she knew him, she is conspicuously absent from her biography. This narrative absence allows her to suggest a mode of perception, a personality in the act of living, rather than a sharply delineated, over-materialized figure. Frequent excerpts from Fry's letters are linked (or, more accurately, insistently *not* linked) sometimes only by recurring metaphors, sometimes by blatantly awkward transitions that emphasize the portrait's fragmentation and temporal discontinuity.

Yet the book coheres, and does so in a way that is, in fact, analogous to music. The Fry that results is at once autonomous and dependent, unique, yet defined by a network of social and intellectual interrelationships. If Woolf has no literary or theoretical model to follow in describing what the self is "born into," she has at least, she writes in "Sketch," a philosophy. She believes that behind daily life is a pattern, that "we are all parts of the work of art." There are no individual artists, and, she insists, no God, but "we are the words; we are the music; we are the thing itself" (*Moments* 72): "If I were painting myself I should have to find some—rod, shall I say—something that would stand for the conception. It proves that one's life is not confined to one's body and what one says and does; one is living all the time in relation to certain background rods or conceptions. Mine is that there is a pattern hid behind the cotton wool" (73). Woolf uses the belief in a pattern and in a contrast between pattern and "cotton wool" to structure her biography of Fry, but she allows the structure to emerge from Fry's own writings, so that Fry's life, mind, and growth all seem part of a single piece of music whose shifting rhythms and themes seem found rather than imposed.

Woolf's concept of the self required an experimental narrative method, but its effect on the sequencing of material was less than her unpublished note would suggest. She does, however, offer a counterplot to the standard story of gradual maturation and achievement. As in *Flush,* she portrays a flight from a Victorian father. She follows it with a rejection of the very idea of maturation, as Fry triumphantly grows younger, rather than older.

In her crucial first chapter, Woolf quotes Fry's description of a family ice-skating expedition which brought a dual revelation—that of his father's joie de vivre and his lack of sympathy for the poor, the "pond loafers with their big red noses and big red neckerchiefs . . . almost like the criminal species of men of which we heard now and then" (22). The men's poverty was, to the Fry family, proof of their immorality, so, when they helped the children with their skates, they were unrewarded—"to pay them a decent tip was truckling to immorality" (22). The logic is reminiscent of Mr. Barrett's reason in *Flush* for not ransoming his daughter's dog.

Fry's father is a slightly more benevolent variety of the domineering Victorian patriarch—alarming, moralistic, inspiring "a mixture of devotion, fear, and bewilderment" (22), complete with busts in the library. Like Mr. Barrett, his paternal authority is closely allied with the status quo of social injustice: "The rights of property were respected," Woolf writes; "class distinctions were upheld; and the pond loafers, with their red neckerchiefs, blowing into their ugly hands, were not to be pitied but blamed" (26). Like Elizabeth Barrett Browning, Roger Fry will escape that authority in part through an 1891 trip to Italy.

"What," a friend asked Fry in 1888, "are you going to be?" (58). Fry never does reply with a terribly precise answer. The notion that, on finishing one's education, one chose a profession, seemed as obvious to his parents as it was inappropriate to Fry himself. Whether because he actually lived this way, or because his biographer was peculiarly likely to construe his life in this way, Fry's vocation is to have no vocation. "His mind," Woolf writes of his experience at Cambridge, "was being unmade rather than made up" (56). Over and over words like *puzzled, bewildered,* and *perplexed* are used to describe his state of mind; his profession is to withhold judgment, to be intensely open to experience, to be an *amateur,* as he said all painters should be (188).

The choice of a vocation for Fry is not, then, a turning point, nor are other ostensibly important experiences. His loss of faith is disposed of in a sentence: "His creed, he noted afterwards, had dropped from him without any shock of pain so far as he was concerned" (48). He remarks "almost casually in the postscript to a letter" that he had won a first; one is reminded of Orlando's parenthetical winning of the Burdett Coutts Prize. Writing of Fry resembles writing of a woman for Woolf, for as in *Orlando,* "everything is out of place—culminations and perorations."

Fry's rejection of the career in science his father would have preferred, his travels, and his unconventional friends are counterpointed by the persistent presence in him of his Quaker ancestors. But his family background is not the only "invisible presence" acting on him. Fry has a particular talent for finding "the people he needed" (53). McTaggart, Middleton, Symonds, Mauron: each provides some pivotal revelation. The Maurons, in fact, were examples of that recurrent phenomenon in his life: the "unknown traveller met by chance" (223). Fry's great gift is for receptivity, even—occasionally—gullibility, so that his mind becomes a meeting ground for innumerable waves of influence.

The biography's plot, then, suggests two contrasting rhythms of flight from and rejoicing in the influence of others. Its images, too, have a musical quality, for as Woolf tells Mrs. Trevelyan, they recur throughout the book. Initially presented as narrated incidents, particular events become condensed into single objects or ideas and resurface, almost as leitmotifs, carrying their associations with them. Thus the first chapter tells of Fry's revelation in the garden at Highgate of his parents' injustice and his own passion for poppies, his Quaker ancestors' contradictory relation to the world, his own attraction to both science and art. All are again evoked when Fry discovers Cézanne: "A red poppy, a mother's reproof, a Quaker upbringing, sorrows, loves, humiliations—they too have their part in moments of vision" (161).

These incidents arise originally from Fry's own autobiographical fragment so that Woolf's images emerge smoothly from her subject's own self-image. The effect is not to dismantle but to open out personality, to portray its internal harmonies. The scene in the garden carries echoes, of course, of every fall since Adam and every conversion since St. Augustine, echoes appropriate to this conversion to beauty from parental authority. It also recalls Pater's "The Child in the House," where Florian discovers the red hawthorne's "plumage of tender, crimson fire" (*Miscellaneous Studies* 185), a passage Woolf praises in a 1920 essay (*Books* 15). The redness, the intensity of his response, the resonance of Pater all make the poppies a powerful image for Fry's awakening sense of self.

Woolf's distinction between cotton wool and pattern becomes, in Fry's terms, life and art. "Art and life are two rhythms, he says [in *Art and Life*]." And she goes on: "This suggests, what the letters also confirm, that there were two rhythms in his own life. There was the hurried and distracted life; but there was also the still life" (214). By "still life" she means something apart and enduring and, more literally, the apples and eggs in Fry's studio, ordinary but untouchable, waiting to be painted. Fry's initial comment in an essay thus becomes a generalization about Fry, and is then replaced by the symbol of the still life. The literal still life of apples and eggs appeared originally many pages before, in the context of Fry's daily life. This apparently unimportant arrangement of objects—noted initially only because the cleaning lady had to be warned not to touch it, despite its untidiness—takes on retrospectively a glow of significance, as the objects are transformed into "symbols of detachment, those tokens of a spiritual reality immune from destruction, the immortal apples, the eternal eggs" (215).

The process by which the ordinary becomes transfigured has been replicated by this movement from narrative fact to symbolic object, and it all seems to have emerged from Fry's own essay and studio, without Woolf's intervention. Woolf's own name for these eruptions of the still life into the ordinary, these glimpses of pattern behind the cotton wool, is moments of vision or being; Josephine O'Brien Schaeffer has discussed their role in Woolf's biographies. Fry himself depicts such a moment, a moonlit conversation with Goldsworthy Lowes Dickinson at Cambridge "while . . . the cuckoo and the nightingale sang," and "we cared only for the now which is the same thing as being eternal" (48). Such moments are, of course, characteristic of Woolf's work, but always she uses Fry's language to describe them, so that her own summations become merely a recapitulation of Fry's own themes. Fry's description, quoted above, becomes, in Woolf's words a few pages later, "Now had become eternal as he sat talking to his friends in a Cambridge room while the moon rose and the nightingales sang" (60). The lyricism emerges from repetition and juxtaposition, not from a narrative persona.

One particularly important image for such an eruption

of the art-rhythm into the life-rhythm comes from a story Fry tells of a column unearthed by him and his wife at Carthage. The column becomes a metaphor for Fry's own process of intellectual growth, as well as a clue to Woolf's handling of chronology. The incident is initially described by Fry in a letter: his wife finds a capital jutting out of the sand and together they dig it out. For a long time they do not know what it is, then all at once the shape is clear. Woolf returns to the image when describing Fry's discovery of Cézanne: "There for a moment Cézanne is seen still half-covered in the sand. But half covered he still was—" (112). Only with the opening of the Post-Impressionist Exhibition was the half-hidden statue fully revealed. The image suggests a mixture of effort sustained over time and sudden revelation; of blind pursuit then suddenly revealed significance. It is a kind of "moment of vision," but one with a history, "when a new force breaks in, and the gropings of the past suddenly have meaning" (161). Woolf describes in somewhat similar terms the effect of reading the Paston letters. Details accumulate gradually over time, each individual one not that important, "and then suddenly they blaze up; the day shines out, complete, alive, before our eyes" (*Common Reader* 21). According to Rose Macaulay, Woolf used an identical image to express her eagerness to hear gossip. "Go on," she would say, "This is enthralling. People keep telling me different bits of this story; I feel as if a buried statue were being dug up piece by piece" ("Reminiscence" 317–18).[6]

The sand-covered capital suggests the mysterious reciprocity of significant events: the statue is there but requires Fry's eager digging if it's to reveal itself; Cézanne is there but cannot affect him until he is ready to be affected. John Ruskin, to whom Fry has been compared, accuses biographers of habitually ignoring this reciprocity:

It is the great error of thoughtless biographers to attribute to the accident which introduces some new phase of character, all the circumstances of character which gave the accident importance. The essential point to be noted, and accounted for, was that I could understand Turner's work when I saw it; . . . not by what chance, or in what year, it was first seen. (26)

Fry had seen Cézanne, his version of Turner, before, but he had not been ready; by 1910, the sand had ceased to obscure its treasure.

This mysterious process by which experience accrues gradually, obscurely, then all at once blazes forth, has a profound effect on the way Woolf orders her material. Woolf was determined not to be one of Ruskin's "thoughtless biographers" oversimplifying the relation between cause and effect. Subterranean influences—the question of why a mind was ready for something at a particular time—fascinate her, but, since they work independently of external events, they offer little help to the connection-maker seeking to explain how and why. To retain the complexity of her idea of human development, she had to deny her narrative the more obvious kinds of continuity.

Throughout the nineteenth century, according to A. O. J. Cockshut, "the fundamental reason for writing a man's life was that he was admirable" (16). The source of admiration was some achievement which inevitably conferred its meaning on the entire life, suggesting, in Hayden White's words, that the story "had a *plot* all along. . . ." "We can comprehend the appeal of historical discourse," White writes, "by recognizing the extent to which it makes the real desirable, makes the real into an object of desire, and does so by its imposition, upon events that are represented as real, of the formal coherency that stories possess" ("Value" 24). Woolf is not so radical as to remove all trace of plot from her biography, but she deliberately allows the premise of continuity and coherence to break down.

One way she does this is through her depiction of Fry's centerlessness. The center is a recurring image in Woolf's work.[7] One thinks of the wick surrounded by flame in *The*

Voyage Out; the dot with flames around it sketched by Ralph Denham in *Night and Day;* the shape Eleanor scribbles in *The Years.* Fry's lack of a center is related to his lack of a well-defined career and, after his wife's madness, of a home-life and is one cause of his extraordinary openness: "He laid himself open to all experiences with a certain recklessness," Woolf writes, "because so many of the things that men care for, as he said later, were now meaningless. The centre which would have given them meaning was gone" (148).

Instead of a center, Fry's daily life has a *texture.* Woolf borrows the word from his comments on Balzac, then makes it her own: "No crust must be allowed to form," she writes, "even if the purely external conditions of life must have a certain solid texture" (245). The lack of a crust facilitates occasional eruptions from the world of the still life, which allow him, "like a water-diviner," to tap "some hidden spring sunk beneath the incrustations that had blocked it" (172). Instead of a unity firmly fixed in a family life and career, Fry's self is a texture superimposed on the reality behind, the pattern behind the cotton wool.

To convey a decentered self, Woolf adopts a disjunctive narrative method, a more extreme version of Forster's "halting narrative." This is what she called her "compiling method," and she worried, oddly, in the same *Diary* passage that it made her biography "too like a novel" (5:215). If compilation felt novelistic to Woolf, it was perhaps because it was so directly opposed to the ordinary aim of history: that of linking events and discerning continuities. These seem to be the grounds on which Leonard Woolf criticized the biography. Woolf writes in her diary of his criticism: "It was like being pecked by a very hard strong beak. The more he pecked the deeper, as always happens. At last he was almost angry that I'd chosen 'what seems to me the wrong method. Its merely anal[ysis], not history. Austere repression. In fact dull to the outsider. All those dead quotations'" (5:271). Leonard urged her to present

Fry from her angle of vision rather than remaining invisible behind an accumulation of quoted letters. Himself a historian, he attacks her refusal to synthesize, to write history.

But this kind of history, as I argued in chapter 5, has tended to be a male domain, a connection suggested by Woolf's imagery in the passage above. Leonard makes his attack aggressively, pecking like a beak, obviously masculine images suggesting Mr. Ramsay's oppressive "beak of brass" in *To the Lighthouse* (58, 59, 60).[8] Synthesis and continuity in the writing of history are consistently associated by Woolf with aggression in its acting out.

"Discontinuity," Foucault writes, "was the stigma of temporal dislocation that it was the historian's task to remove from history" (8). But as Sandra M. Gilbert says of Miss La Trobe, Woolf "seems to want to fragment history in order to ruin it" ("Costumes" 412). Both history and historical writing (which I mean in a broad sense, to include biography) seemed to Woolf—and others—inimical to women. For one thing, historical writing tended to ignore them. For another, history tended to mistreat them. In the late nineteenth and early twentieth century, Avrom Fleishman points out in *The English Historical Novel*, many novels portrayed women as suffering at the hands of history, which was defined, in opposition to more human feminine values, as "mechanical, greed-directed and masculine" (209). Finally, there is, according to Estelle Jelinek, a "continuous female tradition of discontinuity" in the writing of autobiography, at least, in direct opposition to male expectations of coherence and historical explanation (19).

Woolf's "compiling method," then, was a deliberate choice. An effort to demasculinize historical writing, it also reflects Fry's own diffuseness: his decentered quality and also the peculiarly atemporal way in which he grows older. There is no such thing as aging, Woolf wrote in her diary, only "altering one's aspect to the sun" (4:125). Similarly Fry remains very much a child, reborn at the age of forty-four, going through various stages that have nothing to do with chronology and not all that much to do with each other. Rhythmic irregularities, for Woolf, are a more accurate representation of experienced time than the measured ticking of a clock.

Fry himself describes the frogs in a pond at St. Rémy periodically breaking their own croaking rhythm; Woolf, as is her wont, applies the image to its originator (296). *Break* and *fragment* are words that recur frequently to suggest the discontinuities in Fry's life. When his wife becomes ill, for example, Woolf writes, "His emotions were broken and contradictory" (147). But the biggest break comes with the war, and here the narrative breaks down entirely, becoming almost a list, each paragraph beginning with a year and ellipsis, followed by a series of short sentences in the present tense.[9] Fragments of Fry's letters are quoted with scarcely any narrative transition and Woolf comments, "The war years then, as these scattered and incongruous fragments show, broke into many of the lives that Roger Fry lived simultaneously" (213). The disruption of war intensifies Fry's lack of a center, and Woolf's narrative refuses to gloss over the resultant disorder, until it begins to sound like her ridiculing of chronology in *Orlando:* "It was now November. After November comes December. Then . . ." (240).

Woolf's triumph in *Roger Fry* is that she managed to inject a similar element of disruption into what she called "a solid work." In writing the biography she had been troubled by the dichotomy between fact and fiction. How "explain madness and love in sober prose, with dates attached?" she wondered (*Letters* 6 : 267). She worried that she had failed, telling Vita Sackville-West, "Dear me, I'm so tired of correcting Roger and it's so bad. But then how can one make a life out of six cardboard boxes full of tailors' bills, love letters and old picture post cards?" (*Letters* 6 : 374). But finally, she managed to make her own sense of the impossibility of her task express the intangibility of another person: "The muddle in which these old newspaper cuttings lie is perhaps symbolical," she writes in *Roger Fry*. "They are mixed up with passports, with hotel bills, with sketches and poems and innumerable notes taken in front of the picture itself" (116).

Again and again in her letters, Woolf returns to the difficulty of using quotations, of providing transitions so that they blend smoothly into the text. Facts she judges equally resistant to integration. But these are not complaints from an artist loath to submit herself to the trivial. Instead it is the imaginative power, the differentness of each single item that makes synthesis impossible. An accurately depicted self retains all those differences so that its boundaries become a barely discernible line in a gigantic web of contrasting elements. Woolf's mind too is part of that web, and in *Roger Fry* she weaves the encounter between biographer and subject into a single, continuous cloth.

Just as the chaotic state of her source material is symbolic, so also is the picture of Fry the art lecturer pointing at his last slide, a late Cézanne so complex he pronounces himself baffled: "It went, he said, far beyond any analysis of which he was capable" (263). Woolf borrows the image to describe her own silent awe before the core of another being, who cannot be summed up except as possessing a "peculiar quality of reality" (297). The result is a curiously transparent picture of a curiously transparent human being. "The critic of Roger Fry may well drop the stick to the ground and give up pointing" (296), Woolf writes, using Fry's concluding gesture, but neither she nor Fry does stop; both enact again and again an approach, a halt, an expression of helplessness, then a return to the process of seeing "as if for the first time."

What remain, finally, are "certain phrases that recur, that seem to stress the pattern of the whole" (294). Here, at the end of the biography, Woolf provides a recapitulation of themes: poppies, pond loafers, Quakers, centrelessness. All are references to stories taking place amid the cotton wool of daily life and at the same time symbols of that other reality, the pattern behind.

In all her work after *Roger Fry,* Woolf seeks a pattern behind, an all-embracing kind of continuity that relates all of English history, for example, in *Between the Acts,* or all of literary history in *Reading at Random.* She is not in search of a unitary explanation; the urge is rather to stand far back enough, to perceive on a large enough scale, so that implicit patterns may emerge.

To begin with English country before Eth The effect of country upon writers. Hall. Holingshed. The idea of the book is to find the end of a ball of string & wind out. Let one book suggest another. Keep to time sequence. Pass from criticism to biography. (Silver, "Woolf's Last Essays" 373)

So begin Woolf's notes for *Reading at Random,* the book on social history in relation to literature that she began to map out as soon as she finished *Roger Fry* (*Letters* 6 : 430n). In 1937, she had written in her diary, "Were I another person, I would say to myself, Please write criticism; biography; invent a new form for both . . ." (5 : 91). She seems, by 1940, to have thought the work necessary enough to attempt it herself. Commenting on Gibbon in 1937 she had hinted at the broadly sociological and anthropological form her historical interests were taking: "The vanished generations," she writes, "invisible separately, have collectively spun round them intricate laws, erected marvellous structures of ceremony and belief," and descriptions of these structures, she suggests, can be more stimulating even than fiction (*Death* 86). As *Between the Acts* and the notes for *Reading at Random* and "Anon" indicate, the large-scale depiction of English literary and social history fascinated Woolf during the last years of her life.

This fascination is of a piece with her concern in *Roger Fry* and "A Sketch" to capture the social forces that shape the individual life, forces she labels, in *Reading at Random,* "Crot, Ninn, & Pulley," nonsense names which, according to Brenda Silver, designate the economic, social, political, and cultural influences at work on writers (360): "*Crot, Ninn, & Pulley—the 3 influences.* Might (begin) be a fictitious review of a hist of Eng. lit. What it omits. Try to write lit the other way round. define the influences: the affect; the growth; the surrounding, also the inner, current all left out in text books" (Silver, "Woolf's Last Essays" 374).

All of Woolf's last work aims at rewriting history, biography, and literary criticism—all traditionally male domains practiced by her father—from a less self-oriented point of view. Nora Eisenberg argues that in *Between the Acts* and "Anon" Woolf portrays a linguistic alternative to male conventions, a selfless language already the property of women, which is a potentially genderless language of merged sexes (264). Certainly it seems to me her entire concern with biography is to transform it in precisely this way, to find a way, paradoxically perhaps, to write of a single life without singularizing it. The "I" for Woolf is a tyrant, fatal to imagination and endemic to patriarchy. In *Three Guineas* she quotes George Sand, who eloquently makes a similar argument: "Cette individualité n'a par elle seule ni signification ni importance aucune. Elle ne prend un sens quelconque qu'en devenant une parcelle de la vie générale, en se fondant avec l'individualité de chacun de mes semblables, et c'est par là qu'elle devient de l'histoire" (188). Only as individuality merges into interaction with others, does it become the stuff of history, according to Sand. Sociobiography attempts to depict such an individuality in the hopes that history will indeed become a record of intimacies and influence rather than conflict.

VII

Conclusion

*To caricature the pomposity of those who claim
that they are something—was that not in its
way a career?* (Woolf, *Flush* 143)

In his essay on *The Life of Johnson*, Carlyle writes of great
men of the past: "A little row of Naptha-lamps, with its line
of Naptha-light, burns clear and holy through the dead
Night of the Past: they who are gone are still here; though
hidden they are revealed, though dead they yet speak"
(*Critical Essays* 3:80). The suggestion is of order and continuity, of the past enduring into the present and future in
the person of the great man, whose epic life-battle has been
memorialized by his biographer. When Woolf writes in
"Modern Fiction" that "Life is not a series of gig lamps
symmetrically arranged" (*Common Reader* 154), she may
or may not be echoing Carlyle. But she is rejecting, with
her description of the self as "luminous halo" or "semi-
transparent envelope," not merely old-fashioned characterization but a particular view of human achievement.
Those Naptha-lights, post-Victorian experimental biographers insist, lived originally in daylight, as human beings
not prophets, and as human beings their performance was
less stellar. The very concept of the "great man" seemed to
the post-Victorians to condone flawed personal relation-

ships as an acceptable price to pay for divine inspiration. "They who are gone are still here": for Carlyle this was the raison d'être of biography; for Strachey, Forster, Woolf, a nightmarish threat of destruction by the past. These "dead that yet speak" are the targets of the post-Victorian biographers, who insist that they themselves speak about the silent dead. Even James, Lubbock, and Symons, evoking their subjects as ghosts from the past, seem to conjure them up with a kind of protective curiosity devoid of awe.

Like much of late- and post-Victorian fiction, the biographies I have discussed resonate with filial revolt. For biography is always, in some sense, about inheritance. The depiction of a past life incorporates it into the present as a legacy from one age to another. As Carlyle suggests, biographies establish continuities. So do sons. The biographer has tended to play a filial role (as Boswell to Johnson; Lockhart to Scott; Froude to Carlyle), at once admiring from a distance and assimilating the values of his lost father. From *The Way of All Flesh* on, however, with its suggestion that children might profitably follow the example of ants and bees, who "sting their fathers to death as a matter of course" (91), the patrimony is often rejected. Works like *Father and Son* and *A Portrait of the Artist as a Young Man* portray the son's rejection of his inheritance and his virtual self-creation as an artist whose ancestors are literary, not biological; freely chosen, not given. The narrator of modernist biography puts himself in a somewhat similar position.

The twentieth-century biographer, Woolf writes in "The New Biography," "is no longer the serious and sympathetic companion, toiling even slavishly in the footsteps of his hero," but an equal free to shape the life as he sees fit: "He chooses; he synthesizes; in short, he has ceased to be the chronicler; he has become an artist" (*Granite* 152). Even when, in "The Art of Biography," Woolf announces that biography is not in fact an art, she allows the biographer to retain this freedom and importance. This aestheticization of biography, which I mentioned in chapter 1 as a major feature of modernist biography, involves a rejection of filiality, whether in regard to the subject, to the notion of "great men," to the past in general, or even to the sacred authority of historical data. Biography moves in the direction of play, becoming a self-contained system based on internal consistencies rather than such external concerns as usefulness (i.e., Stephen's dictum that it should teach morality) or verifiability. The presence of this playful element is not restricted to outright parody; it is present even in Scott's somber *Portrait of Zélide* or Lubbock's affectionate *Calderon,* in our constant awareness of artifice, which brings with it, no matter how sad the story, a comic element. The subject died, but, we are reminded, the artist still lives. This awareness of the biographer as artist, as interpreter, as decision-maker (even Woolf's suppressed narrative persona in *Roger Fry* represents a decision) injects a gigantic loose end into biography. The pretense of absolute authority associated with a life predestined by God, lived by man, then recorded by biographer is gone, along with the satisfying finality of the death bed scene. A mere biographer is left with the last word.

Psychologization, an increasing interest in the intangibles of motivation, personality, and perception, was the other major feature of modernist biography mentioned in chapter 1. Post-Victorian biographers answer the question, How would it feel to be X? rather than What did X do? Mendilow's description of the modern novel remains apt: "More importance is being attached to what the characters think and how they think, less and less to what they do" (202). There is a new tendency to see the boundaries of the self as debatable, not given: whether self-limiting, satisfyingly self-defining, or radically permeable, they seem a product of the subject's own imagination. The self is no longer a static object to be depicted but a continual activity, and the biography must be, to some extent, a mis-en-abîme: a portrayal of a self in the act of creating itself.

Conclusion

Faced with the challenge of depicting an activity rather than an object, biographers are liable to use their own activity as a model, mirroring the subject's self-creation with their own biographical quest. Whether directly portrayed, as in mediated biography, or touched on briefly, as in novelistic and psychosociobiography, the biographical process itself is very much in evidence.

There is, then, a great deal that my three categories have in common. All the biographers embrace to some extent the "indirect method" praised by Lubbock in *The Craft of Fiction*, simply because the act of biographical narration is not, for them, something to take for granted. Strachey attacking his subjects from the side rather than head-on, Woolf and Forster, eliciting from their subjects' own texts a pattern of selfhood rather than drawing it themselves, Nicolson recreating his childhood self to observe his uncle's life: all are acutely aware of their role as interpreters and make that awareness evident in their angle of approach. All reject any claim to absolute narrative authority, and all question the value of traditional historical explanation. Even the novelistic biographers, with their apparent omniscience, make it clear that they are arranging the evidence in a possible and pleasing configuration, not presenting a definitive interpretation. For all, the self is in part an imaginative construct, in part defined by that "underlife" James Hafley calls typically Georgian (13): a meeting-place of primal forces shared by all human beings, not yet fully understood. The whirlpool image that Woolf derives from her reading of Freud, Pater's "tremulous wisp constantly re-forming itself on the stream" (*Renaissance* 236), Forster's "lower" personality "with something general about it" (*Anonymity* 16), and Lawrence's nonindividualized ego (75) are closely related images that dominate novelistic and psychosociobiography but also appear less prominently in mediated biographies.

My various categories, then, are distinguished more by shifting emphases than rigid boundaries. Similarly, the various influences I and others have discerned operating on English biography between the wars cannot be isolated and traced, for the most part, to a single kind of biographical experiment. Lubbock's Jamesian biographies and Nicolson's self-consciously Proustian one are exceptons; for the most part that absurdly varied list of influences—Pater, Freud, Conrad, Proust, World War I, Einstein, James, post-Impressionism, Dostoievski, and feminism—must simply be seen as a conglomeration of ideas pervading the intellectual atmosphere and rendering traditional accounts of lives unconvincing. The ideas surface in varying combinations to varying extents in the works I have discussed, but my aim has not been to trace specific lines of influence. As Woolf wrote *Orlando* she read Ruskin, Proust, James, and Dostoievski (Silver, *Reading Notebooks* 84). Clearly they affected her understanding of how human experience can best be recorded. But my interest has been in the effects of that influence, not in its constituent parts. For the same reason I have not attempted to isolate a "Bloomsbury" biography. What matters is that the impact on life-writing of ideas—whether literary, philosophical or political—be acknowledged. Understanding that conventional schemata underlie the depiction of reality is essential to our understanding of ourselves. Analysis of how English biographers between the wars responded to changing schemata clarifies how particular narrative choices and concepts of time, selfhood, and human nature interact.

Since 1940, there have been few biographers who have continued the revolt and experimentation so characteristic of the twenties and thirties. The most lasting impact was probably made by novelistic biography. Certainly few life-writers would now take their subject's self-image at face value; Edel's suggestion that biographers look for a "figure under the carpet," a hidden myth behind the self-image, has been taken seriously (Pachter 26). His life of James, with its repetitions and anachronies, clearly diverges from traditional biographical structure. There is general agreement, though, that over-long, overly dry compilations of data have made a comeback in recent years and that biography has not yet received the careful critical attention it deserves.

The last ten years have brought a change, however: a new awareness that biographies are made, not found. As early as 1970, Roland Barthes wrote of a "fundamental ideological transformation" taking place in the writing of history, as structural analysis replaced chronological narrative (155), and he detected widespread rejection of the "referential illusion," whereby an absent narrator tries to suggest the "referent is speaking for itself" (149). Lionel Gossman discerns a similar trend in the work of Lucien Febvre and Ferdinand Braudel (24–25). Feminism, too, has had an impact on the subject matter and methodology of history and biography. "As long as historians held to the traditional view that only the transmission and exercise of power were worthy of their interest," writes Gerda Lerner, "women were of necessity ignored" (349). The answer is to move in the direction of social history, as Woolf's Merridew does in *The Journal of Mistress Joan Martyn*, as Eileen Power did in her 1924 *Medieval People*, where she announces, "This book is chiefly concerned with the kitchens of History" (16), and as feminist historians are now, increasingly, doing.[1]

As history changes, so too does biography. Contemporary theoreticians such as Ira Nadel, Park Honan, and Leon Edel question the need for a strictly chronological presentation; James Clifford *fils* challenges traditional notions of the self, proposing an "ethnobiography" that recognizes the sociality and fragmentation of the ego and rejects the "myth of personal coherence" which has long shaped and stunted biographical writing (45).[2] The extent to which we are not ourselves, but a meeting ground for the influence of friends and family, for social and economic pressures, is precisely what so fascinates Woolf in her late work. Fittingly, Clifford borrows the title for his essay from Woolf's 1939 "Art of Biography": "'Hanging up Looking Glasses at Odd Corners': Ethnobiographical Prospects." Feminist biography has burgeoned, and with it discussion of how gender affects the shape of a life and how biographical subjects can best be chosen.[3] Again Woolf is a precursor.

The future of biography is uncertain. One element in its evolution, though, is sure to be a rediscovery of earlier experiments. In responding to a recent questionnaire, scholars and writers of biography predicted, among other things, more coauthored works on multiple subjects, more innovative biographies by women, and an "*avant garde*" biography employing stream of consciousness, authorial uncertainty, and collage (Friedson 83–96)—methods already evident in Strachey, Symons, and Enfield. Biography is the terrain on which each generation works out crucial questions about its relation to the past, its conception of time, selfhood, and achievement. The post-Victorian experimenters are worth examining not only because they provide evidence of biography's responsiveness to literary innovation, but also because they provide a precedent and a wider range of options than we may realize is available for the working out of these questions.

They also serve the vital purpose of injecting into the writing and discussion of biography what Woolf in *Flush* calls "the potent spirits of truth and laughter," encompassing a distrust of anything asserted with too oppressive or too self-important an authority. As biography receives more critical attention, the biographies written in England between the wars will gain, I suspect, a new prominence. In the process, it is to be hoped that biographers and critics of biography will see themselves in Woolf's terms: as miners' canaries on guard against the noxious air of outmoded schemata and unexamined assumptions.

Notes

Bibliography

Index

Notes

1. Introduction

1. The 1973 *Encyclopedia Britannica* describes the new biography as "often the record of the inner life, the revelation of previously unsuspected aspects of character," and lists among its practitioners André Maurois, Philip Guedella, David Cecil, and Harold Nicolson. One particularly precise description is George A. Johnston's, who links Strachey, Maurois, and Emil Ludwig, all of whom, he writes: adopt novel or drama rather than history as model; emphasize design, detachment, psychology; refer frequently to fate; are stylistically brilliant; suggest an "enduring humanity"; use historical tableaux; and provide smooth transitions. (334–40).

2. Numerous other classification systems have been devised, generally too arbitrary or prescriptive to be useful. Among the more frequently cited are Nicolson's distinction between "pure" and "impure" (*Development*); Clifford's "objective," "scholarly-historical," "artistic-scholarly," "narrative," "novelistic," and "miscellaneous" (*Puzzles* 85); Edel's three categories: the traditional, heavily documented "chronicle," full of the subject's letters; the "pictorial," based on the subject's essential traits with less emphasis on chronological development; and the "narrative pictorial or novelistic," where the biographer serves as narrator with access to the subject's mind (*Literary Biography* 82–83). Ira Nadel has recently contributed another system; he names three traditional forms: dramatic/expressive, objective/academic, and interpretive/analytic (the first related to my mediated; the last to novelistic) (*Biography* 170). He lists three twentieth-century forms as well: psychobiography, group biography, and contextual biography—my psychosociobiography being a combination of first and last categories (186).

3. Olney's *Autobiography: Essays Theoretical and Critical* includes a useful bibliography as well as Starobinski's "The Style of Autobiography" (73–83).

4. Among the historical overviews are Nicolson's *Development;* Waldo H. Dunn's *The History of English Biography*, Robert Gittings' *The Nature of Biography*, Altick's *Life and Letters*, Paul Murray Kendall's *The Art of Biography*, and John A. Garraty's *The Nature of Biography.* Anecdotal discussions include Hesketh Pearson's *Ventilations*, Catherine Drinker Bowen's *Biography*, and Richard Ellmann's *Golden Codgers.* Leon Edel's recent *Writing Lives: Principia Biographica* is essentially a reworking of previously published material, particularly of *Literary Biography.*

5. On reading Nadel's book, after completion of this one, I found that we had reached some similar conclusions independently. His general sense of modern biographical trends parallels mine as does his emphasis on tropes and narrative strategy, though we pursue our interests quite differently. (Nadel's discussion of Strachey's *Eminent Victorians* appeared earlier and is discussed in chapter 2.)

6. See also Toulmin, 94.

2. The Revolt against Victorianism

1. Gosse's *Father and Son* is generally treated by historians of biography as biography, while critics of autobiography tend to label it autobiography. This generic ambiguity indicates that one aspect of its impact on biography may have been its infusion of such autobiographical conventions as confession and revelation into biographical writing. I mention it here not because I believe it to be generically definable as biography but because its impact on biographers (of whom Gosse, after all, was one) was indisputable.

2. Frank Manuel describes a similar propensity among German philosophers, who turn history into biography and write "elitest dramas of the passions of great men's souls" (192).

3. Leslie Stephen in his *Swift*, for example, confesses his ignorance of his subject's actual feelings about marriage, then adds, "But we may still ask what judgment is to be passed on Swift's conduct" (143). Lionel Gossman describes the nineteenth-

century tendency to make story and discourse appear unitary; unlike the eighteenth-century narrator who cultivates complicity with his reader, the nineteenth-century narrator suppresses himself, according to Gossman, thereby asserting the autonomy of his story (22–41).

4. For example: "Reticence about his personal sufferings was at no time one of his virtues. Dyspepsia had him by the throat" (*First Forty Years* 62).

5. John Clubbe also points out Froude's use of Greek dramatic conventions (317–53). He cites as well Spenser's *Faerie Queen* and Goethe's *Faust* as sources of imagery.

6. Throughout late Victorian and Edwardian literature, eighteenth-century literature has an anti-Victorian resonance, as when Sue Bridehead reads Gibbon in *Jude the Obscure*. In Woolf, on the other hand, who is already reacting to the reaction against Victorianism, Gibbon suggests an enlightened but intrusive and relentlessly dry intellect. (See her "The Historian and 'The Gibbon'" in *Death* 82–93.)

7. See, for example, Humphrey House's attack on David Cecil's expressivist biography (260).

8. There is no evidence of a direct Freudian influence on Strachey until *Elizabeth and Essex*, though Martin Kallich, in *The Psychological Milieu of Lytton Strachey*, detects Freudian preoccupations throughout Strachey's oeuvre.

9. Nadel points out that this contrast between "naming" and interpretation comes from Park Honan (109–20).

10. See, for example, Christopher Saltmarshe (193); Louis Kronenberger (376); and Charles Smyth (655).

11. Paul Hernadi has pointed out the flexibility of *style indirecte libre*, which he calls "substitutionary narration." The same technique, he argues, has been used by Flaubert to achieve ironic distance, and by Joyce to gain emotional intensity ("Dual Perspective" 35–37). Perry Meisel suggests that Strachey's "hyperbolic demeanor" seems to have been learned from his subjects; the narrator's incorporation into his own voice of his subjects' voices, he argues, sets up a "counterplot," a "self-subverting" element that throws the narrator's claim to authority into question ("Counterplot" 8–11).

12. "We can comprehend the appeal of historical discourse by recognizing the extent to which it makes the real desirable," White writes, "makes the real into an object of desire, and does so by its imposition, upon events that are represented as real, of the formal coherency that stories possess. . . . Insofar as historical stories can be completed, can be given narrative closure, can be shown to have had a *plot* all along, they give to reality the odor of the *ideal*" ("Value" 24).

13. Meisel cites Nightingale's "Demon" as an example of Strachey's deliberate and virtually self-parodic use of hyperbole ("Counterplot" 6).

14. Similarly, Harriet Martineau, unwilling to live with her mother, found invalidism useful; Theodora Bosanquet writes, "her only respectable resource was to fall ill" (131).

3. Weaving the Self: Novelistic Biography

1. George A. Johnston points out a similar connection between Forster's *Aspects* and the New Biography (333).

2. Hayden White argues that the very idea of entering into the mind of a dead person is characteristically modern, derived especially from Collingwood ("Politics" 123).

3. See Hans Meyerhoff (89–117) on the "modern" conception of time. Jerome Buckley attributes similar characteristics to time in "The Eternal Now," a chapter in his *The Triumph of Time*.

4. Meisel also suggests, though without elaborating, that Pater's *Imaginary Portraits* gave rise to the New Biography, particularly influencing Strachey, Nicolson, and Woolf in *Orlando* (44–45).

5. Frederic Jameson writes of the same problematic in the psychological novel, which, like novelistic biography, substitutes "unity of personality for the unity of action." Such novels, he writes, gain their coherence from a "feeling of identity or permanence in time of the monad or point of view," but behind the point of view are the "isolation and juxtaposition of closed subjectivities" (13).

6. Somewhat similarly, Paul Ricoeur distinguishes between composite unity and dramatized narration as two aspects of his-

torical narration (*History and Truth* 39) and Gossman writes of a polarity in narrative between syntagmic (empirical) and paradigmatic (rational) elements (19–20).

7. Carolyn Heilbrun in *Toward a Recognition of Androgyny* argues that Victoria and Albert, in conforming to traditional sex roles, lose effectiveness as rulers and parents (145).

8. "Defiantly they insisted upon the pre-eminence of human personality," Harold Nicolson writes of the Victorians in his biography of Tennyson, suggesting that this insistence turned their heroes into "whitewashed effigies" (4–5).

9. R. W. B. Lewis, in *Edith Wharton*, provides a list of the limited material available on Scott (564).

10. Nicolson and Lewis differ on the precise date.

11. On Scott's importance as a commentator on Boswell, see Passler, who writes that Scott destroyed the old image of Boswell and revealed him to be a deliberate artist (xiv).

12. The comparison to Strachey has also been made by Michael Swan (240), the *Times Literary Supplement* ("The Portrait of Zélide," 12 March 1925, 168), and John St. Loe Strachey (811). See also Nicolson's imitation of Victoria's end in his *Tennyson* (88).

13. The death scene was also important to the Victorians, but it was depicted externally, from an eyewitness's point of view, not from within the mind of the dying man. See, for example, Carlyle's description of the death of Sterling: "The faint last struggle was ended, and all those struggles and strenuous often-foiled endeavours of eight-and-thirty years lay hushed in death" (261).

14. See, for example, Lily Briscoe's meditation on the pear tree in *To the Lighthouse* (41).

4. Omniscience Rejected: Mediated Biography

1. In Genette's terms, Lubbock's "panorama" becomes "diegesis," while "scene" is "mimesis" (163).

2. Roland Barthes' "Historical Discourse" does point the way toward a linguistic analysis of historical discourse.

3. In addition to James's biography of William Wetmore Story, see his unfinished novel *The Sense of the Past*.

4. Symons "reluctantly" accepted modern psychological theory's description of the unconscious, his brother Julian says in *A. J. A. Symons: His Life and Speculations* (115).

5. Symons's curiosity is similarly deadly, so great he is "half-stifled," suggesting that such ravenously inquisitive pursuit of dead lives may result finally in role reversal.

6. He also wrote works on Elizabeth Barrett Browning and Pepys, but both predate the period under discussion.

7. Flaubert, he writes, does not suggest historical truth, as does a Defoe narrative, but makes his effect through his relation to the story (*Craft* 62, 66).

8. The downplaying of Wharton's accomplishment is extreme enough for R. W. B. Lewis to write of its "subtly distributed malice toward its subject" (516).

9. Symons, unpublished letter, 27 November 1936, Henry W. and Albert A. Berg Collection, The New York Public Library, Astor, Lenox and Tilden Foundations.

10. Symons, unpublished letter, 16 November 1936, Henry W. and Albert A. Berg Collection, The New York Public Library, Astor, Lenox, and Tilden Foundations.

11. This quality results when the letters describe the writer's circumstances in increasingly elaborate detail with explanations that shift and multiply in the course of the letter, clearly emerging from, rather than predating, the act of composition. Symons's own letters have much the same quality.

5. Feminism and Biography: *Orlando* and *Flush*, Virginia Woolf's "Jokes"

1. The Post-Impressionism Exhibition, organized by Woolf's friend Roger Fry, which opened in November 1910, is often proposed as an explanation for her choice of that year. Phyllis Rose suggests the explanation was more personal: Woolf's participation in the Dreadnought Hoax (102). James Hafley, on the other hand, associates the date with the influence of such varied factors as Henry and William James, Bergson, Freud, and Dostoievski (10).

2. Nina Auerbach argues a similar point in broader terms in *Woman and the Demon*. "Mr. Bennett and Mrs. Brown," she writes,

links literary characterization with woman's power to create herself, equating the "magic of character with a personification of womanhood" (225).

3. Woolf described both *Orlando* and *Flush* as jokes that went on for too long; see *Diary* 3 : 177 and *Letters* 5 : 177.

4. See Harper (168–96) for a contrasting interpretation of the tapestry's significance.

5. Elizabeth Shore argues that *Orlando* is Woolf's most Proustian work (232–45), and James Hafley also emphasizes its Proustian flavor (101).

6. A. R. Louch writes that the goal of history is to "fill in the gaps and provide a smooth flow of change" (54).

7. Susan Squier, in her insightful analysis of *Flush* in *Virginia Woolf and London,* published after the completion of this discussion, argues similarly that Woolf exposes a "phallocratic world of material uniformity, consistency, and authority" (126) by juxtaposing patriarchal London with maternal Florence. Stephen Trombley emphasizes the relation between Flush and Virginia Woolf herself as Potto, the "dog-self" created in her letters to Sackville-West, and in relation to Clive and Vanessa Bell, her version of Barrett and Browning (272).

8. Thomas S. W. Lewis notes another Stracheyan passage—in Flush's dreamy memories of his past—on page 167 (311).

6. Unweaving the Self: Psycho- and Sociobiography

1. Forster's *Marianne Thornton: A Domestic Biography,* about his great-aunt, is another, somewhat more innovative experiment in biography, but outside the scope of this discussion since it was published in 1956.

2. See also Jeffrey Mehlman on Freud's "psychical reality" and its blurring of the distinction between truth and falsehood (17).

3. Freud writes in similar terms of the plasticity of the sexual instinctual impulses: "One of them can take the place of another, one of them can take over another's intensity; if the satisfaction of one of them is frustrated by reality, the satisfaction of another can afford complete compensation. They are related to one another like a network of intercommunicating canals filled with a liquid" (*Psychological Works* 16 : 345).

4. See, for example, Jeanne M. McNett, Lawrence A. Garber, and Thomas Chalfant.

5. Edel revises his view in his talk at the National Gallery, reprinted in Pachter (19). Edel also has praise for *Roger Fry* in "Biography: The Question of Form" (356).

6. Leonard Woolf writes of his own life in similar terms: "Looking back over one's life, one of the curious things one notices is how two or three small events happened years and years ago, then for years the consequences disappear beneath the surface of one's life like underground springs or streams, and then, like streams breaking out of the ground as tributaries to form a great river, years later the events reappeared with important consequences in one's life" (*Journey* 173).

7. This point is also noted by Sarah Gallagher (97).

8. Lewis also makes this connection between Leonard's "beak" and Mr. Ramsay ("Combining" 320).

9. Woolf's treatment of the war as a major interruption in Fry's life contrasts with the more casual treatment afforded by Frances Spalding in her *Roger Fry*.

7. Conclusion

1. See, for example, Linda Gordon, Carroll Smith-Rosenberg, and Carolyn Heilbrun ("Women's Biographies").

2. Clifford names Erik Erikson, R. D. Laing, and Jacques Lacan as some of those recognizing the incoherence of the self; all, he says, "inject sociality into the most individual expressions of an ego conceived as continually 'outside' itself" (47). Edward Mendelson, writing in the same volume as Clifford, also rejects past biography's excessively narrow focus on the inner workings of the individual self. He suggests future biographers seek inspiration not from Freud, but from Weber (Aaron 25).

3. "Until the last decade," Carolyn Heilbrun writes, "a biography of a woman writer written by a woman was an anomaly." Only now, she argues, are reevaluations of women's lives being made that place, at the heart of their achievement, their "displacement . . . from the center of established institutions" (Heilbrun, "Women's Biographies" 343).

Bibliography

Aaron, Daniel, ed. *Studies in Biography.* Cambridge, MA: Harvard UP, 1978.

Altick, Richard D. *Lives and Letters: A History of Literary Biography in England and America.* New York: Knopf, 1965.

Annan, Noel. *Leslie Stephen: The Godless Victorian.* New York: Random House, 1984.

Auerbach, Nina. *Woman and the Demon: The Life of a Victorian Myth.* Cambridge, MA: Harvard UP, 1982.

Bakhtin, M. M. *The Dialogic Imagination.* Ed. Michael Holquist. Trans. Caryl Emerson and Michael Holquist. Austin: U Texas P, 1981.

Baldanza, Frank. "*Orlando* and the Sackvilles." *PMLA* 70 (March 1955): 274–79.

Barthes, Roland. "Historical Discourse." *Introduction to Structuralism.* Ed. Michael Lane. New York: Basic, 1970. 145–55.

Benedict, Ruth. *Patterns of Culture.* 1934. Boston: Houghton Mifflin, 1959.

Blackmur, R. P. Review of *Quest for Corvo. New Republic* 80 (12 Sept. 1934): 135.

Blain, Virginia. "Narrative Voice and the Female Perspective in Virginia Woolf's Early Novels." Patricia Clements and Isobel Grundy, eds. *Virginia Woolf: New Critical Essays.* London: Vision and Barnes and Noble, 1983. 115–36.

Bosanquet, Theodora. *Harriet Martineau.* London: Frederick Etchells and Hugh MacDonald, 1927.

Boswell, James. *Life of Johnson.* London: Oxford UP, 1904.

Bowen, Catherine Drinker. *Biography: The Craft and the Calling.* Boston: Little Brown, 1969.

Bower-Shore, Clifford. *Lytton Strachey.* London: Fenland Press, 1933.

Brown, Ashley. "Homage to Percy Lubbock." *Southern Review* 15 (January 1979): 22–25.

Buckler, William. *The Victorian Imagination*. New York: New York UP, 1980.

Buckley, Jerome. *The Triumph of Time*. Cambridge, MA: Belknap P of Harvard U, 1966.

———. *The Victorian Temper*. New York: Vintage, 1951.

Butler, Samuel. *Ernest Pontifex, or the Way of All Flesh*. 1903. Ed. Daniel F. Howard. Boston: Houghton Mifflin, 1964.

Carlyle, Thomas. *Critical and Miscellaneous Essays*. 5 vols. London: Chapman and Hall, 1899.

———. *The Life of John Sterling*. London: Chapman and Hall, 1897.

———. *On Heroes, Hero-Worship and the Heroic in History*. London: Chapman and Hall, 1897.

Cecil, David. *The Fine Art of Reading*. Indianapolis: Bobbs-Merrill, 1957.

———. *Hardy the Novelist*. Indianapolis: Bobbs-Merrill, 1943.

———. "Mr. Hugh Walpole and the Modern Novel." *Eton Review* 2 (July 1918): 47.

———. *The Stricken Deer or the Life of Cowper*. London: Constable & Co., 1929.

Chalfant, Thomas H. "The Marriage of Granite and Rainbow: Virginia Woolf as a Biographer." Diss. U of Wisconsin, 1971.

Clifford, James. "'Hanging Up Looking Glasses at Odd Corners': Ethnobiographical Prospects." *Studies in Biography*. Ed. Daniel Aaron. Cambridge: Harvard UP, 1978. 41–56.

Clifford, James L. *From Puzzles to Portraits*. Chapel Hill: U of North Carolina P, 1970.

Clubbe, John. "Grecian Destiny: Froude's Portraits of the Carlyles." *Carlyle and His Contemporaries*. Durham, NC: Duke UP, 1976. 317–53.

Cockshut, A. O. J. *Truth to Life: The Art of Biography in the Nineteenth Century*. New York: Harcourt Brace Jovanovich, 1974.

Collingwood, R. G. *The Idea of History*. 1945. New York: Oxford UP, 1946.

Colmer, John. *E. M. Forster: The Personal Voice*. London: Routledge & Kegan Paul, 1975.

Conrad, Joseph. *The Nigger of the Narcissus*. New York: Doubleday, 1924.

Bibliography

Culler, Jonathan. *The Pursuit of Signs: Semiotics, Literature, Deconstruction.* Ithaca: Cornell UP, 1981.

Daiches, David. "What Was the Modern Novel?" *Critical Inquiry* 1 (June 1975): 813–20.

Delattre, Floris. *Le roman psychologique de Virginia Woolf.* 1932. Paris: Librairie Philosophique J. Vrin, 1967.

DeSalvo, Louise. "Shakespeare's 'Other' Sister." *New Feminist Essays on Virginia Woolf.* Ed. Jane Marcus. Lincoln: U of Nebraska P, 1981. 61–81.

DeVoto, Bernard. "The Skeptical Biographer." *Harper's,* 166 (1933): 182–92.

DiBattista, Maria. *Virginia Woolf's Major Novels: The Fables of Anon.* New Haven: Yale UP, 1980.

Dunn, Waldo H. *The History of English Biography.* New York: Dutton, 1916.

Edel, Leon. "Biography: The Question of Form." *Friendship's Garland: Essays Presented to Mario Praz.* Ed. Vittorio Gabrieli. Rome: Edizioni di Storia E Letteratura, vol. 2: 243–60.

———. *Henry James the Master, 1901–1916.* New York: Avon, 1972.

———. *Literary Biography.* Toronto: U of Toronto P, 1957.

———. *Writing Lives: Principia Biographica.* New York: Norton, 1984.

Eisenberg, Nora. "Virginia Woolf's Last Words on Words: Between the Acts and 'Anon.'" *New Feminist Essays on Virginia Woolf.* Ed. Jane Marcus. Lincoln: U of Nebraska P, 1981. 253–66.

Ellmann, Richard. *Golden Codgers: Biographical Speculations.* New York: 1973.

Enfield, D. E. *A Lady of the Salons: The Story of Louise Colet.* New York: Scribner's, 1923.

———. *L. E. L.: A Mystery of the Thirties.* London: Hogarth, 1928.

Epstein, William. "Recognizing the Life-Text." *Biography* 6 (Fall 1983): 283–306.

Flaubert, Gustave. *Madame Bovary.* Paris: Ed. Garnier Frères, 1961.

Fleishman, Avrom. *The English Historical Novel.* Baltimore: Johns Hopkins UP, 1971.

———. *Figures of Autobiography.* Berkeley: U of California P, 1983.

Bibliography

Forster, E. M. *Abinger Harvest*. 1936. New York: Harcourt Brace Jovanovich, 1964.
———. *Albergo Empedocle and Other Writings*. Ed. George H. Thomson. New York: Liveright, 1971.
———. *Anonymity*. London: Hogarth, 1925.
———. *Aspects of the Novel and Related Writings*. 1927. Ed. Oliver Stallybrass. London: Edward Arnold, 1974.
———. *Goldsworthy Lowes Dickinson and Related Writings*. 1934. Ed. Oliver Stallybrass. London: Edward Arnold, 1973.
———. *Marianne Thornton: A Domestic Biography*. New York: Harcourt, Brace Jovanovich, 1956.
———. *Two Cheers for Democracy*. New York: Harcourt Brace Jovanovich, 1951.
Foucault, Michel. *The Archaeology of Knowledge*. Trans. A. M. Sheridan Smith. New York: Pantheon, 1972.
Fox, Alice. "Virginia Liked Elizabeth." *Virginia Woolf: A Feminist Slant*. Ed. Jane Marcus. Lincoln: U of Nebraska P, 1983. 37–51.
Freud, Sigmund. *Moses and Monotheism*. Trans. Katherine Jones. London: Hogarth Press and the Institute of Psychoanalysis, 1939.
———. *Standard Edition of the Complete Psychological Works*. Trans. and Ed. James Strachey. Vol. 16. 1916–1917. London: Hogarth Press and the Institute of Psychoanalysis, 1963.
———. Vol. 11. 1910. London: Hogarth Press and the Institute of Psychoanalysis, 1957.
Friedländer, Saul. *History and Psychoanalysis*. Trans. Susan Suleiman. New York: Holmes and Meier, 1978.
Friedson, Anthony. *New Directions in Biography*. Honolulu: UP of Hawaii, 1981.
Froude, James Anthony. *Thomas Carlyle: A History of the First Forty Years of His Life*. 1882. 2 vols reprinted as 1. New York: Scribner's, 1897.
———. *Thomas Carlyle: A History of His Life in London*. 1884. 2 vols. New York: Scribner's, 1898.
Fussell, Paul. *Abroad*. New York: Oxford UP, 1980.
———. *The Great War and Modern Memory*. New York: Oxford UP, 1975.
Gallagher, Sarah Van Sickle. "The Fiction of the Self: Virginia Woolf and the Problem of Biography." Diss. SUNY Buffalo, 1979.

Garber, Lawrence A. "Bloomsbury Biography." Diss. U of Toronto, 1971.

Garnett, David. "Keynes, Strachey and Virginia Woolf in 1917." *London Magazine* 2 (September 1955): 48–55.

———. Review of *Quest for Corvo*. *New Statesman and Nation* 7 (17 February 1934): 230.

Garraty, John. "The Interrelation of Psychology and Biography." *Psychological Bulletin* 51 (November 1954): 569–82.

———. *The Nature of Biography*. New York: Knopf, 1957.

Genette, Gerard. *Narrative Discourse: An Essay in Method*. Trans. Jane Lewin. Ithaca: Cornell UP, 1980.

Gerhardie, William. *God's Fifth Column*. New York: Simon and Schuster, 1981.

Gilbert, Sandra M. "Costumes of the Mind: Transvestism as Metaphor in Modern Literature." *Critical Inquiry* 7 (Winter 1980): 391–418.

Gittings, Robert. *The Nature of Biography*. Seattle, U of Washington P, 1978.

Gombrich, E. H. *Art and Illusion: A Study in the Psychology of Pictorial Representation*. 1960. Princeton: Princeton UP, 1972.

Goodman, Nelson. "Twisted Tales; or, Story, Study, and Symphony." *Critical Inquiry* 7 (Autumn 1980): 103–20.

Gordon, Linda. "Towards a Feminist History." *Female Studies* 5:49–52.

Gordon, Lyndall. *Virginia Woolf: A Writer's Life*. New York: Norton, 1984.

Gosse, Edmund. *Father and Son: A Study of Two Temperaments*. London: Heinemann, 1907.

———. *The Naturalist of the Sea Shore: The Life of Philip Henry Gosse*. London: Heinemann, 1896.

———. *Some Diversions of a Man of Letters*. London: Heinemann, 1919.

Gossman, Lionel. "History and Literature." *The Writing of History: Literary Form and Historical Understanding*. Ed. Robert H. Canary and Henry Kozicki. Madison: U of Wisconsin P, 1978. 22–41.

Grushow, Ira. "Biography as Literature." *Southern Humanities Review* 14 (Spring 1980): 155–60.

Guiget, Jean. *Virginia Woolf and Her Works*. Trans. Jean Stewart. New York: Harcourt Brace and World, 1965.

Gusdorf, Georges. "Conditions and Limits of Autobiography." *Autobiography: Essays Theoretical and Critical.* Ed. James Olney. Princeton: Princeton UP, 1980. 28–48.

Hafley, James. *The Glass Roof: Virginia Woolf as Novelist.* Berkeley: U of California P, 1954.

Halperin, John. "Eminent Victorians and History." *Virginia Quarterly Review* 56 (Summer 1980): 433–54.

Harper, Howard. *Between Language and Silence: The Novels of Virginia Woolf.* Baton Rouge: Louisiana State U, 1982.

Hawkes, Ellen. "Friendship's Gallery." *Twentieth Century Literature* 25 (Fall/Winter 1979): 270–302.

———. "Woolf's Magical Garden of Women." *New Feminist Essays on Virginia Woolf.* Ed. Jane Marcus. Lincoln: U of Nebaska P, 1981. 31–60.

Heilbrun, Carolyn. *Toward a Recognition of Androgyny.* New York: Knopf, 1973.

———. "Virginia Woolf in Her Fifties." *Twentieth Century Literature* 27 (Spring 1981): 16–33.

———. "Women's Biographies of Women: A New Genre." *Review* 2 (1980): 337–45.

Hernadi, Paul. "Clio's Cousins: Historiography Considered as Translation, Fiction, and Criticism." *New Literary History* 7 (1976): 247–57.

———. "Dual Perspective: Free Indirect Discourse and Related Techniques." *Comparative Literature,* 24 (1972): 32–43.

Hill, Katherine C. "Virginia Woolf and Leslie Stephen: History and Literary Revolution." *PMLA* 96 (May 1981): 351–62.

Holland, Norman. "Human Identity." *Critical Inquiry* 4 (Spring 1978): 451–69.

Holroyd, Michael. *Lytton Strachey.* 2 vols. New York: Holt, Rinehart, and Winston, 1968.

———. ed. *Lytton Strachey by Himself: A Self-Portrait.* New York: Holt, Rinehart, and Winston, 1971.

Honan, Park. "The Theory of Biography." *Novel* 13 (Fall 1979): 109–20.

Houghton, Walter E. *The Victorian Frame of Mind: 1830–1870.* New Haven: Yale UP, 1975.

House, Humphrey. *All in Due Time.* London: Rupert Hart-Davis, 1955.

Huxley, Thomas H. *Evolution and Ethics and Other Essays.* New York: D. Appleton and Co., 1898.

Isherwood, Christopher. *Lions and Shadows: An Education in the Twenties.* London: Hogarth Press, 1938.

James, Henry. *The Altar of the Dead, The Beast in the Jungle, The Birthplace, and Other Tales.* New York: Scribner, 1922.

————. *The Ambassadors.* 2 vols. New York: Scribner, 1909.

————. *Letters.* 2 vols. Ed. Percy Lubbock. London: Macmillan, 1920.

————. *Literary Reviews and Essays.* Ed. Albert Mordell. New York: Grove, 1957.

————. *The Princess Cassamassima.* 2 vols. New York: Scribner, 1908.

————. *William Wetmore Story and His Friends.* 2 vols. Boston: Houghton Mifflin, 1904.

Jameson, Frederic. "Metacommentary." *PMLA* 86 (1971): 9–18.

Jehlen, Myra. "Archimedes and the Paradox of Feminist Criticism." *Feminist Theory: A Critique of Ideology.* Eds. Nannerl O. Keohane, Michelle Z. Rosaldo, and Barbara C. Gelpi. Chicago: U. of Chicago P, 1981. 189–217.

Jelinek, Estelle, ed. *Women's Autobiography: Essays in Criticism.* Bloomington: Indiana UP, 1980.

Johnston, George A. "The New Biography." *Atlantic* 143 (March 1929): 333–42.

Johnstone, John K. *The Bloomsbury Group.* New York: Noonday, 1954.

Joseph, David I. *The Art of Rearrangement: E. M. Forster's Abinger Harvest.* New Haven: Yale UP, 1964.

Kahane, Claire. "The Nuptials of Metaphor: Self and Other in Virginia Woolf." *Literature and Psychology* 30 (1980): 72–82.

Kallich, Martin. *The Psychological Milieu of Lytton Strachey.* New York: Bookman, 1961.

Kendall, Paul. *The Art of Biography.* New York: Norton, 1965.

Kingsmill, Hugh. *Matthew Arnold.* New York: Dial, 1928.

Kronenberger, Louis. "Lytton Strachey." *Bookman* 71 (July 1930): 375–80.

Landow, George, ed. *Approaches to Victorian Autobiography.* Athens: Ohio UP, 1979.

Lawrence, D. H. *Selected Letters.* Ed. Diana Trilling. New York: Farrar, Straus, and Cudahy, 1958.

Lee, Sidney. "The Perspective of Biography." *Elizabethan and Other Essays.* Ed. Frederick Boas. Oxford: Clarendon, 1929. 58–82.

———. *Principles of Biography.* Cambridge: Cambridge UP, 1911.

Lejeune, Philippe. "Le Pacte autobiographique." *Poétique* 14 (1973): 137–62.

Lerner, Gerda. "New Approaches to the Study of Women in American History." *Liberating Women's History.* Ed. Bernice A. Carroll. Urbana: U of Illinois P, 1976. 349–56.

Lewis, R. W. B. *Edith Wharton.* New York: Harper Colophon, 1975.

Lewis, Thomas S. W. "Combining 'The Advantages of Fact and Fiction': Virginia Woolf's Biographies of Vita Sackville-West, Flush, and Roger Fry." *Virginia Woolf: Centennial Essays.* Ed. Elaine Ginsberg and Laura Moss Gottlieb. Troy, NY: Whitston Pub. Co., 1983. 295–324.

Longaker, Mark. *Contemporary Biography.* Philadelphia: U of Pennsylvania P, 1934.

Louch, A. R. "History as Narrative." *History and Theory* 8 (1969): 54–70.

Lubbock, Percy. *The Craft of Fiction.* 1921. New York: Viking, 1964.

———. *George Calderon: A Sketch from Memory.* 1921. London: Grant Richards, 1971.

———. *Mary Cholmondeley: A Sketch from Memory.* London: Jonathan Cape, 1928.

———. *Portrait of Edith Wharton.* London: Jonathan Cape, 1947.

Macaulay, Rose. "Reminiscence of Virginia Woolf." *Horizon* 3 (May 1941): 317–18.

———. *The Writings of E. M. Forster.* New York: Harcourt Brace and Co, 1938.

Maitland, Frederic William. *The Life and Letters of Leslie Stephen.* New York: Putnam, 1906.

Manuel, Frank E. "The Use and Abuse of Psychology in History." *Daedalus* 100 (Winter 1971): 192–213.

Marcus, Jane. "Thinking Back through Our Mothers." *New Feminist Essays on Virginia Woolf.* Lincoln: U of Nebraska P, 1981. 1–30.

Mariano, Nicky. *Forty Years with Berenson.* New York: Knopf, 1966.

Maurois, André. *Aspects of Biography*. Trans. Sydney Castle Roberts. New York: D. Appleton and Co., 1929.

McNett, Jeanne M. "Virginia Woolf on Biography: Theory and Praxis." Diss. U of Massachusetts, 1980.

Mehlman, Jeffrey. *A Structural Study of Autobiography*. Ithaca: Cornell UP, 1974.

Meisel, Perry. *The Absent Father: Virginia Woolf and Walter Pater*. New Haven: Yale UP, 1980.

———. "Strachey's Counterplot." *Structuralist Review* 1 (Winter, 1978): 3–12.

Mendilow, A. A. *Time and the Novel*. New York: Humanities Press, 1966.

Meyerhoff, Hans. *Time in Literature*. Berkeley: U of California P, 1960.

Mill, John Stuart. *Autobiography and Literary Essays*. Eds. John M. Robson and Jack Stillinger. Toronto: U of Toronto P, 1981.

Miller, Nancy. "Emphasis Added: Plots and Plausibilities in Women's Fiction." *PMLA* 96 (January 1981): 36–48.

Monsman, Gerald. *Pater's Portraits*. Baltimore: Johns Hopkins UP, 1967.

Moore, Madeline. "Virginia Woolf's *Orlando:* An Edition of the Manuscript." *Twentieth Century Literature* 25 (Fall/Winter 1979): 303–46.

Nadel, Ira Bruce. *Biography: Fiction, Fact, and Form*. London: Macmillan, 1984.

———. "Strachey's 'Subtler Strategy': Metaphor in *Eminent Victorians*." *Prose Studies* 4 (September 1981): 146–52.

Naremore, James. *The World without a Self: Virginia Woolf and the Novel*. New Haven: Yale UP, 1973.

Nettels, Elsa. "Henry James and the Art of Biography." *South Atlantic Bulletin* 43 (November 1978): 107–24.

Neuman, Shirley. "*Heart of Darkness,* Virginia Woolf and the Spectre of Domination." Patricia Clements and Isobel Grundy, eds. *Virginia Woolf: New Critical Essays*. London: Vision and Barnes and Noble, 1983. 57–76.

Nicolson, Harold. *The Development of English Biography*. New York: Harcourt Brace and Co., 1928.

———. *Diaries and Letters 1930–1939*. Ed. Nigel Nicolson. London: Collins, 1966.

———. *Helen's Tower*. New York: Harcourt Brace and Co., 1938.

————. *Some People.* 1927. New York: Atheneum, 1982.

————. *Tennyson.* London: Constable, 1923.

Nicolson, Nigel. *Portrait of a Marriage.* New York: Atheneum, 1973.

Olney, James. ed. *Autobiography: Essays Theoretical and Critical.* Princeton: Princeton UP, 1980.

————. *Metaphors of Self: The Meaning of Autobiography.* Princeton: Princeton UP, 1972.

Origo, Iris. *Images and Shadows: Part of a Life.* New York: Harcourt Brace Jovanovich, 1971.

Pachter, Marc, ed. *Telling Lives: The Biographer's Art.* Washington DC: New Republic Books/National Portrait Gallery, 1979.

Pascal, Roy. *Design and Truth in Autobiography.* Cambridge, MA: Harvard UP, 1960.

Passler, David L. *Time, Form and Style in Boswell's Life of Johnson.* New Haven: Yale UP, 1971.

Pater, Walter. *Miscellaneous Studies: A Series of Essays.* 1895. London: Macmillan, 1924.

————. *The Renaissance.* London: Macmillan, 1904.

Pearson, Hesketh. *Ventilations: Being Biographical Asides.* Philadelphia: Lippincott, 1930.

Petrie, Dennis W. *Ultimately Fiction: Design in Modern American Literary Biography.* West Lafayette, IN: Purdue UP, 1981.

Philipson, Morris. "Virginia Woolf's *Orlando:* Biography as a Work of Fiction." *From Parnassus: Essays in Honor of Jacques Barzun.* Ed. Dora B. Weiner and William Keylor. New York: Harper and Row, 1976. 237–48.

"The Portrait of Zélide." *Times Literary Supplement,* 12 March 1925, 168.

Power, Eileen. *Medieval People.* New York: Doubleday, 1924.

Raymond, John. *England's on the Anvil.* London: Collins, 1958. 161–67.

Read, Herbert. *Wordsworth.* London: Jonathan Cape, 1930.

Reed, Joseph W., Jr. *English Biography in the Early Nineteenth Century 1801–1838.* New Haven: Yale UP, 1966.

Ricoeur, Paul. *History and Truth.* Evanston: Northwestern UP, 1965.

Rose, Phyllis. *Woman of Letters: A Life of Virginia Woolf.* New York: Oxford UP, 1976.

Rosenbaum, S. P. "*Aspects of the Novel* and Literary History." *E. M.*

Forster: Centenary Revaluations. Ed. Judith Scherer Herz and Robert K. Martin. Toronto: U of Toronto P, 1982. 55–83.

———. "An Educated Man's Daughter: Leslie Stephen, Virginia Woolf and the Bloomsbury Group." *Virginia Woolf: New Critical Essays.* Ed. Patricia Clements and Isobel Grundy. London: Vision and Barnes and Noble, 1983. 32–56.

———. "Virginia Woolf and the Intellectual Origins of Bloomsbury." *Virginia Woolf: Centennial Essays.* Eds. Elaine K. Ginsberg and Laura Moss Gottlieb. Troy, New York: Whitston Pub. Co., 1983. 11–26.

Rosenthal, Michael. *Virginia Woolf.* New York: Columbia UP, 1979.

Ruskin, John. *Praeterita.* Boston: Dana Estes and Co., 1885.

Saltmarshe, Christopher. "Lytton Strachey." *Scrutinies* 2. Ed. Egell Rickword. London: Wishart and Co., 1931. 183–202.

Sartre, Jean-Paul. *La Nausée.* Paris: Gallimard, 1938.

Schaefer, Josephine O'Brien. "Moments of Vision in Virginia Woolf's Biographies." *Virginia Woolf Quarterly* 2 (Summer/Fall 1976): 294–303.

Scholes, Robert, and Robert Kellogg. *The Nature of Narrative.* New York: Oxford UP, 1978.

Scott, Geoffrey. *The Architecture of Humanism.* 1914. New York: Scribner, 1969.

———. "The Making of the Life of Johnson." *The Private Papers of James Boswell from Malahide Castle,* vol. 6. New York: Privately printed by Ralph Isham, 1929.

———. *The Portrait of Zélide.* New York: Scribner, 1926.

Scott, P. J. M. *E. M. Forster: Our Permanent Contemporary.* London: Vision and Barnes and Noble, 1984.

Shore, Elizabeth. "Virginia Woolf, Proust, and *Orlando.*" *Comparative Literature* 31 (Summer 1979): 232–45.

Silver, Brenda R. *Virginia Woolf's Reading Notebooks.* Princeton: Princeton UP, 1983.

———. ed. "'Anon' and 'The Reader,' Virginia Woolf's Last Essays." *Twentieth Century Literature* 25 (Fall/Winter 1979): 356–424.

Smith-Rosenberg, Carroll. "The New Woman and the New History." *Feminist Studies* 3, 185–98.

Smyth, Charles. "A Note on Historical Biography and Mr. Strachey." *Criterion* 8 (July 1929): 647–60.

Spacks, Patricia Meyer. *The Female Imagination.* New York: Knopf, 1975.

Spalding, Frances. *Roger Fry: Art and Life.* Berkeley: U of California P, 1980.

Squier, Susan. "The London Scene: Gender and Class in Virginia Woolf's London." *Twentieth Century Literature* 29 (Winter 1983): 488–500.

———. *Virginia Woolf and London: The Sexual Politics of the City.* Chapel Hill: U of North Carolina P, 1985.

Squier, Susan M., and Louise A. DeSalvo, eds. "Virginia Woolf's *The Journal of Mistress Joan Martyn.*" *Twentieth Century Literature,* 25 (Fall/Winter, 1979): 237–269.

Stephen, Leslie. *Men, Books, and Mountains.* Ed. S. O. A. Ullmann, Minneapolis: U of Minnesota P, 1956.

———. *Swift.* New York: Harper, 1882.

Strachey, John St. Loe. "A Book of the Moment, *Portrait of Zélide.*" *Spectator* 16 May 1925, 811.

Strachey, Lytton. *Biographical Essays.* New York: Harcourt, Brace, Jovanovich, nd.

———. *Eminent Victorians.* 1918. New York: Harcourt Brace and World, nd.

———. *Elizabeth and Essex.* New York: Harcourt Brace and Co., 1928.

———. *Queen Victoria.* Harcourt Brace and Co., 1921.

———. *The Really Interesting Question and Other Papers.* Ed. Paul Levy. London: Weidenfeld and Nicolson, 1972.

Stratford, Jenny. *"Eminent Victorians." British Museum Quarterly* 32 (Spring 1968): 93–96.

Suleiman, Susan R. and Inge Crossman, eds. *The Reader in the Text: Essays on Audience and Interpretation.* Princeton: Princeton UP, 1980.

Swan, Michael. *A Small Part of Time.* London: Jonathan Cape, 1957.

Symons, A. J. A. *Essays and Biographies.* Ed. Julian Symons. London: Cassell, 1969.

———. *The Quest for Corvo: An Experiment in Biography.* 1934. New York: Penguin, 1979.

Symons, Julian. *A. J. A. Symons: His Life and Speculations.* London: Eyre and Spottiswoode, 1950.

——— and Vyvyan Holland. "A. J. A. Symons: 1900–1941." *Horizon* 4 (October 1941): 258–71.

Toulmin, Stephen. "The Construal of Reality: Criticism in Modern and Postmodern Science." *Critical Inquiry* 9 (September 1982): 93–112.

Trombley, Stephen. *All That Summer She Was Mad.* New York: Continuum, 1982.

Weinstein, Mark. "The Creative Imagination in Fiction and History." *Genre* 9 (Fall 1976): 263–77.

Weintraub, Karl. "Autobiography and Historical Consciousness." *Critical Inquiry* 1 (June 1975): 821–48.

White, Hayden. *Metahistory.* Baltimore: Johns Hopkins UP, 1980.

———. "The Politics of Historical Interpretation: Discipline and De-Sublimation." *Critical Inquiry* 9 (September 1982): 113–38.

———. "The Value of Narrativity in the Representation of Reality." *Critical Inquiry* 7 (Autumn 1980): 5–28.

White, William Hale. *The Autobiography of Mark Rutherford.* 1881. London: T. Fisher Unwin, 1893.

Wilson, Edmund. "Lytton Strachey." *Shores of Light.* New York: Noonday, 1967. 550–54.

Woolf, Leonard. *The Journey not the Arrival Matters.* New York: Harcourt Brace Jovanovich, 1969.

——— and James Strachey, eds. *Virginia Woolf and Lytton Strachey: Letters.* New York: Harcourt Brace and Co., 1952.

Woolf, Virginia. *Books and Portraits.* New York: Harcourt Brace Jovanovich, 1977.

———. *The Captain's Deathbed.* New York: Harcourt Brace Jovanovich, 1950.

———. *The Common Reader.* New York: Harcourt Brace Jovanovich, 1953.

———. *Contemporary Writers.* London: Hogarth, 1965.

———. *The Death of the Moth.* 1942. New York: Harcourt Brace Jovanovich, 1970.

———. *Diary.* Vol. 1, Ed. Anne Olivier Bell. New York: Harcourt Brace Jovanovich, 1977; Vol. 2, Ed. Anne Olivier Bell assisted by Andrew McNeillie. New York: Harcourt Brace Jovanovich, 1978; Vol. 3, 1980; Vol. 4, 1982; Vol. 5, London: Hogarth, 1984.

———. *Flush.* New York: Harcourt Brace and World, 1933.

————. *Granite and Rainbow.* 1958. New York: Harcourt Brace Jovanovich, 1975.

————. *The Haunted House.* New York: Harcourt Brace and World, 1949.

————. *Jacob's Room and the Waves.* New York: Harcourt Brace and World, 1959.

————. *Letters.* Ed. Nigel Nicolson and Joanne Trautmann. New York: Harcourt Brace Jovanovich, Vol. 2, 1976; Vol. 5, 1979; Vol. 6, 1980.

————. *Moments of Being.* Ed. Jeanne Schulkind. New York: Harcourt Brace Jovanovich, 1976.

————. *Night and Day.* 1919. New York: Harcourt Brace Jovanovich, 1920.

————. *Orlando.* 1928. London: Hogarth, 1960.

————. *The Pargiters.* Ed. Mitchell Leaska. New York: Harcourt Brace Jovanovich, 1978.

————. *Roger Fry: A Biography.* 1940. New York: Harcourt Brace Jovanovich, 1976.

————. *A Room of One's Own.* New York: Harcourt Brace and World, 1929.

————. *The Second Common Reader.* 1932. New York: Harcourt Brace and World, 1960.

————. *Three Guineas.* New York: Harcourt Brace and World, 1938.

————. *To the Lighthouse.* 1927. New York: Harcourt Brace Jovanovich, 1955.

————. *The Voyage Out.* 1915. New York: Harcourt Brace Jovanovich, 1948.

Index

Altick, Richard, 2, 4–5
Annan, Noel, 180
Aristotle, 7, 74, 104, 140
Arnold, Matthew: and heroes, 26; "Sohrab and Rustum," 147–48
Autobiography, 15, 102

Bakhtin, M. M., 143, 146, 147, 155
Barthes, Roland, 203
Benedict, Ruth, 180–81
Berenson, Mary, 77
Blackmur, R. P., 129
Boswell, James, 101, 102; *Life of Johnson*, 5–6, 81, 198; Scott's views of, 76–77; Strachey's views of, 5–6
Bower-Shore, Clifford, 166
Brown, Ashley, 106
Browning, Robert, 11
Buckler, William, 11
Buckley, Jerome, 72
Butler, Samuel: as Strachey's precursor, 12, 34–35; *The Way of All Flesh*, 21, 33–35, 199

Carlyle, Thomas: on biography, 147–48, 199; on heroes, 29, 198; military metaphors of, 27; Strachey's treatment of, 135; on Victorian biography, 29; Woolf's treatment of, 135–37, 154–55. Works: *On Heroes, Hero-Worship, and the Heroic in History*, 25; "On History," 11; *The Life of John Sterling*, 27–28, 29, 43
Cecil, David, 61, 83–90; as expressivist, 86; on modern novel, 84–85; on Pater, 83; and Strachey, 84; and Woolf, 88. Works: *Hardy the Novelist*, 83–84; *The Stricken Deer*, 61, 84–90; *The Young Melbourne*, 61, 90
Character study, 120–21
Charrière, Madame de. *See* Scott, Geoffrey, *Portrait of Zélide*
Clifford, James, 1, 4
Clifford, James (son), 203–4
Cockshut, A. O. J.: on autobiography in relation to biography, 15; on Froude's *Carlyle*, 31; *Truth to Life*, 16; on Victorian biography, 8, 28, 34, 105, 151, 191

229

Strachey, Lytton (*continued*)
183. Works: *Elizabeth and
Essex*, 53, 54, 92, 162–71,
183; *Eminent Victorians*, 24,
37–57, 164: Gordon, 49–
52; Manning, 43, 44–45,
47–48; Nightingale, 53,
54–57, 58–59, 165; preface
to, 5, 39–42; *Landmarks of
French Literature*, 65; *Queen
Victoria*, 54, 59, 60–61, 63,
64–73, 164, 165: ending of,
69, 82, 116, 158; Woolf's
view of, 183
Symons, A. J. A., 100–109,
121–32; as bibliographer,
122; biographical theory of,
123–24; on Burton, 125;
and Carlyle, 124, 129; and
Conrad, 130–31; as fin-de-
siècle figure, 124–25, 130;
and Freud, 108, 129; on
Hook, 125; and James, 122;
The Quest for Corvo, 122–32;
on Stanley, 124, 131; and
Strachey, 121–22, 125–26,
130; subjects, relationship
to, 123–26, 130
Symons, Julian, 124, 127, 129,
130

Tennyson, 26. *See also* Nicolson, Harold, *Tennyson*

Victoria, Queen. *See* Strachey,
Lytton, *Queen Victoria*
Victorian biography, 8, 10–
12, 25–28; the revolt
against, 21–57; Woolf's
view of, 144

Wharton, Edith. *See* Lubbock,
Percy, *Portrait of Edith
Wharton*
White, Hayden, 43–44, 46,
52, 59, 164, 191, 210n.2
White, William Hale, 24
Wilson, Edmund, 71
Woolf, Leonard, 3, 182,
192–93
Woolf, Virginia, 82, 133–60,
161–63, 179–97, 198; anti-
Victorianism of, 135–36,
155; on Carlyle, 135–37;
on characterization, 4, 85,
139–40; on DeQuincey,
150; and Forster, 171–73,
178–79, 182; and Freud,
180; on Gibbon, 135, 196;
on hero-worship, 29; on
history, 133; importance of
biography to, 134, 137, 142,
183–84; on Lee, 9; and mediated biography, 144–45;
on "new biography," 6–7,
91, 199, 144; on Nicolson,
6–7, 99; and novelistic biography, 144–45, 154; and
Pater, 62–63, 144, 188; and
Proust, 95, 150, 151, 202;
on Scott, 75–76; the self,
view of, 152–54, 179–182;
on Stephen, 32, 135–38,
146; and Strachey, 35, 143–
45, 158–59, 183; on Vic-
torian biography, 3, 144; on
women in relation to his-
tory, 3–4, 14, 134–35, 141.
Works: "The Art of Biog-
raphy," 4, 183, 184, 199;
Flush, 136, 143, 154–60,

Ruth Hoberman received her B.A. in French from Oberlin College and her M.A. and Ph.D. in English from Columbia University. She has taught at Columbia University and Queens College in New York City and is now Assistant Professor of English at Eastern Illinois University. She is co-author (with David Engel and Frank Palmeri) of *The McGraw-Hill Guide to World Literature*.